PLATO'S ATLANTIS STORY
TEXT, TRANSLATION AND COMMENTARY

Plato's Atlantis Story

*Text, Translation
and Commentary*

Christopher Gill

LIVERPOOL UNIVERSITY PRESS

First published 2017 by
Liverpool University Press
4 Cambridge Street
Liverpool
L69 7ZU

British Library Cataloguing-in-Publication data
A British Library CIP record is available

ISBN 978-1-78694-016-2 cased
ISBN 978-1-78694-015-5 limp

Typeset by Carnegie Book Production, Lancaster
Printed and bound by CPI Group (UK) Ltd, Croydon CR0 4YY

Contents

Preface

This book aims to provide, in a single volume, the materials needed to explore Plato's Atlantis story in some depth. It contains the two relevant Greek texts (the start of Plato's *Timaeus* and the incomplete *Critias*), using the Oxford Classical Text (Burnet 1902),[1] which has been supplied in digital form by the Thesaurus Linguae Graecae, and a new translation of these texts. It also offers a full interpretative introduction, a medium-length commentary and a vocabulary. Different kinds of readers can use the book in various ways. Those, including scholars and students of ancient philosophy and general readers, who want to gain a better understanding of Plato's story without knowing Greek can focus on the translation and introduction. Readers with knowledge of Greek can use all parts of the book.

The book may also be useful for students (whether specializing in ancient philosophy or not) wanting to study an intriguing Greek prose text of moderate length (34 pages in the Oxford Classical Text). The text contains an unusual combination of dialogue, exposition, narrative and description, and is less philosophically technical in style than many Platonic dialogues. The commentary provides considerable help on translation and grammar, referring to several widely used Greek textbooks, and there is a complete vocabulary of Greek words. To make the book as useful as possible for this purpose, the Greek text and commentary have been interleaved, rather than printed separately. The text is printed in short sections, immediately followed by notes commenting on that section. Anyone preferring to read the Greek text continuously can use Burnet's Oxford Classical Text alongside this book.

---

[1] See the bibliography for works cited by author and date.

The present volume is based on one first prepared for the Bristol Classical Press series of texts with commentary, which was subsequently taken over by Duckworth; it was first published in 1980 and reprinted in 1996, but then fell out of print. This second edition uses the same Greek text (which is still the current Oxford Classical Text). The commentary has been updated and modified in various ways but retains the original aim of providing concise exegetical comment and guidance on translation, and the vocabulary is largely the same. The translation has been specially prepared for this book. The introduction is almost wholly new, much fuller than in the 1980 book and offers an interpretative reading of Plato's presentation of the story in both *Timaeus* and *Critias*.

In 1980, the Atlantis story was a subject of relatively limited interest among scholars of classics or ancient philosophy.[2] Apart from consideration of this topic in commentaries on the *Timaeus*,[3] the most notable contribution was an article by Pierre Vidal-Naquet, 'Athènes et l'Atlantide' (1964), which argues for the importance of understanding the contemporary (fifth- and fourth-century BC) Athenian connotations of the story. This article had a strong influence on the previous edition of the present book, and has continued to shape much subsequent discussion. However, since 1980, the Atlantis story has become a more widely discussed subject. The most substantial contributions have been a translation of *Timaeus-Critias* with introduction and notes by Luc Brisson (1992); a full-scale interpretative monograph by Jean-François Pradeau (1997); a comprehensive commentary on the *Critias* by Heinz-Günther Nesselrath (2006); and a monograph on the reception of the Atlantis story by Vidal-Naquet (2007). A good deal of recent work, including that of Brisson and Pradeau, has aimed to locate the Atlantis story more firmly in its context in the *Timaeus-Critias*, and to examine thematic links with Timaeus's cosmological account. This is also the aim of monographs by Thomas

[2] Of course, throughout the modern period, as in previous centuries, there have been general books claiming to 'find' Atlantis somewhere in the world. On the ancient and modern reception of Plato's story, see the latter part of the introduction, including the Appendix on the hypothesis of Luce 1970 that Atlantis was based on Minoan Crete or Thera.

[3] See Rivaud 1927; Taylor 1928; Cornford 1937.

Johansen (2004) and Sarah Broadie (2012); Broadie's work has been especially influential on the reading offered here. There have been many articles and chapters by other scholars, treating all aspects of the story – its literary-philosophical character, its factual or fictional status and links with Platonic thought more generally, including his political ideas. The new introduction takes full account of this recent work, and the commentary has been modified in the light of the interpretation it offers.

I am grateful to Simon Baker and Anna Henderson, of the University of Exeter Press, for their encouragement to write this book (and their patience in waiting for me to do so), and, more recently, to Alison Welsby of Liverpool University Press, for her help in bringing the book to completion. I would like to thank Sarah Broadie for sharing the Atlantis chapter of her book (2012) in advance of publication and for reading the introduction, and also Christopher Rowe and Thomas Johansen for providing detailed comments on the introduction. Thanks are due too to the anonymous reader for Liverpool University Press. I am also grateful to Oxford University Press for permission to use Burnet's Oxford Classical Text, and to the Thesaurus Linguae Graecae for supplying a digital file of Burnet's text, which is printed here.

I would also like to thank, very warmly, my son Ralph, for invaluable assistance in preparing the book, notably by keying in the commentary and vocabulary, and providing technical assistance of various kinds. The book is dedicated to the many people with whom I have studied and discussed Plato over the years, including the scholars I have just mentioned and others with whom I have debated in the meetings of the International Plato Society, and the many students with whom I have explored Plato's texts and ideas.

C.G.
University of Exeter
May 2016

Introduction: Plato's Atlantis Story

Setting the scene

[1][1] Few stories have captured the popular imagination as much as that of Atlantis, the vast island with an ancient but highly advanced civilization which disappeared beneath the Atlantic Ocean. Atlantis is so famous that many people suppose that its legend is based on a wide variety of sources, found in the literature of several countries and ages. In fact, this is not so. The story of Atlantis is derived from one source, and one only, which is contained within the covers of this book. Plato (*c.* 429–347 BC) outlined the story in one of his late dialogues, the *Timaeus*, and started to tell it in full in the uncompleted sequel, the *Critias*. There is no reference to Atlantis in ancient literature before Plato, and later ancient references are based on his account. The story of Atlantis originates from Plato alone.

[2] Did Plato obtain the story from some source now lost to us or did he make it up himself? If he invented it, did he, nonetheless, have a factual model in view? Plato's presentation is highly ambiguous, and offers conflicting indications about its status and basis. Many of Plato's modern readers have thought that the story must have had a factual basis and have tried to 'find' Atlantis in an extraordinarily wide range of locations. However, Platonic scholars, ancient and modern, have generally believed that the story is Plato's invention, and that it is based primarily on his own philosophical ideas, even if he also alludes to historical or mythological

---

[1] The paragraphs in this introduction are numbered: any references elsewhere in this book to numbers in square brackets, for example, [2] or [16], are to these paragraphs. References to Platonic works use the standard Stephanus page and paragraph numbers found in all texts and translations of Plato.

material for this purpose.[2] There was a period (from the late 1960s to the late 1970s), when some scholars explored the idea that the Atlantis story was based on reports of the volcanic eruption at Thera in the middle of the second millennium BC, which, as it was supposed, had ended the early but advanced culture of Minoan Crete. However, this line of enquiry has, as far as I am aware, been largely abandoned.[3] Although there has been quite extensive scholarly discussion of the Atlantis story in recent decades, this has focused on interpreting Plato's presentation of the story, on the assumption that it is his invention and that his motives in composing it were philosophical. This is also the assumption made in this book.

[3] I now outline Plato's presentation of the story, before setting out the interpretative questions raised by this presentation, which are addressed in the rest of the introduction. At the start of the *Timaeus* (17c–19b), Socrates offers a résumé of most of the main features of the ideal state in the *Republic*. These include the institution of a large military or guardian class, living separately from the rest of population, but exclude the important and innovative idea that this state should be ruled by philosophers. Socrates then asks his companions to tell a story that will illustrate the character of this ideal by representing it in some great action, such as war with a worthy opponent (19b–20c). The obvious implication is that the story will be a narrative invention based on philosophical ideas, of which there are many instances of different kinds in Plato's dialogues, usually called his 'myths'.[4] However, Critias, who undertakes this task, offers to do so by narrating a story allegedly based on historical facts. This is to be an account of a very ancient conflict (over 9,000 years earlier) between ancient Athens and the maritime empire of Atlantis, in which Athens defeated a much larger opponent, before the whole island of Atlantis was submerged under the sea by earthquakes and floods. This story, provided by the sixth-century BC statesman Solon, was preserved in Critias's family, but was previously unknown to anyone else. In his retelling, Critias has primaeval Athens play the role of Socrates's ideal state, while Atlantis serves as its formidable but defeated enemy (20c–26e).

---

[2] See [40–45].

[3] See [46–53].

[4] On Platonic 'myths', see [36–39].

[4] Critias's offer to satisfy Socrates's request with a factually based story is unexpected, though Socrates accepts it readily. Even more surprising is Critias's next move, explaining that his story will be preceded by an account from another speaker, Timaeus, of the origin of the universe and of the human race, considered as part of the universe (26e–27b). This long exposition, not included in this edition, takes up the rest of the *Timaeus* (27c–92c). It is an immensely famous account which has received detailed analysis in both antiquity and modern times. It has often been discussed separately from the Atlantis story, though some recent treatments have studied both parts and considered what implications each has for understanding the other.[5] Critias takes over as spokesman in the *Critias*, and begins to tell the story of the great war that he sketched in the *Timaeus*. His focus is on illustrating the different characters of the two states in a series of ways. These include reference to the physical environment (both natural and built), political and military organization, and, in the case of Atlantis, public buildings and other material structures, such as canals, ditches and roads. At the end of this preliminary description Critias is about to narrate the story of the great war between these two states; but then, surprisingly, breaks off in mid-sentence. At this point the Atlantis story comes to an end (*Critias* 106a–121c).

[5] I now consider in more detail the different parts of this presentation and the interpretative questions raised by each. My aim is to clarify the character of the Atlantis story and its significance in the context of Plato's philosophy. I begin by listing a number of puzzling or problematic questions raised by the presentation: 1) Why does Socrates's opening summary of the institutions of the ideal state omit reference to philosopher-rulers, such a striking and distinctive feature of Plato's ideal? 2) Why does Critias offer an allegedly historical story when we might expect a philosophical fable, and why does he insist on its (factual) 'truth', even though this claim is not credible, for a number of reasons? 3) Why is Timaeus's account of cosmology placed between Critias's summary and the full version of his story, and what implications, if any, does this have for interpreting the full version? 4) Why are there certain important

---

[5] See Johansen 2004; Broadie 2012.

differences – at least in emphasis and approach – between Critias's summary of his story and its full version? 5) Why does Plato abandon the full version of the story in mid-sentence, just as Critias is reaching the core of the subject, the account of the war between primaeval Athens and Atlantis? In the course of this introduction, I outline answers to all these questions, while also highlighting scholarly discussions where they are pursued much further than I can do here.

Dialogue form

[6] Before looking at each stage in the presentation of the story, I consider a question which bears on each of the stages, namely the significance of the dialogue form for making sense of Plato's philosophical objectives. Plato is famous for his innovative and creative deployment of the dialogue form or philosophical drama. It has often been supposed that this was a feature only of his early and middle works, and that his later dialogues were, in effect at least, straightforward theoretical exposition; but some recent scholarship has underlined the role of the dialogue form in the late works too.[6] In the *Timaeus-Critias*, there is relatively little dialectical interchange and most of the text consists of narrative or exposition by one speaker. However, as brought out shortly, the question of form is quite important for making sense of the content and objectives of the work, and a salient aspect of this is the kind of dialogue presented between different figures and the viewpoints they hold. I will also suggest that the sequence and unfolding of the exposition carries with it a quasi-dialectical exploration of the subject, analogous to that conducted wholly in dialogue form in most other Platonic writings. These three points are taken in turn.

[7] The form of the work is significant for interpretation of its philosophical content in several ways. First, and most obviously, the *Timaeus-Critias*[7] as a whole consists of a series of quite different parts;

---

[6] See for example Gill and McCabe 1996.

[7] I refer to the *Timaeus-Critias* (rather than *Timaeus* and *Critias*) since the two dialogues are presented as a single (long) discussion, conducted on one day, following the discussion of the ideal state 'yesterday' (*Ti.* 17a). See Broadie 2012, 115 on this point.

and the question arises how they are interrelated. On the one hand, there is Critias's summary of his story, preceded by an account of its transmission (*Ti.* 20c–26d), and then his full (but incomplete) version, also preceded by a discussion of historical exploration of the past (*Criti.* 108e–119a). On the other hand, there is Timaeus's lengthy cosmology and anthropology (*Ti.* 27c–92c), and also dialogic interchange between figures linking these various parts.[8] One can ask whether the two main parts (Critias's Atlantis story and Timaeus's creation story) are essentially distinct in aim and philosophical approach as well as in form, or whether they are conceptually linked. An associated question is how both these parts are related to Socrates's original request, to see the ideal state of the *Republic* represented in action (*Ti.* 19b–20c). As explained later, I think that Critias's full version of his story is informed in content and, to some extent, conceptual approach by Timaeus's creation story, which it follows. Also, his full version responds more fully and thoughtfully to Socrates's original request than his initial summary.[9] So the overall form is quite important for making sense of the content.

[8] Is it important that the Atlantis story unfolds in these various stages, formulated by different named individuals? Do these individuals have 'characters' in a way that matters for interpretative purposes? Who are these figures and how are they presented to us? Socrates is, of course, the main speaker in most Platonic dialogues, though not in a number of late ones. Here, the Socrates-figure is closely linked with the political themes of the *Republic* through the (partial) summary of its content in *Ti.* 17c–19a. The other three figures are all presented by Socrates as, exceptionally, expert in both philosophy and politics (*Ti.* 19e–20b). Timaeus of Locris (an Italian city) is especially praised in this respect, while the commendation of Critias of Athens and Hermocrates is rather more qualified. Of these three figures, Timaeus, who is otherwise quite unknown, is generally taken to be a Platonic invention. Since cosmological speculation of this kind is not linked with the Socrates-figure elsewhere in Plato's dialogues, it is plausible to think that Timaeus has been invented

---

[8] *Ti.* 17a–20d, 26c–27b; *Criti.* 106a–108d. I use the shortened forms *Ti.* and *Criti.* for the *Timaeus* and *Critias* throughout.

[9] For this view, see also Broadie 2012, 148.

for this role. Although Hermocrates is not explicitly linked with any city, it is generally assumed that he is the Syracusan politician and general who played a key role in the defeat of Athens in the Sicilian expedition in 415–413 (all dates in this book are BC unless indicated otherwise). The identity of Critias is more problematic and has aroused much scholarly discussion. Was he the intellectual and politician (*c.* 460–403) who was a leading figure in the notorious '30 tyrants' who briefly took over Athens after its defeat by Sparta which ended the Peloponnesian War (404–403)? Or was he his grandfather, with the same name, about whom we know nothing beyond the fact of his existence? The older figure would make a more credible chronological bridge between the era of Socrates and the time of Solon (the alleged source of the story).[10] However, the younger Critias is, for several reasons brought out later, a highly appropriate person to provide this story and to present it as he does. If the figure is meant to be taken as the younger, famous Critias, has Plato slipped up chronologically or has he deliberately telescoped the time between this discussion and the age of Solon?[11]

[9] A more fundamental question, which has been much less discussed, is whether the *Timaeus-Critias* is actually located in a precise historical

---

[10] Solon lived *c.* 630–*c.* 558; his reforms of the Athenian constitution, apparently alluded to in *Ti.* 21c6–7, are usually dated to 594/593, and Plato puts his journey to Egypt earlier. Socrates's dates are 469–399. If Critias the speaker is the grandfather of Critias the tyrant (born *c.* 520), *his* grandfather (Critias, born *c.* 600) could have heard the story from his father, Dropides (born *c.* 630). Critias, the grandfather could, as a very old man, have told Socrates and others the story in 430–425, when Hermocrates would have been able to visit Athens. For this genealogical schema and the dates suggested, see Brisson 1982, 32–38, 1992, 328–35. Other features matching this scenario are that the poems of Solon are described as 'new' in *Ti.* 21b5, though they were not in fact new at the time of the grandfather of Critias the tyrant, and that Critias refers to himself as 'old' in *Ti.* 26c1, although Critias the tyrant died aged 54 and so did not reach old age.

[11] For the view that Plato deliberately telescoped the time between Solon and Critias (the tyrant), reducing five generations to three, see Davies 1971, 325–26. On the extensive (and inconclusive) scholarly debate on the identity of the speaker Critias, see Nesselrath 2006, 43–50, including discussion of anachronisms in Plato's dialogues on pages 47–48.

setting at all, so that it makes sense to ask exactly who these figures are in real life and whether they could have had this discussion in Athens in Socrates's lifetime. Certainly, some of Plato's dialogues are historically and dramatically located with great care in this way (for instance, the *Protagoras* and *Symposium*) and in those cases the historical context matters for philosophical interpretation. However, in several late dialogues, although the choice and juxtaposition of speakers continues to have conceptual significance, there is no attempt to locate the dialogue plausibly in a precise time period.[12] The *Timaeus-Critias* seems to be intermediate in this respect. The opening presentation of the figures is quite unspecific as regards the timing of the discussion;[13] there is more precision in the account of the transmission of the story (*Ti.* 20e–21d), but, as indicated, this still leaves the question of Critias's identity ambiguous. Sarah Broadie has recently argued that the dialogue's context is meant to be taken as fictional and not matching any specific time period. Her main reason for this suggestion is that Critias's summary of the Atlantis story evokes, unmistakably, the defeat of the great empire of Persia by Athens at the battle of Marathon in 490.[14] However, none of those present, oddly, comments on this resemblance; and she takes this as an indication that this is a setting in which the battle of Marathon has not taken place. That is to say that this is a purely fictional context, even though at least three of the figures are real and have specific historical connotations. Some may find this proposal too bold to accept, though it is powerfully argued.[15] However, we may still accept one of her claims, namely that 'Critias' was chosen as speaker primarily for the historical connotations of the younger man (the tyrant) even if the dialogue does not establish a specific chrono-logical setting in which we can locate the speaker as the tyrant. Indeed,

---

[12] For example, *Parmenides, Philebus, Laws.*

[13] See *Ti.* 17a, 19e–20c. On the question of the date of the conversation (assuming we can identify this), see Nesselrath 2006, 55–59.

[14] *Ti.* 25b–c evokes Marathon (490), rather than Salamis (480), since the battle is presented as one between an army and a force invading by sea (i.e. a land battle, rather than the sea battle of Salamis). On historical allusions of this kind in the Atlantis story, see also [22, 30–33].

[15] Broadie 2012, 130–40.

we can suppose that the chronology suggested by *Ti.* 20e–21a points to the speaker being Critias the grandfather rather than Critias the tyrant, and recognize that the connotations of the younger man colour our impressions of the speaker.[16] This, at any rate, is the view assumed here.

[10] This leads naturally to the third point, the idea that the sequence of speeches forms a quasi-dialectical exploration of its topic, in which conceptual progress is made. In Plato's dialogues in general, dialectical exploration of a topic or question, conducted through argument-based question-and-answer, is the standard mode of presentation. The *Timaeus-Critias*, on the face of it, takes a rather different form. However, it is possible to read the speeches and dialogic interchange as forming an intellectual exploration analogous to that normally conducted through dialogue.[17] This exploration centres, at one level, on finding an appropriate response to Socrates's original request, to see the ideal state depicted in action (*Ti.* 19b–20c). Critias's initial response, with a historical story which forms a kind of eulogy of (primaeval) Athens (*Ti.* 20c–26d), is not really, despite initial appearances, what Socrates wants. The second version, presented after Timaeus's creation story and in some ways informed by it (*Criti.* 108e–119a), is much closer to what is required. Among other salient features, we find a more considered treatment of historiographical method and a more reflective approach to the question of what makes a given state more or less effective in action. At another, deeper, level, the sequence of speeches examines, in two different ways, what it means for an ideal to be given concrete form, that is, to be specified or embodied. Timaeus's creation story does this in terms of the cosmos and human race, while the Atlantis story does it in terms

---

[16] For the view that the identity of Critias the speaker is ambiguous in this way, see Brisson 1982, 37; this is also, in effect, the view of Davies 1971, 325–26.

[17] For the view that Platonic dialectic is continued in the late dialogues, though sometimes in different modes, see Gill and McCabe 1996, esp. Gill 1996a. See also Gill 2002, 150–53, 2006, 144–47. On the relationship between form and philosophical content in the *Timaeus-Critias*, see also Osborne 1996; Johansen 2004, ch. 9. Johansen suggests that it is significant that Timaeus's creation story is in monologue form, a single complete speech presenting a single, complete universe (Johansen 2004, 197; see also Osborne 1996, 207, 210–11).

of the ideal state (or one version of the ideal state).[18] All the elements in the two texts (the dialogue and interchange between figures, as well as the different kinds of speech) contribute to this sequence of thought – which has perhaps reached a kind of conclusion by the end of the *Critias*, despite the appearance of incompleteness.

Socrates's original request – a philosophical fable

[11] The sequence begins at the start of the *Timaeus* with Socrates's request. He starts by summarizing certain key features of the ideal state as set out in Books II–V of the *Republic* (*Ti.* 17c–19a).[19] This summary includes the establishment of a separate guardian class to govern the state, their education (briefly noted) and their social arrangements: men and women alike to be guardians, marriage to be abolished, and women and children held in common. However, the summary excludes another striking feature of the ideal state, the idea that the supreme rulers should be philosophers (of both genders), selected for their exceptional character and intellect from the larger guardian class, and given a further education centred on mathematics and dialectic, combined with practical experience in governing (Books VI–VII). Socrates goes on to say that he feels a desire to see this state exhibiting its special qualities in some great action involving war and diplomacy. He claims that he lacks the skill to provide this kind of representation, and he is not confident that the poets or sophists of his day could do so either. However, he says that the three men present (Timaeus, Critias and Hermocrates) have the required combination of philosophical and political expertise and experience to carry out this task, and asks that they do so in return for his account of the ideal state (*Ti.* 19b–20c).

[12] The main puzzle in this section is the omission of the idea of philosopher-rulers from the summary of the ideal state of the *Republic*. One response to this problem would be to suppose that, since writing

---

[18] See further [15 and 24–25].

[19] However, it is also indicated that 'yesterday's' discussion, summarized by Socrates, and that of the *Republic* are not identical. See n. 28.

the *Republic* – the *Timaeus* is normally thought to be significantly later[20] – Plato has changed his mind about what makes the best possible state. There are, in fact, certain statements in other dialogues later than the *Republic* which point in this direction. For instance, we find the suggestion in the *Statesman* and the *Laws* that no, or at least only an exceptional, human being can exercise supreme power and not be corrupted. Hence, government by a code of well-designed laws is preferable to unfettered rule by individuals.[21] Since the *Republic*'s philosopher-rulers appear to have such unfettered power, the fact that they do not figure explicitly in Plato's later political theorizing has sometimes been taken to signal a change of mind by Plato since the *Republic*. This might then also explain the absence of philosopher-rulers from Socrates's summary in the *Timaeus*.[22]

[13] However, there are a number of objections to this line of explanation. For one thing, just after his summary in the *Timaeus* itself, Socrates seems to allude to this idea, saying that he is looking for those individuals who (exceptionally) combine philosophical and political expertise, that is, people who are like his philosopher-rulers.[23] In the *Seventh Letter* (if this is authentically Platonic), Plato himself presents the idea of philosopher-rulers as his own distinctive contribution to political theory and one he feels obliged to try to put into practice in his involvement in the political life of Syracuse.[24] In the *Statesman*, Plato's spokesman (the Eleatic Stranger) affirms his belief that the best kind of rule is that based on genuine political expertise, even though he also expresses doubt about human beings' capability to exercise unfettered power without being corrupted. Although political expertise is not explicitly said to be based on philosophical knowledge in the *Statesman*,

---

[20] The chronology of Plato's works is largely conjectural; however, on stylometric grounds, the *Timaeus-Critias* is normally placed in the last group, and the *Laws* (perhaps followed by the *Epinomis*) is taken to be his last work. See Kahn 2002.

[21] See *Statesman* 300–303, especially 301c–d; *Laws* 691–692, 713c–714a, 875a–e.

[22] For this view of Plato's development, see Vlastos 1981, 212–17; Klosko 1986, chs 11–13; and, applied to the Atlantis story, with some qualifications, Gill 1979a, 158–60.

[23] *Ti.* 19e–20b. See also Schofield 1997, 213–15.

[24] *Seventh Letter* 325c–326b. If authentic, this letter was written later than the *Republic*. On the question of its authenticity, see Schofield 2006, 13–19.

it is not ruled out either.²⁵ Even in the *Laws*, although the version of
the ideal state presented there is based on an elaborate law code, Plato
retains a role for an exceptional group of people (the nocturnal council),
who combine philosophical understanding and political expertise, and
use it to maintain the good government of the state (*Laws* 961–69). These
points, taken together, do not support the hypothesis that Plato has
decisively abandoned the *Republic*'s ideal of the philosopher-ruler in his
later political theory, and that this explains their absence from Socrates's
summary in *Timaeus* 17b–19b.²⁶

[14] This subject raises a broader interpretative point, which may take
us closer to resolving this puzzle. Scholars have often interpreted Plato, on
this topic and others, as acting like a modern philosophical author, using
his publications as a means of working towards, and making known,
his or her definitive position on a certain issue. However, for various
reasons, this approach may not be suitable for interpreting Plato. For one
thing, apart from the letters (if they are genuine), Plato does not speak in
his own voice but through dialogues consisting of reasoned arguments
between a wide variety of speakers. Although there is nearly always a
single main speaker, mostly Socrates but sometimes someone else, it is not
clear that we can simply identify the words of this speaker (which usually
take the form of a series of questions rather than exposition) with Plato's
own views. Also, different ideas are put forward by the main speakers
in different dialogues; and there is normally no explicit reference in one
dialogue to another. In general, I think, variations between works are
better explained by the hypothesis that Plato is using different dialogues
to carry out different philosophical projects or different enquiries, rather
than that he has, straightforwardly, changed his mind on a specific topic.²⁷

[15] The inclusion of a summary of a substantial part of the *Republic*
at the start of the *Timaeus* is quite exceptional (even so, it is made clear
that the two conversations are not identical).²⁸ The exclusion of the

---

²⁵ *Statesman* 293a–302b. See Rowe 1995, 15–18, 230–31, 1996, 165–71; also Gill 1995,
292–97; Schofield 1997, 220–30.

²⁶ See also, in support of this conclusion, Rowe 1997, 2004.

²⁷ See Gill 1995, 301–04, 2002, 153–61, 2006, 140–47; also Schofield 1997, 216–21.

²⁸ Although the summary unmistakably recalls (part of) the *Republic*, it is also

philosopher-rulers here may be an early indication of the special focus of the *Timaeus-Critias*, one indicated in different ways in Timaeus's creation story and in the full version of Critias's Atlantis story. In the *Republic* and also in the *Symposium* and *Phaedo*, in different ways, a prominent place is given to attempts to outline the kind of intellectual progress that would lead towards complete knowledge of the ideal (the Forms). Much less attention is given to reflection on what would be involved in putting ideal knowledge into practice.[29] The *Timaeus-Critias* takes a different approach. Timaeus's creation story is centred on the project of putting knowledge of the ideal into practice, in the creation of a cosmos that matches an ideal model and of the human race, viewed as, at least, an approximation of this ideal.[30] In his opening request, Socrates, summarizing his ideal state, asks those with the required expertise to put it into practice, in the sense of illustrating its character and education through appropriate action (*Ti.* 17b–20b). The opening summary of the *Republic* may omit the philosopher-rulers to mark this shift of emphasis and to show that the role allocated to philosopher-rulers there is to be carried out here, in a different form, by Socrates's (allegedly) expert interlocutors. The omission of the philosopher-rulers from the summary also concentrates attention on the social structure of the ideal state, rather than the advanced educational programme designed to lead to complete philosophical knowledge.[31] In

made clear that the two discussions (that of the *Republic* and the one summarized in *Ti.* 17a–19b) are different. The participants are different people and the dialogues took place at different festivals, those of Bendis (*Republic* 327a, 354a) and Athena (*Timaeus* 21a, 26e). This follows the Platonic convention that different dialogues do not refer explicitly to each other, except when they are presented as part of a connected discussion (e.g. *Theaetetus, Sophist, Statesman*); see Gill 2002, 153–61. See also Nesselrath 2006, 55–59.

[29] See *Republic* Books VI–VII; *Symposium* 210a–212b; *Phaedo* 64a–67b, 73b–76e. *Phaedo* 97c–98b envisages the kind of teleological conception of cosmology offered in *Timaeus* 27a–92c, but does not explore this further.

[30] See *Ti.* 29e–31a, 41a–42e. See also Johansen 2004, chs 4, 5, 7; Sedley 2007, ch. 4; Broadie 2012, chs 3–4.

[31] In *Ti.* 17b–19b, Socrates focuses on the class structure of the ideal state, especially the guardian class, and its distinctive way of life (no use of money, women and children held in common). In *Ti.* 18a9–10, Socrates refers only to cultural and physical

his full version of the Atlantis story (as far as it goes), Critias too will focus on social and governmental structures, along with other kinds of structure, such as the physical environment. So, in both the creation account and the Atlantis story, there is a special focus on structure and embodiment, as a way of representing what is involved in putting the ideal into practice.[32] In these respects, Socrates's summary of the ideal state and his request prefigure key features of the intellectual project of the *Timaeus-Critias* as a whole, both in what is included and what is left out.

Critias's 'true account'

[16] The next stage of the discussion centres on Critias's summary of a long-ago war between primaeval Athens and an invading power (Atlantis) and the process by which Critias came to be in possession of this account. He offers the summary to Socrates to see whether it meets his requirements, with a view to recounting it in full later on (*Ti.* 20c–27b). Socrates accepts this with apparent readiness (26e). However, there are a number of reasons for being cautious about whether this story, as Critias summarizes it here, actually matches what Socrates has in mind. These reasons for caution centre on three interrelated features: the treatment of history or historiography, the claims about truth and the focus on Athens and Critias's own family. Also potentially significant are certain nuances of expression in the dialogue between Socrates and Critias, which, taken with the other factors, indicate that the two men are not really on the same conceptual wavelength. Overall, then, we are left with the impression that this phase of the discussion only takes us a quite limited distance in the dialectical exploration of the project of the *Timaeus-Critias* as a whole.

education (*mousikē* and *gumnastikē*), the two components of the first phase of the educational programme (for all future guardians) in *Republic* 376e–412a. Socrates mentions other types of learning (*mathēmata*), but there is no reason to think of the elaborate programme of advanced education in *Republic* Books VI–VII, based on mathematics and dialectic.

[32] See also [10 and 24–25].

[17] Socrates's original request leads us to expect a philosophical fable or 'myth' (like other Platonic myths), based on the structural features of the ideal state that Socrates has outlined. It is a surprise, then, that Critias responds by offering what is presented as a historical account (*Ti.* 20e–21a). In his exposition, historiographical themes are very prominent, while what one might expect to be the core content (the social structure of the equivalent of the ideal state and the great war, designed to show the character of this state in action) are dealt with more briefly.[33] Critias focuses especially on two aspects of the transmission of the account. One is the process by which records about Athens as it was over 9,000 years earlier, including its political organization and the defeat of an invading power (Atlantis), were preserved in Egypt although knowledge of them had been lost in Athens itself. Greek knowledge of its past had been interrupted by discontinuities in civilization brought about by natural disasters such as earthquakes and floods, which Egypt, with its very different geographical location, had avoided (21e–23c). The other aspect is the process by which the account was conveyed, we are told, from Egyptian priests to the sixth-century statesman Solon and thus to the family of Critias, within which it has been preserved to this day (20d–21d, 23d–24a, 25e–26c).

[18] In some ways, this historiographical focus might seem to be a positive point in meeting Socrates's request. Although interest in historiography is not evident in most of Plato's dialogues, it figures, rather more credibly handled, in Critias's full version of the story and in *Laws* Book III. In both cases, especially *Laws* Book III, historiography is used to make a serious attempt to recover the past, and to chart good forms of social and political structure.[34] The broader project of the *Timaeus-Critias*,

---

[33] Historiographical themes, including the transmission of the story, are to be found at *Ti.* 20d–24a, also 26a–c; social structure at 24a–d; great war at 24e–25d. Only the latter two themes match Socrates's request (19b–c). The historiographical themes include interest in reconstructing the past in spite of periodic disasters (22c–23c), and comparison between the social structures of different states as a way of gauging past historical contacts and influences (24a–d).

[34] See *Criti.* 109d–110b (inferences about the past, in spite of discontinuities in civilization), and 110d–111d, 112d (evidence of past soil erosion and changes in water

correlating the ideal and the actual, by way of the themes of structure and embodiment, could indeed be advanced in this way (and is advanced in Critias's full version). However, Critias's treatment of this theme in *Ti.* 20d–26e is problematic in several ways. By this stage in Greek culture, there was already a highly sophisticated understanding of historiographical method, and of the difficulties of gaining accurate knowledge about the past, especially the distant past. Hence, both Herodotus and Thucydides focus on trying to provide a reliable account of quite recent events, based on a variety of sources, preferably eyewitness accounts (including that of the historian himself in Thucydides's case). Thucydides especially recognizes that gaining such knowledge about the distant past is a much less feasible objective.[35] Judged by these standards, Critias's methodology is both more casual and overconfident. He claims to provide evidence about a distant period of history which falls far outside the normal limits of ancient historiography. His account is, supposedly, based on a single line of transmission, uncorroborated by any other sources: from Egyptian priests to Solon, Solon to the older Critias and so down to the speaker. Critias repeatedly stresses the cultural and military importance of the events he reports (like Herodotus and Thucydides).[36] However, this stress is, bizarrely, out of line with the fact that, according to him, no one in this lengthy sequence of transmission, in Egypt or Greece, saw fit to make these facts more widely known, to open them up to general scrutiny or to use them for public benefit.[37]

---

supply). In *Laws* III, we have a study of prehistory and early Greek history (676–683) and of more recent history (684–706d), designed to establish the nature of the best, or at least best achievable, political structure (702b–c, 739a–b). On a new interest in historiography as a distinctive feature of the Atlantis story, see Gill 1977, 301–02; Pradeau 1997, 43–54, 156–89; Broadie 2012, 120–21. On Plato's interest in early history, see also Weil 1959.

[35] Thucydides begins his account with a review of early Greek history, but stresses the difficulty of gaining accurate information about this, in the way he has tried to do in connection with recent history (that of the Peloponnesian War); see 1.1, 1.21–22. See also Ephorus, fr. 9 in Jacoby 1923. For more on this point, see Johansen 2004, 42–43.

[36] See *Ti.* 20e, 21d, 23c, 24d–25d; also Herodotus 1.1; Thucydides 1.1, 1.21.

[37] *Ti.* 20e, 21b–d, 25e–26c. Broadie 2012, 164–66 stresses this incongruity.

[19] These features of Critias's account render especially questionable his emphatic and repeated claim to be providing 'a true account' and not a made-up story (*Ti.* 20e–21a, 26c–d). There are two main problems. One is that, for the reasons given, and others, Critias's account is most unlikely to be 'true' in a factual, historical sense.[38] Also, it is far from clear that Socrates, at least, is primarily concerned with the question of whether the story is true in this empirical sense. It is surely significant that, a few pages later, Timaeus offers a very different conception of truth. According to this view (which is close to the ideas of Plato's *Republic*), only statements about the intelligible realm (such as the Forms) have any chance of achieving 'truth' in a real sense. Statements about the physical world can only achieve 'likelihood' at best, because they are describing what is only a 'likeness' of intelligible being.[39] Of course, we need not assume that Socrates has quite this idea of truth in mind when putting his request to the interlocutors, though his enthusiastic intervention in response to Timaeus's opening claims about truth is very striking.[40] However, the fact that his summary of the *Republic* is entirely focused on arguments about the social structure that would enable the best kind of communal life (*Ti.* 17c–19a) gives us a clear view of where his intellectual priorities lie. In other words, the kind of 'truth' in which Socrates is primarily interested is that of ideas based

---

[38] There are other troubling features. These include: 1) minor inconsistencies (was Athens founded 9,000 years ago (*Ti.* 23e), or was this the date of the war which destroyed it (*Criti.* 108e)? Is Critias's story based on written records (*Criti.* 113b) or memory (*Ti.* 26b–c)?); 2) the substantial role played by gods in an allegedly historical account (*Ti.* 23d–e, 24c–d; *Criti.* 109b, 113b–114c, 121b–c); 3) the pastiche of Herodotean and Thucydidean historiography, suggesting that this is *pseudo*-history; 4) the precision and profusion of detail (esp. *Criti.* 115c–118e) despite the remoteness of the events and the slender line of transmission of the story. See also Gill 1977, 292–93; Clay 1999.

[39] *Ti.* 28a–29d. Compare *Republic* 508d–511e. On this passage, in the context of Timaeus's cosmology, see Johansen 2004, ch. 3; Broadie 2012, ch. 2. In the context of the Atlantis story, see Gill 1977, 290–91. On the contrast between Timaeus's conception of truth and Critias's, see also Osborne 1996, 183–91.

[40] *Ti.* 29d. This is Socrates' only intervention during Timaeus's exposition and is markedly more enthusiastic than his response to Critias's claim to offer a 'true' account (*Ti.* 26e).

on argument (and centred especially on the question of what is involved in putting the ideal into practice) rather than the factual or empirical 'truth' that is so important for Critias. Critias does not overlook the need for his story to match Socrates's ideas about the ideal state. However, his discussion of the social structure of ancient Athens in the *Timaeus* is quite sweeping, and is not explicitly presented as explaining Athens's success in warfare against Atlantis.[41] So, if Socrates was looking for an account which brought out the 'truth' of his philosophically based claims in the *Republic* about the best kind of state, he has not yet received it. More precisely, Socrates does not clearly have an interlocutor who recognizes this objective – at least not yet.[42]

[20] A third, related, feature of Critias's presentation is a strong focus on Athens, and on his own family (which may be closely linked in his mind). Nothing in Socrates's request prepares us to think that the intended story will centre on Athens, or indeed, any specific state; the ideal state of the *Republic* is a purely conceptual one. However, Critias repeatedly stresses that the story he will tell reflects wonderfully well on Athens, his home city state.[43] His (rather brief and impressionistic) account of the war with Atlantis is strongly evocative of praise of Athens's remarkable defeat (almost single-handedly) of the much larger forces of the Persians at Marathon in 490. The style echoes the kind of eulogy of the city standardly offered in funeral speeches, and parodied in Plato's own *Menexenus*.[44] Critias's focus on Athens is coupled with that on his own family, a highly distinguished and aristocratic one. He stresses the closeness between the famous statesman Solon and his own

---

[41] *Ti.* 24a–d. The social structure is not cited as a factor in the victory over Atlantis in 24e–25d. For instance, Critias does not cite the unity of the ideal state, as contrasted to the disunited character of other states, a factor presented as making the ideal state effective in warfare in *Republic* 422a–423a; however, this contrast does form part of Critias's full version of the story (see [29]).

[42] For this view, see also Broadie 2012, 157–66, 2013, 261–68.

[43] *Ti.* 20e, 21d, 23c, 24d–25c.

[44] *Ti.* 25b–c. For similar characterizations of the role of Athens in the Persian Wars, see Herodotus 7.139.5–6; Plato, *Menexenus* 240d–e (referring to Marathon); Isocrates, *Panegyricus* 52, 66–68. On these links, see also Loraux 1986, 302–03; Otto 1997; Morgan 1998, 104–06. On *Menexenus*, see also Pradeau 1997, 191–205, 2002, 14–42.

grandfather (also named Critias), and the fact that this closeness afforded his grandfather and, in turn, Critias himself privileged access to this remarkable story.[45] As noted earlier, as Critias presents the situation, neither Solon nor anyone in Critias's family had seen fit till this moment to share this story with anyone else, despite his now claiming that it was an event of huge significance in the history of the world, especially, of course, for the Athenians.[46] Critias's partiality of viewpoint is notably different from Socrates's concern with what makes *any* state as good as possible and what actions would illustrate that character (*Ti.* 17b–20b). Critias's standpoint is also in jarring contrast to Timaeus's much more general project, of which Critias is fully aware and which is supposedly linked to his own, to explain 'the origin of the universe and concluding with the nature of human beings' (*Ti.* 27a5–6).

[21] The latter point especially bears on a question noted earlier: the identity of the speaker Critias. We need to be aware that the younger (well-known) Critias (460–403) is likely, at best, to have been a highly ambivalent figure for Plato. Although he was a member of Plato's family (his mother's cousin) and for a while one of Socrates's (many) associates, we are told that he later quarrelled with Socrates and did what he could to harm him. As one of the '30 tyrants' in 404–403, he tried to incriminate Socrates by ordering him to arrest a citizen, Leon, with a view to seizing his property (Socrates ignored the order). He also passed a law prohibiting 'teaching the art of *logoi* (arguments)' which seems to have been primarily directed at Socrates.[47] His earlier association with Critias, and also with Alcibiades, was highly damaging to Socrates's reputation and seems to have been instrumental in leading to his trial and execution in 399.[48] A further relevant point is that, as one of the pro-Spartan junta set up to run Athens after its defeat in the Peloponnesian War, and perhaps its most brutal member, Critias represented an extreme position in the

---

[45] *Ti.* 20e, 21b–d, 25e–26c. See also Tulli 2013, 275–77, who underlines that this family is also Plato's.

[46] See text to n. 37.

[47] Xenophon, *Memorabilia* 1.2.29–31; Plato, *Apology* 32c–d.

[48] Xenophon, *Memorabilia* 1.2.12. Aeschines, *Against Timarchus* 173 shows that this association was still current in 345. See also Broadie 2012, 153–55, 2013, 253–54.

long-standing movement by aristocratic Athenians from the late fifth century onwards to modify or subvert the fully democratic system set up by Pericles.[49] A recurrent theme in this movement, which extended into the mid-fourth century, was that Athens should go back to its 'ancestral (pre-democratic) constitution', which was sometimes identified with the framework set up by Solon, and which provided the basis, with further modifications by Cleisthenes (late sixth century), for the Athenian constitution at the time of the battle of Marathon (490).[50]

[22] Why is all this relevant for the presentation of the Atlantis story? If the speaker 'Critias' is Critias the tyrant, it gives an added (dark) resonance to his evident concern to link himself and his aristocratic family to Solon and to the 'ancestral constitution' associated in his story with primaeval Athens (and Egypt).[51] Since idealization of Marathonic Athens (as distinct from later, more fully democratic, Athens) formed part of this complex of political attitudes,[52] the presentation of the victory of primaeval Athens as a yet more splendid 'pre-Marathon' fits in with this viewpoint. Even if, on chronological grounds, the speaker is taken to be the grandfather of Critias the tyrant, the reputation of the younger Critias

[49] Pericles (*c.* 495–429) is generally seen as completing the movement towards full democracy (by restricting the powers of the Areopagus council in 462), which started with the reforms of Solon (594/593) and Cleisthenes (508). There was a short-lived oligarchic coup in 411, in which power was given to a council of 400.

[50] For example, in the mid-fourth century, Isocrates (436–338) advocated a return to the Solonian (more moderate) form of democracy in *Areopagitus* 7, 15–16, 22–24. However, Solon was a contested figure, and those reviving democracy after the regime of the '30 tyrants' in 404–403 also claimed to be recovering the laws of Solon. See Finley 1971, 1, 11–14; Morgan 1998, 111–14.

[51] The link to Egypt in the Atlantis story (*Ti.* 21e–26e) may form part of this complex of associations since Egypt was famous in the fourth century for the unchanging (conservative) character of its social structure and customs. See Isocrates, *Busiris* 15–16; Plato, *Laws* 656d–657b. See also Morgan 1998, 110, 113.

[52] On the linkage between Athens's victory against the Persians and her constitution at that time, see Isocrates, *Panegyricus* 39–40, 66–68, 78–79, *Panathenaicus* 42–44, 120 (see also Morgan 1998, 105–106). Plato, *Laws* 698b–e links the Athenian constitution with the victory of Marathon (but on this point, see further n. 93). On the Athenian political connotations of the Atlantis story, see also [30–33].

may still colour – or stain – the characterization of Plato's interlocutor, especially since the older man seems to have been little more than a name for most Athenians.[53]

[23] This broader background may be significant for the final topic of this section. There are certain striking nuances in the interchange between Socrates and Critias, following the latter's summary, which, taken with the other points noted, underline the gap between their viewpoints. For one thing, Critias is immensely enthusiastic about the extent to which the story summarized matches Socrates's original request, even though, as I have suggested, he has not – not yet at least – really shown that this is the case. He says at one point, in a comment that might seem rather patronizing, that, by some supernatural chance, Socrates's ideas were not 'off-target' (*apo skopou*) in matching the story that Solon told – which puts things the wrong way round, since his task is to find an equivalent for Socrates's ideas.[54] Secondly, he comments, rather naïvely, that while his childhood memory of Solon's story has become indelibly etched in his mind, he is not sure he can remember everything that Socrates said yesterday (*Ti.* 26b–c). Given that his agreed role is to match Socrates's account of the ideal state with concrete and detailed representation of it, this is not very reassuring. How does Socrates himself respond to Critias's proposal? On the surface, he accepts it positively (26e); but there are some disturbing notes. Socrates starts by commenting that this story is appropriate for the festival of the goddess Athena, but this was not part of his earlier motivation (19b–e), and he may just be underlining Critias's strongly pro-Athenian attitude. Second, he says that the fact that Critias's story is not a 'made-up story but a true account' is 'all important, perhaps' (26e5). The combination of the rather exaggerated 'all important' (*pammega*) with a deflationary 'perhaps' (or 'I suppose', *pou*) may be seen as undercutting Critias's enthusiasm for this point. After all, in the way Socrates set up the original request, there was nothing to indicate that it made any difference to him whether the story was based on fact. The key point was the correspondence between Socrates's political ideal and the (imaginary?) specific actions and words that would bring out the

---

[53] See text to nn. 10–11, 16.

[54] *Ti.* 25e4–5; see also 26a, d. See the commentary on 25e4–5.

character of this ideal. So, in spite of the surface harmony on this point, Socrates may well feel that, so far, there has been only limited progress in taking his project forward.[55]

Critias's full version

[24] After the first surprise, Critias's offer to provide a 'true account', comes the second, the news that Critias's story will be preceded by Timaeus's exposition of the origin of the universe and of human beings (*Ti.* 27a). Despite its unexpectedness, Socrates greets this with enthusiasm and is even more positive in his response to Timaeus's opening comments, on the truth status of his account – in contrast to his more qualified response to Critias's offer of a 'true account'.[56] This indicates that, in spite of the rather indirect relationship of Timaeus's topic to Socrates's original request, Timaeus plays a crucial role in responding to it.[57] Underlying Socrates's request, I suggested earlier, is the desire to explore the idea of putting the ideal into practice, rather than simply working towards knowledge of the ideal. A key means of doing this is finding appropriate structures, of various kinds, in which the ideal can be embodied. This explains the fact that Socrates's summary of the *Republic*'s ideal state focused on social and political structure rather than on the philosopher-rulers' progress towards ideal knowledge; and his subsequent request was to have the character of that political structure expressed in specific actions such as war and diplomacy. Timaeus's cosmological account (*Ti.* 27c–92c), not included in this edition, can be seen as undertaking this

---

[55] For these points, see also Johansen 2004, 45–46 (on 26e4–5); Broadie 2012, 157–66, 2013, 262–68. On negative elements in Plato's characterization of Critias in the *Timaeus-Critias*, see also Welliver 1977.

[56] *Ti.* 27b7–9, 29d4–6; contrast 26e2–5.

[57] It is perhaps significant that Socrates's opening conversation, including the summary of the ideal state of the *Republic*, is conducted with Timaeus, whose approval is requested by Socrates before Critias is invited to outline his story (*Ti.* 20d4–5). Also, Socrates's praise for Timaeus's intellectual qualities is much warmer than for the other two men (20a).

task on a broad cosmic and human level. He aims to chart the structures by which the ideal (the model adopted by the divine craftsman and his assistant gods) is translated into concrete form, and embodied in the universe as a whole and in the human race, conceived as a psychophysical whole, in particular.[58]

[25] Because of the way in which the series of speeches has been arranged, Timaeus's cosmological account falls between Critias's summary of his story and his full version (as far as this gets), rather than following the latter, which one might have expected. This may encourage us to read Critias's full version with the creation account in mind, especially if we are reading the whole work in sequence.[59] In broad terms, Critias's full version simply develops the theme outlined earlier, describing the contrasting states, primaeval Athens and Atlantis, which are to go to war (*Ti.* 24e–25c), and thus meeting Socrates's request (19b–c). However, there are a number of ways in which Critias's full version differs in approach and implications from the earlier summary, making it a much more effective response to Socrates's request. For one thing, Critias brings out here the contrasting social and political structures of the two states, which underlie their subsequent success or failure in warfare, and also shows how one of the two states, primaeval Athens, matches Socrates's summary of the institutions of the ideal state. Also, Critias broadens the scope of his treatment to include elements not covered in Socrates's summary. These centre on the natural environment and topographical layout of the two cities, and the way in which these were used or modified, in the case of Atlantis, by the inhabitants. Critias also indicates how the use of natural resources and the city's environment are linked with the political character of the two states and, in Atlantis, with the evolution and change of that character. In these respects, Critias's full version seems to pick up some of the breadth of perspective of Timaeus's account, which locates humanity in the context

---

[58] For similar suggestions about the relationship between the themes of Timaeus's cosmology and the Atlantis story, see Pradeau 1997, 314–17, 2002, 114–17; Broadie 2001, 22–26, 2012, 123–26; Johansen 2004, 16–23.

[59] On the significance of the position of Timaeus's account, see also Johansen 2004, 9–23.

of nature as a whole.[60] It also responds more effectively to the underlying aim of Socrates's request, to see the ideal and its opposite translated into embodied structures. As for the problematic features of Critias's presentation of the story noted in the preceding section, these have either disappeared or become incorporated into a more credible and coherent analysis. For instance, the (inappropriate) stress on the story's factual 'truth' has gone, along with the emphasis on its preservation by Critias's family. The historiographical interest in reconstructing the past from available evidence is retained, but presented more plausibly. The eulogistic characterization of Athens as victorious has been replaced by analysis of its salient political and environmental features, and a more neutral, or at least fair-minded, contrast with those of its opponent. Critias also draws on specific features of historical Athens, drawn from different periods, as well as those of other states, especially as described by Herodotus. The significance of these allusions for gauging the character and objectives of Plato's Atlantis story as a whole is considered later. However, taken as a whole, I think Critias's full version takes what I called the 'quasi-dialectical exploration' of Plato's main theme much further than his first response.[61]

[26] Critias's initial reaction to Timaeus's creation account is not, in fact, very promising. This consists of a – rather unconvincing – plea for his audience's indulgence in judging his speech because of the greater difficulty in providing a convincing likeness of human action than of the gods' work in creating the universe. The plea is still less convincing because Critias is concerned only with making his representation seem lifelike to his audience, whereas Timaeus's comments (to which he refers) centre on the much more profound question of the truth status of an account of the physical world.[62] However, when Critias moves into his

---

[60] On this point, see Pradeau 1997, part 3 (235–313), 2002, 115–19.

[61] On these differences in the characterization of Critias, and of his contributions, in the two dialogues, see also Broadie 2012, 146–53, esp. 148.

[62] See *Criti.* 106c–108a, referring back to *Ti.* 27e–29d (on the contrast with Timaeus's comments, see Gill 1977, 288–91, Osborne 1996, 187–91); also [37–38]. Socrates's response to Critias's plea (*Criti.* 108b3–7), reiterating his enthusiastic praise of Timaeus's opening comments (*Ti.* 29d4–6), is not wholly reassuring.

actual exposition, things improve. In the first instance, we find a more thoughtful or credible treatment of motifs that also figured in his earlier summary. As in the summary, we find the traditional Greek idea of specific gods as patrons or founders of specific states.[63] However, we also find here two modifications of tradition. First, it is claimed that the distribution of states to specific patron gods did not involve strife or contention, contradicting certain well-known myths to that effect.[64] Second, gods are presented as divine shepherds, who guide their human flocks by persuasion rather than force, that is, by influencing their minds or characters. This provides a more psychologically credible version of the idea of gods founding states.[65] Next, Critias returns to the topic of trying to recover evidence of the distant past, despite discontinuities in civilization caused by natural disasters. This theme is also treated in a more considered and plausible way than in Critias's earlier claim to have recovered, via Egypt and Solon, reports of Athens of over 9,000 years before. Critias refers to observations and inferences that could indeed be taken as reliable indicators of past events, such as names that are no longer in use and evidence of soil erosion, deforestation and the drying up of streams.[66] Although the methodology involved is different from that of Timaeus's analysis of the universe and the human race, it represents a parallel form of investigation of nature.

[27] If we move to the main subject, the comparative account of the two competing states, we find broadly the same topics being dealt with in

---

[63] See *Ti.* 21e, 23d–e, 24c; *Criti.* 109b–c, 113b–114c, 121a.

[64] *Criti.* 109b1–6, 113bb7–c4. The contrast is with the famous myth that there was a contest between Athena and Poseidon for possession of Attica.

[65] *Criti.* 109c1–4, c6–d2. See also 121a8–b1, referring to inherited divine character, which is progressively weakened over several generations. On this idea of divine control, compared with other Platonic uses of the image of gods as divine shepherds, see Gill 1979a, 154–61.

[66] *Criti.* 109d–110b, 110d–111d, 112d. Timaeus's earlier comments on natural catastrophes and discontinuity in civilization, and on comparative social structure (*Ti.* 22a–23c, 24a–d), also indicate Platonic interest in prehistory (and history) in his later works (see Gill 1977, 299–303, 1979a, 161–62). However, the value of this is qualified by Timaeus's incredible claim to provide accurate details about a very remote time period (see also [18]).

each state, though not in quite the same order or fullness. In the case of Athens, the historiographical introduction just noted includes reference to the original inhabitants, or at least first rulers (*Criti.* 109e–110c); it also leads into the account of the natural environment of the city and the resources it offers (110d–111e). Then follows a description of the city, which is linked with the organization of the groups in the community and their way of life (at least, that of the guardian class of about 20,000 men and women, 111e–112e). In the case of Atlantis also, after an excursus on the use of Greek names (113a–b), we are told about the original inhabitants or rulers, stemming from a liaison between the god Poseidon and a human woman, combined with an account of the territory and its (very rich) natural resources (113c–115b). Then we have a long description, taking up much of the rest of the text, of the way the royal family transformed the original layout of the island, and created an elaborate network of canals, roads and bridges, as well as splendid temples (115c–117e). This description focuses on the capital and the civic structures built by the royal family; it is followed by an account of the surrounding natural environment, and of the way this too was transformed by a network of canals (118a–e). Critias then enumerates the huge military resources of Atlantis (118e–119b), and recounts in detail an elaborate ritual designed to avoid internal conflict between the ten kings of Atlantis (119c–120d). He ends by reporting that, after many generations of stability and virtuous behaviour , there was a sharp moral decline among the Atlanteans, leading to divine intervention by Zeus (120e–121c).[67] This intervention would, presumably, have led to Atlantis's invasion of Europe and their defeat by primaeval Athens just before both were destroyed by natural disasters (*Ti.* 24e–25d). However, the account breaks off just as Zeus is about to begin his speech on the subject to the other gods.

[28] Several features bring out how this version responds more fully and directly to Socrates's original request, and its underlying point, while also being indirectly informed by Timaeus's creation story. Critias's description includes an account of the social and governmental structure of the two states, presented in a way that invites comparison between

---

[67] On the structure of themes, see Pradeau 1997, 328–29, 2002, 122, 125–26.

them.[68] He also shows, in each case, how the sociopolitical structure is closely linked with the natural and built environment, and with the use of resources.[69] The description meets Socrates's request by locating the large guardian (or auxiliary) class of the *Republic*[70] in an appropriate civic and natural context, and by contrasting the community centred on this class with its rival on a series of key points. More generally, the account not only presents specific kinds of embodied social structures but also provides the materials, at least, for analysis of what constitutes an effective community or its opposite. By contrast with the highly eulogistic characterization of primaeval Athens in his summary (*Ti.* 20e–21a, 24d–25c), Critias's description is largely even-handed in considering the same topics in each case and in the language used, at least until the final paragraphs on the moral decline of Atlantis (*Criti.* 120e–121c). However, the account conveys a sharp contrast on three major points, which carry broader implications about what makes a community effective or not.

[29] One is the contrast between unity and (structured) plurality or complexity. Primaeval Athens is highly unified especially in its large, socially cohesive, guardian class; and this is mirrored in the uniform layout of the city (centred on an enlarged Acropolis) and the surrounding area. Atlantis constitutes a contrasting framework of structured complexity in every respect: the ruling families, the layout of the capital city and its temples, and the surrounding countryside.[71] The plurality is structured and not chaotic or random: a recurrent pattern is the alternation of even and odd numbers, and circular and straight lines.[72] However, this plurality contains scope for internal division (as indicated in the ritual and legal arrangements of the ruling family), and for loss of central

---

[68] *Criti.* 110b–d, 11e, 112b–c, d (Athens); 114a–e, 119c–120d (Atlantis).

[69] *Criti.* 110d–111a, 111d–112d (Athens); 113c–114a, 114d–118e (Atlantis). On this dimension of the story, see Pradeau 1997, 235–83.

[70] See Socrates's summary of the main features of this class in *Ti.* 17c–19a; and see the commentary for corresponding passages in the *Republic*. The Atlantis story, like the summary, leaves out the distinction between 'auxiliaries' and 'guardians' in the full sense, who will go on to become philosopher-rulers (*Republic* 413d–414a).

[71] Contrast *Criti.* 111e–112e with 113c–114c, 115c–119b.

[72] See for example 113d6–8, 115e2–116a1, 117d6–e4 (rings), 118a6–7, c2–3 (oblong or rectangle), 119b, 119d1–4 (making explicit the odd-even alternation).

control or unified communal action and way of life.[73] A related contrast is between stability and expansion or change generally. Athens, we are told, maintained unchanged its governmental structure (including the number of guardians), its urban and rural layout. In Atlantis, by contrast, the description emphasizes the radical transformation of the original layout of the central island, the surrounding islands and the countryside on the main island, especially through large-scale engineering and architectural projects.[74] These contrasts in turn underlie the final one, which is framed in terms of lifestyle, attitudes and ethical character. In Athens, Critias stresses the moderation of the guardians' lifestyle and their avoidance of gold and silver (110d, 112c, e). In Atlantis, he emphasizes the vastness of the natural and mineral resources, and the extravagant splendour of the royal palaces and temples (114d–118e). In the final paragraphs, he explains that, though they had for some time borne with moderation the weight of this great wealth, they became increasingly less able to do so as the original divine element in their character was reduced over successive generations (120e–121c). These interrelated contrasts give specific content to the sociopolitical contrast originally requested by Socrates; they also carry broader implications about what makes for unified, stable and virtuous communal life and its opposite.[75]

[30] The contrast between the two states is also conveyed by a rather complex web of allusions to fifth-century Greek history. Critias's summary of the story alludes, unmistakably, to Athens's defeat of Persia at Marathon, and this allusion persists in the full version. The large and cohesive guardian class in primaeval Athens recalls the unified hoplite army that inflicted this defeat on a much larger, but less united, opponent, and perhaps also evokes the political structure of Athens in the late sixth or early fifth century.[76] Atlantis, by contrast, has many connotations of

---

[73] 119c–d, e, 120a, c–d, 120e5–6; these passages imply the scope for internal division which may form part of the moral decline sketched in 121b.

[74] Contrast 111e–112e with 114d–118e.

[75] On these contrasts, see Brisson 1970; Pradeau 1997, 235–306 (esp. 277–83, on this mode of description as a form of implicit political theory); Pradeau 2002, 121–22, 127–31.

[76] Primaeval Athens could be seen as a version of the 'hoplite democracy' or mixed

the large-scale, politically more diffuse, Persian empire, including great wealth, large-scale engineering projects, temple and civic architecture and massive armed forces.[77] On the other hand, primaeval Athens has also been transformed into a state that is more like Sparta, with a large military ruling class, and a land-based power, with no naval force.[78] At the same time, Atlantis is strongly evocative of Athens in the later fifth century (rather than at the time of Marathon). Its engineering projects evoke the construction of the Peiraeus in the mid-fifth century, with elaborate town planning, harbours and Long Walls, while its temple architecture echoes features of the Parthenon (dedicated in 438) (115c–117a). Atlantis, like later fifth-century Athens, is predominantly a sea-based power, and its engineering projects, as in Athens, serve to enhance its role as a maritime rather than a land-based power (117d–e). The echoes in Atlantis of Athenian maritime expansion (prefiguring Atlantis's invasion of Europe and Asia) may also remind readers of the disastrous Sicilian expedition of 415–413 that hastened the end of Athens's military hegemony and her eventual defeat (in 404). The fact that Hermocrates, the main Syracusan architect of Athens's defeat in the Sicilian expedition, is standing waiting to play his part in telling the story, reinforces this echo.[79]

[31] These various allusions to historical settings, and especially to Athenian history, can certainly be seen as complementing the central

---

constitution (combining oligarchy and democracy) set up by Solon in 594/593. In fact, this was already modified by the time of Marathon (490) by Cleisthenes (508); but the modification was sometimes ignored by those who linked the victory at Marathon and the 'ancestral constitution'. Plato's *Laws* characterizes the Athenian constitution as 'ancient' and based on four property classes (698a–b), that is, the Solonian constitution (see also Morrow 1960, 83–84). On echoes of Marathon in the Atlantis story and on the idealization of the 'ancestral constitution', see nn. 44, 50. On Plato's political attitudes, see [34].

[77] *Criti.* 115c–117a, 118a–119b. See the commentary for allusions to the Persian empire.

[78] Primaeval Athens is also presented as having much more land than historical Athens (lost by soil erosion and other natural processes) and in this respect too as more of a land-based power (*Criti.* 110d–111d, 112a, d). The absence of any mention of maritime or naval resources or power in primaeval Athens is in sharp contrast to those highlighted in Atlantis (115c–116a, 117d–e).

[79] On these features of the story, see Gill 1977, 294–98.

contrast between the two states as regards unity, stability, virtue and their opposites. Should we also infer that the strong echoes of Athenian history carry more pointed, and localized, political messages? In fact, a series of suggestions along these lines have been made by scholars. It has been suggested that the Atlantis story is, in a rather strong sense, *about* fifth-century Athens. For instance, the contrast built into the story between early Marathonic Athens and later fifth-century (maritime, imperialistic) Athens has been seen as implying a negative view about the development from one to the other and a preference for the earlier Athens.[80] It is also sometimes thought that the story was designed to have a special message for Athenians in the mid-fourth century, when we generally suppose the *Timaeus-Critias* was written. The message is that fourth-century Athens should not repeat the mistakes of the fifth century and seek to restore her maritime empire, as she had started to do earlier in the fourth century.[81] The story is also sometimes seen as implying a politically conservative attitude, within the spectrum of Athenian views current in the mid-fourth century. The idealization of Marathonic (rather than Periclean Athens) can be seen as linked with a preference for the 'ancestral constitution', which was in operation prior to the full-scale democratic structure of later fifth-century Athens. In effect, then, the message of the Atlantis story would be to go back to this kind of political structure as well as to avoid the maritime expansion linked with Athens's democratic constitution in the late fifth century.[82] Attributing these messages to Critias would be especially apposite if he were taken to be Critias the tyrant or even if his characterization is coloured by that link. As well as being an extreme conservative, his role as a member of the pro-Sparta junta (the 30 tyrants) set up after the defeat of Athens in the Peloponnesian War associates him with many of these attitudes.

[32] These views have been strongly argued by a number of scholars. However, if one accepts the main thrust of my reading of the Atlantis

---

[80] This view was presented in an influential article by Vidal-Naquet (1964, reprinted 1981); it was anticipated by Bartoli 1779 (on which see Pradeau 1997, 71–82, Vidal-Naquet 2007, 92–95). See also Pradeau 1997, 102–10, 190–224.

[81] See Pradeau 1997, 224–29, 2002, 123–24; Morgan 1998, 114–18.

[82] See Pradeau 1997, 190–206; Morgan 1998, 108–14. See also nn. 44, 50.

story here, one would be cautious about the idea that Plato's message is as strongly Athens-centred as is implied in these interpretations. I have suggested that the sequence of speeches implies a kind of quasi-dialectical exploration of the subject, in which there is a movement towards an increasingly direct and thoughtful response to Socrates's original request and its underlying concern with correlating the ideal and the practical through description of embodied structures. I have also maintained that Critias's first response fell short of meeting this request, in part because it claimed to provide a historically factual account, when this was not asked for, and also because it was strongly centred on Athens as well as on the preservation of the story in Critias's own (highly aristocratic) family. I have also taken the view that the full version cuts deeper in part because it reflects a more analytic approach, which views the two states in a more even-handed way, and which, by implication at least, identifies general features which enable states in general to function in a unified, stable and virtuous way.[83] Although I accept fully that the characterization of these two states is also enhanced by allusions to fifth-century Greek history, especially that of Athens, I do not think that the full version, at least, should be read as being *about Athens* in a strong sense. For the same reason, I am cautious about the view that the story should be seen as having a special message about the direction of policy in the mid-fourth century (opposing the revival of the Athenian empire) or that the story should be seen as a political 'pamphlet'.[84] The localization of focus implied in these suggestions goes in the opposite direction to the kind of reading of the sequence of speeches I have offered here.[85]

[33] What about the idea that Critias is an appropriate mouthpiece for a narrative which has these connotations, given his (extreme) political conservatism? This is more plausible, I think. Critias's initial summary implies admiration for Marathonic Athens (*Ti.* 25a–c). Such admiration naturally goes along with a negative view of Athenian maritime expansion (seen as linked with full-scale democracy) and an emphasis on the disastrous outcome of Athens's maritime expansion – that is, with the

---

[83] See [10, 19–20, 25, 28–29].

[84] For this view see the works referenced in n. 81.

[85] For a similar approach to that taken here, see Broadie 2012, 140–46.

historical connotations of Critias's full version of the story.[86] These features help to explain why Plato chose Critias the tyrant as speaker (or at least as a symbolic presence, if the speaker is his grandfather) along with Hermocrates.[87] However, this linkage needs to be qualified, I think, in two ways. One is that, in the full version of the story, the Athenian connotations, and the implied oligarchic attitudes, are submerged in, and subordinate to, a more broadly conceived contrast between two types of state, and one that implies a more analytic and reflective approach. To this extent, we can say that Critias's mind has been changed by the intervening cosmology of Timaeus, thus enabling what I am calling the quasi-dialectical progress of the dialogue.[88] If this is so, it helps to counter an objection sometimes made to the idea that Plato's 'Critias' can be taken to be the tyrant, namely the improbability of Plato using a figure with such negative connotations as the mouthpiece for his story.[89] The 'Critias' who delivers the full version of the Atlantis story no longer presents (to the same extent, at least) the problematic features evident in the initial summary, namely a strongly Athens-centred viewpoint and a narrowly conservative outlook.

[34] This suggestion, however, raises a further question. It is often assumed that Plato himself was a political conservative in terms of Athenian attitudes. This assumption is based partly on the fact that his

---

[86] In fifth-century Athens (though not of course Atlantis), maritime expansion was associated with democracy because democratic leaders such as Themistocles and Pericles promoted this expansion and because the Athenian people (*dēmos*) played a key role in providing rowers in the navy. The Sicilian expedition (415–413), which hastened Athens's defeat in the Peloponnesian War, was widely seen as a disastrous decision by the Athenian popular assembly. The linkage between maritime expansion and Athenian democracy is underlined by the pseudo-Xenophontic *Constitution of the Athenians*, the 'Old Oligarch' (on which, see Marr and Rhodes 2008). For comparison between the approaches of this political 'pamphlet' and the Atlantis story, see Pradeau 1997, 211–24.

[87] Critias, as one of the '30 tyrants', is said to have performed the symbolic (oligarchic) act of turning the dais (*bēma*) in the Pnyx to face the land instead of the sea (Plutarch, *Themistocles* 19), reflecting the 'land versus sea' ideology of this period.

[88] For the view that there is a significant difference between the approaches of the speaker Critias in the *Timaeus* and the *Critias*, see Broadie 2012, 148 and [25].

[89] See Nesselrath 2006, 49–50.

background was aristocratic (he was from the same family as Critias), and that the dialogues include criticism of democracy as a system as well as of the maritime imperial expansion of late fifth-century Athens.[90] However, we should not be too quick, I think, to identify Plato as a conservative for these reasons. There is the obvious problem, applying to Plato's views on all topics, that his writings are all in dialogue form and that the main speakers and their interlocutors are given their own specific projects and viewpoints.[91] The nature of Plato's direct involvement in the politics of the fourth century is quite murky; and there is no scholarly consensus about whether the key document (the Seventh Letter) is authentic.[92] If one judges Plato's approach not just by specific passages culled from specific dialogues, but by the overall approach reflected in the political dialogues, the impression is not that of someone whose views can be readily identified with a specific, localized, standpoint. The *Republic*, *Statesman* and *Laws* all advocate views and ideals which are quite different from those of specific political standpoints in Athens or in Greek thought generally. Plato, one might say, deliberately situates himself at an oblique angle to typical political attitudes, including that of Athenian conservatism.[93]

---

[90] See, for example, Plato's criticism of the democratic state (and corresponding personality type) as part of the review of these types (*Republic* VIII 555–561) and also of oligarchy (*Republic* VIII 551–554); his criticism of Athenian democratic leaders for fostering the growth of Athens's maritime empire, walls, dockyards and public buildings (*Gorgias* 515c–519a); criticism of Athenian democracy for deviating from the moderate version of the constitution current at the time of the Persian Wars (*Laws* 698b–701e). The view of Plato as anti-democratic (and totalitarian) was proposed influentially by Popper 1961.

[91] On this point see [14].

[92] See n. 24.

[93] For a thoughtful treatment of Plato's political theory, which brings out this dimension, see Schofield 2006. I have mainly in mind the broad lines of Plato's approach; but this tendency may also extend to smaller points. For example, in his discussion of the factors underlying Athens's victory in the Persian Wars, while noting briefly its constitution at that time (698b), the Athenian Stranger gives more attention to the factors of hope and fear, including 'fear' of the laws of the state (698b–699d) (see Schofield 2013, 293–96; Broadie 2012, 141, n. 49). So, although Plato seems, at first glance, to be making the standard conservative linkage between Marathon and the 'ancestral constitution', his line of thought, when closely examined, is rather different.

The more thoughtful, analytic approach to political structures which is implied in Critias's full account, in partial contrast to his initial summary, is thus fully representative of Platonic political thought in general.

[35] The last point may go some way towards explaining why Plato, unexpectedly, breaks off his story in mid-sentence. If Critias's opening description of the two competing states in 108–210 has already gone quite a long way towards meeting Socrates's original request and its underlying project (that of finding structures that embody the ideal in specific form), one can see why Plato's motivation for completing the story may have waned. It is, of course, striking that the text breaks off exactly when Critias approaches the project as Socrates first outlined it: the representation of war and diplomacy between the ideal state and its opponent and other states.[94] However, it is at this moment that the shift to a more dramatic and narrative mode would have needed to take place, and, presumably, on a large scale comparable at least with Timaeus's creation story. Plato may have come to think that Critias's description of the two states, with its clear implications about what makes for excellent communal life or its opposite, was as far as he now wished to go within the framework of the Atlantis story. It is probably also relevant that in the *Laws*, which seems to have been Plato's next (and last) major piece of writing, there are many points of contact with the underlying themes of the Atlantis story, especially as presented in Critias's full account. In the *Laws*, there is a focus on the sociopolitical structure in which the best (or best possible) ideal could be embodied, rather than on the progress towards knowledge of the ideal (the theme of *Republic* Books VI–VII, omitted from Socrates's summary in the *Timaeus*). Here too the discussion is extended from social and political structures to material ones, including the influence of natural environment (the moral dangers of proximity to the sea), the use of natural resources and the physical organization of the state.[95] *Laws* Book III offers a reflective history of

---

See also Rowe forthcoming chapter 'Plato on Equality and Democracy', which challenges the common view of Plato as anti-democratic.

[94] See *Ti.* 19b–c and *Criti.* 120d–121c.

[95] See, for example, *Laws* 704a–707a (moral dangers of proximity to sea). On this aspect of *Laws*, see Morrow 1960, ch. 4; Pradeau 2002, 148–51.

political forms. This includes a reconstruction of the distant past, which takes account of discontinuities of civilization, as well as considering the strengths and weaknesses of the states whose history is evoked in the Atlantis story (Athens, Sparta and Persia).[96] The *Laws*, however, takes the form of a sustained, discursive discussion about the best (or best achievable) state and about what promotes or hinders this,[97] though it is couched in unusually down-to-earth language, by Platonic standards.[98] It is possible that this is the idiom in which Plato decided to couch the themes that he would have had to address if he had completed the Atlantis story as planned. The *Laws* also includes imagined speech-making of different types (for instance, the address by the founder to the colonists of the ideal state and the preludes to the laws framed for the moral education of the citizens).[99] To this extent, the *Laws* contains imagined discourse of the kind Plato would have had to compose for the continuation of the Atlantis story.[100] But he may have decided it was more worthwhile to do so as part of the philosophical discussion he sets up in the *Laws*, explicitly devoted to questions of political theory, than in the imagined drama and narrative of the Atlantis story.[101]

The Atlantis story as myth

[36] I close this reading of the Atlantis story by considering, though briefly, the overall character of the story from another standpoint. I have discussed it with reference to the ideas it contains or implies and its

---

[96] See Gill 1977, 301–02.

[97] *Laws* 702a–b, 739a–e.

[98] On the form of the dialogue in *Laws*, see Gill 2003.

[99] *Laws* 716a–718c, 723c–724b, 726a–734e.

[100] See *Ti.* 19c7–8, e1–2, 6–8 for the role of speeches, as well as appropriate actions, in the story that Socrates requests.

[101] For other versions of this suggestion, see Nesselrath 2006, 39–40; for *Laws* as the (planned) continuation of the Atlantis story, see Naddaf 1994, 190, 202–09. For an alternative explanation of why the story breaks off at this point – Critias, assumed to be the tyrant, is not equal to telling this story in full form properly – see Johansen 2004, 196–97.

historical allusions. However, is it also, or alternatively, to be taken as a myth, of a traditional or Platonic kind?[102]

[37] The Atlantis story contains a number of features we normally regard as typical of Greek myths, such as the divine foundation of states and divine intervention.[103] There are also obvious allusions to a number of well-known Greek myths, notably that of Atlas, and Zeus's punishment of the Titans, including Atlas, along with the gardens of the Hesperides and Homer's Phaeacia.[104] The main effect of these mythical touches is to underline that the story is not factually true, as Critias maintains (*Ti.* 20d), though I think this is already clear on other grounds.[105] However, more suggestive for gauging the character of the story is the question of how it relates to Plato's discussion of poetry ('poetry' meaning, in effect, representational literature)[106] in the *Republic*, and to his own use of narratives for philosophical purposes, which we call his 'myths'. A key theme of Socrates's critique of poetry in *Republic* X is that poets imitate the external appearance of things, including human actions in politics and warfare, without having the basis required for doing this, namely expertise in these subjects, demonstrated independently of their compositions.[107] The start

---

[102] Two ideas not explored in this short section are: 1) that the Atlantis story should be seen as a 'noble lie' (see *Republic* 382a–d, 414b–415d), or 'charter-myth' supporting the ideal state of the *Republic*, or reinforcing the idea that fourth-century Athens should return to its 'ancestral constitution'); and 2) that the Atlantis story is an early experiment in the genre of (self-conscious) fiction. For discussion of these ideas, on 1): see Gill 1993, 52–54, 64–66; Morgan 1998, 103–08, 2000, 264–71; and (critical of this idea) Broadie 2012, 142–45; on 2), see Gill 1979b, 1993, 63–66.

[103] See [26].

[104] Atlas and the punishment of the Titans (Hesiod, *Theogony* 506–735; see *Ti.* 24e, 25d, *Criti.* 121b–c.); Garden of the Hesperides and Homer's Phaeacia (*Theogony* 211–17, Homer, *Odyssey* 7.112–132; see *Criti.* 115a–c, 118e). On the Atlantis story and traditional Greek myths, see Fredericks 1978.

[105] See [18] and n. 38.

[106] At this stage of Greek culture, the main established genres of representational or 'imitative' literature were poetic, especially Homeric epic and tragedy or comedy; prose fiction only emerged in the later Hellenistic and Roman periods.

[107] *Republic* 598d–603b. See also Gill 1993, 47–51. On Plato on poetry, see further Ferrari 1989.

of the *Timaeus* echoes this critique, identifying Socrates's interlocutors as the kind of people, with expertise and experience in politics and philosophy, who have the ability to provide the kind of representation Socrates has in view, unlike most poets and sophists (*Ti.* 19b–20b). Critias's characterization of his task, at the start of the *Critias*, also seems to evoke this critique of imitative poetry. However, in sharp contrast, Critias's comments make him seem like the kind of poet criticized by Socrates in *Republic* X. He sounds like someone who is preoccupied with giving a convincing surface appearance of human action in politics and warfare rather than being concerned with the question of whether he has the requisite knowledge of his subject matter.[108]

[38] I focus first on the implications of the first passage and then on those of the second. Socrates's request for knowledge-based imitation at the start of the *Timaeus* does not only evoke the critique of mimetic poetry in *Republic* Book X. It also recalls Socrates's requirements for cultural training (*mousikē*), including poetic representation, in the early education of guardians in the ideal state. Socrates stipulates that this should express true norms of virtuous character and action.[109] A related passage, in *Republic* Book VI, suggests that the philosopher-rulers of the ideal state should act like (knowledge-based) imitative artists, looking both at ideal models (the Forms of justice, moderation and so on) and the raw material (human character and action) in which these ideals can be realized.[110] Also, central to Timaeus's cosmological account is the idea of a divine craftsman shaping the universe as a whole and, as far as possible, the human race, in the light of an ideal model.[111] These passages, taken together with Socrates's opening request, may provide the

---

[108] See *Criti.* 106c–108a, esp. 107b5–e3; and compare *Republic* 598b–c. The comments also evoke the contrast between the imitator who is only concerned with appearances and the one who aims at capturing the true lineaments of his subject (*Sophist* 235e–236c). See Gill 1977, 288–89, 1979b, 73–74.

[109] *Republic* 398a–402c. Socrates's summary of *Republic* Books II–V notes briefly this phase of the educational programme at *Ti.* 18a9–10; on this phase, see Gill 1993, 42–44, 1996b, 267–71.

[110] *Republic* 500c–501c, also 499a–c.

[111] *Ti.* 27d–29a, 41a–42e.

best indication of the kind of representation which Plato has in mind in conceiving his Atlantis story. This is planned to be a story which rests on genuine understanding of its subject matter (the character and basis of the ideal state and its opposite), and which conveys the kind of actions and words in which this character would plausibly be expressed. Initially, and judging from his summary of the story (*Ti.* 20d–25d), it seems that Plato's narrator Critias is unlikely to grasp or carry out this project effectively, despite his confidence in doing so. As underlined earlier, his initial presentation of the story focuses on features (the alleged factual truth of the story, eulogy of Athens and the importance of Critias's own family as a vehicle for the transmission of the story) which seem very far from Socrates's concerns.[112] Also, Critias's focus on surface mimetic skill at the start of the *Critias* is rather troubling, and stands in pointed contrast to the (much more profound) subsequent comments of Timaeus about the epistemological status of his enterprise.[113] However, Critias's comments here are perhaps best taken as a throwback to his characterization in the *Timaeus*, which indicates the presence of *amour propre* (pride in his own family and city), uncritical self-confidence (regarding the status of his story) and intellectual superficiality.[114] By contrast, when Critias gets into the story itself, at least as far as the description of the two states, he seems to respond more fully to the spirit of Socrates's request, and is perhaps inspired by the high-level analysis and breadth of viewpoint in Timaeus's speech. So, his full version can be seen as presenting substantive and well-judged claims about what constitutes a good state and its opposite, though couched in terms of the characterization of imagined city states and their physical environments.[115] Thus, we can see the Atlantis story, at least in its full version, as meeting Platonic conditions of knowledge-based representational composition.

[112] See [19–20, 23].

[113] See text to n. 62.

[114] See works referenced in n. 112.

[115] See [28–29]. On the echo of *Republic* X, and for the idea that the *Timaeus-Critias* is designed to provide, by contrast, knowledge-based 'imitation' (in spite of the implausibility of Critias's claim to provide a 'true story'), see also Johansen 2004, 32–47.

[39] In these respects, the Atlantis story is in line with Plato's general use of myths in his dialogues. These Platonic myths cover a wide variety of topics, including life after death, cosmic world views or cycles of change, the nature of the psyche (or soul) and the foundations of ethical life in human societies.[116] Although scholars have sometimes suggested that Plato uses myth when rational argument has exhausted its scope,[117] a more convincing view is that Plato uses myths as an alternative means of carrying forward philosophical enquiry and speculation.[118] As I have suggested, the Atlantis story plays a quasi-dialectical role in leading us gradually towards – at least some way towards – a better understanding of its subject, the nature of the ideal state and its opposite. Although stories and exposition are used in the *Timaeus-Critias*, rather than, or in conjunction with, dialogic interchange, the overall aim is the same as Plato's standard method of dialectical argument.

Reception

[40] Given Plato's complex and ambiguous presentation of the Atlantis story, it is unsurprising that it has produced a wide range of reactions, in antiquity and in more recent times. Our evidence for ancient responses is actually quite limited.[119] In fact, the first surviving ancient commentary is very late, that of the Neoplatonist thinker Proclus (fifth century AD), who discusses the story in his treatment of the *Timaeus*. Proclus outlines some previous ancient philosophical readings as well as offering his own.

---

[116] On life after death see Gorgias 523a–526d; *Phaedo* 107c–108c, 113d–114e; *Republic* 614b–621d. On cosmic world views or cycles see *Phaedo* 108c–113c; *Statesman* 269c–274e. On the nature of psyche see *Phaedrus* 244a–257a. On the foundations of human ethical life see *Protagoras* 320d–322d.

[117] This is often suggested in connection with the myth in *Phaedo* 107c–113c, which comes after a long series of arguments for the immortality of the soul.

[118] For this view, see Gill 1993, 51–66; Rowe 1999, 263–64, 278. On Plato's myths in general, see Morgan 2000, chs 5–9, esp. 281–89, on the relationship between myth and *logos* (argument or reason) in Plato.

[119] On ancient reception, see Ramage 1978b, 20–27; Vidal-Naquet 2007, ch. 2; Tarrant 2007, 60–84. See also the résumé of ancient comments in Pradeau 1997, 330.

In addition, we have some brief comments about Atlantis by ancient geographers, though these do not seem to be based on close reading of Plato's story. None of the evidence we have suggests that anyone else had privileged access to Plato's motives; and the ancient comments seem to be based, largely or wholly, on Plato's text, rather than on a range of sources. So it seems that in antiquity people were in much the same position as we are in terms of making sense of the story.

[41] What range of interpretations do we find? The geographer Strabo (*c.* 64 BC–AD 21) records a comment: 'He who invented it obliterated it like the poet in the case of his Achaean wall'. This was applied both to an incident in the Trojan War in Homer's *Iliad* and to Plato's Atlantis story, referring to the fact that Atlantis was eventually submerged. Although the evidence is not unequivocal, it looks as though Aristotle (384–322), Plato's long-time pupil, applied the line both to Homer and the Atlantis story, thus expressing scepticism about the historical status of the latter. Aristotle, in fact, never discusses the story in his extant writings, though he alludes to one of the geographical details at one point.[120] However, the Stoic Posidonius (*c.* 135–50), followed by Strabo, thought it possible that such an island had existed and been submerged.[121] Pliny the Elder refers to the submergence of Atlantis, adding the qualification, 'if we believe Plato' (*Natural History* 2.204–5). Thus, on the geographical side, we have little more than bare references to Plato's story, ranging between scepticism and readiness to accept its factual truth. Another strand worth noting is that of allusions to the Atlantis story in two fantasy or utopian histories by Greek writers who also wrote serious history. One is Theopompus (*c.* 378–320) and the other Didorus Siculus (*c.* 80–30). Although they did not actually discuss the Atlantis story, their allusions to it imply that, for them, it was a fantasy.[122]

[42] Proclus is an informative source for earlier Platonic treatments. According to him, Crantor (*c.* 335–275) wrote the first commentary on

---

[120] *Meteorologica* 2, 354a22, referring to mud blocking the Atlantic (*Ti.* 25d).

[121] Strabo 2.3.6, 13.1.36. The Homeric reference is to *Il.* 12.1–33 (see also 7.433–53); on the destruction of Atlantis, see *Ti.* 25d3. On this comment, see also Proclus, *Commentary on Timaeus* 1.190.4–8.

[122] See Vidal-Naquet 2007, 35–36, 39–40.

the Atlantis story. Crantor describes the story as a 'pure history' (*psilē historia*); this is sometimes taken to mean a historically factual account, especially as he also refers to the Egyptian origin of the story. However, *historia* has by Proclus's time acquired quite a broad range of meanings ('story', 'account', 'history'); and what Proclus seems to be stressing is Crantor's focus on the explicit content of the story, rather than the heavily symbolic readings which became standard in later Platonic writings on this subject. As for the reference to Egypt, it seems that Crantor was highlighting thematic links between the institutions of the ideal state (summarized by Socrates in *Ti.* 17b–19b), which some critics had claimed were borrowed by Plato from the Egyptian social structure, and Plato's decision to make the Atlantis story a transmission from Egypt. Crantor emerges as someone who traces links between different parts of the Atlantis story in a way that is not fundamentally different from modern interpretative readings.[123] Plutarch (*c.* AD 50–120), commenting on the Atlantis story in his biography of Solon, described it, rather broadly, as an 'account' (*logos*) or 'fable/myth' (*muthos*). While claiming to clarify various historical points, he does not seem much concerned with whether the story was factually true or not.[124] Proclus himself, like previous late Platonist thinkers who discussed the story, assumed that it was symbolic or allegorical. Hence, the war between Athens and Atlantis was interpreted by different Platonists in terms of various cosmic or metaphysical oppositions, which were also seen as the key themes in Timaeus's cosmological account. The terms of the oppositions included those of two kinds of soul (good and bad), the fixed stars and the planets,

---

[123] Proclus, *Commentary on Timaeus* 1.75.30–76.10. In the reading offered earlier in this introduction, for instance, there is also much discussion of the relationship between the different parts of the account (i.e. Socrates's partial summary of the *Republic*, Critias's outline of the Atlantis story and his fuller version) and the significance of this relationship. Contrast Proclus's summary of typical later Platonist views: 'Others say that it is a myth and an invention, something that never actually happened but gives an indication of things which have either always been so, or always come to be, in the cosmos' (75.10–12). See Tarrant 2007, 63–70.

[124] *Solon* 26.1, 31.6–32.2. Plutarch places Solon's visit to Egypt after his political legislation (contrast *Ti.* 21c–e) and says that Plato did not complete the story due to old age.

the one and the indeterminate dyad, same and other, limit and unlimited, rest and movement. The thinkers adopting these interpretations either assumed that Plato's story was made up or argued that it was 'true' in a deeper, symbolic sense.[125]

[43] If in antiquity the Atlantis story attracted rather little attention outside specialist circles, the opposite is true in modern (post-Renaissance) Western culture. Theories, speculations or retellings of the story have been pervasive from the late fifteenth century onwards. However, within classical scholarship, the Atlantis story, by contrast with Timaeus's cosmology, has aroused much less interest until quite recently. In the many preceding centuries, only two scholars produced work that is still regarded as making a significant contribution to the subject. One is Giuseppe Bartoli, whose book on Atlantis (1779) prefigured the view that Plato's story is crucially informed by his responses to fifth-century Athenian history. Bartoli anticipated the influential proposal by Pierre Vidal-Naquet that the story has strong echoes of Athens both at the time of Marathon and the Peloponnesian War, and that historical Athens thus underlies both primaeval Athens and Atlantis.[126] The second significant contribution was by Thomas-Henri Martin (1841), in a long essay on the story which formed part of his commentary on Plato's *Timaeus*. Martin's thorough study concluded that it was, in effect, pure fiction and that the feverish efforts in preceding centuries to 'find' Atlantis all over the globe were entirely futile.[127]

[44] The many speculative treatments of the story have been reviewed in an illuminating book by Vidal-Naquet (2007). As he brings out, there have been wide variations in the extent to which those writing on Atlantis have studied Plato's text in any detail; and in most cases, the approach has been

---

[125] See Pradeau 1997, 67–71; Vidal-Naquet 2007, 46–50; Tarrant 2007, 70–84, including discussion of the Neoplatonist Longinus, whose approach was closer to Crantor. Of modern studies, Brisson 1970 is perhaps closest to the Neoplatonist standpoint. On the idea that such contrasts (e.g. unity and plurality) underlie Critias's full version of the story, see [29].

[126] Bartoli 1779. See also Pradeau 1997, 71–82; Vidal-Naquet 2007, 92–94. On this approach, see also text to nn. 79–80.

[127] Martin 1841. See also Ramage 1978b, 32; Vidal-Naquet 2007, 13–14.

syncretistic, combining Platonic evidence with other material drawn from many different fields and sources (geographical, mythological, religious, historical and so on).[128] The focus has been very much on Atlantis, rather than on primaeval Athens or on the contrast between the two. The features that have attracted most interest include Plato's massive extension of known geographical space (into the Atlantic) and the claim of the story to uncover the long-lost origins and early history of one's own culture from remote sources (Egypt, in Plato's case). The project of 'finding' Atlantis has been linked with other major preoccupations of the age. These have included the European discovery of America and other remote lands, both western and eastern.[129] Another preoccupation has been with finding the ten lost tribes of Israel, identified with the ten kingdoms in Atlantis; for this purpose Atlantis has been relocated in Palestine.[130] The link with finding primaeval origins for one's home state attracted those looking for myths to support nationalism of various kinds, though Atlantis, rather than Athens, tended to be the favoured place of origin. A notable example was Sweden at the time of its military and political ascendancy; but there have been many other attempt to appropriate Atlantis, including that of the Nazis.[131]

[45] The overall outcome of all this is that:

> by the nineteenth century the Atlanteans had ... been connected with people as widely different in race and time as Goths, the Gauls, the Druids, the Egyptians, and the Scyths and had been discovered in many [other] parts of the world: the Mediterranean, the Sahara, the Caucasus, in South Africa, Ceylon, Brazil, Greenland, the British Isles, the Netherlands, and Prussia.[132]

---

[128] Striking examples of syncretism include Jean-Silvain Bailly (late eighteenth century) and Ignatius Donnelly (1882). See Ramage 1978b, 31–36; Vidal-Naquet 2007, 85–86, 138–41.

[129] Vidal-Naquet 2007, 58–64, 82–83.

[130] Vidal-Naquet 2007, 57–58, 81–82. See also *Criti.* 113e–114c.

[131] The main exponent of the Swedish theory was the late seventeenth-century Olof Rudbeck. See Vidal-Naquet 2007, 65–71, also 107–09, 120–26 on other versions of nationalism.

[132] Ramage 1978b, 31, also 37 for a further list, including various sites in North and South America.

A further line of modern enquiry, drawing on the techniques of geology and marine archaeology, has been to try to locate Atlantis in land masses in the Atlantic (or elsewhere) now submerged. However, this line of enquiry seems not to have proved fruitful; there is no geological evidence to show that any such land mass sank in the Atlantic as recently as 9600 BC.[133] The one hypothesis that has attracted significant scholarly interest in recent years is the Minoan theory, linked with work on the volcanic eruption at Thera (Santorini), discussed in the following Appendix.[134]

Appendix: the Minoan hypothesis

[46] The one attempt in recent years to 'find' Atlantis that generated serious scholarly interest is the Minoan hypothesis.[135] During the late 1960s and 1970s especially, some scholars (notably J. V. Luce) argued that we should look to Minoan Crete for the origin of Plato's Atlantis. Like Atlantis, Minoan Crete was an island-based naval power with high technological development and, like Atlantis, its civilization suffered a sudden decline at the height of its power (in the fifteenth century BC). Those who saw Minoan Crete as the model for Atlantis pointed to certain parallels between the two cultures, which were underlined by the results of twentieth-century archaeology. Following Sir Arthur Evans's excavations at Cnossos, it became clear that Minoan Crete was a highly developed civilization, notably in its art, architecture, engineering and plumbing (in this respect, it was like Atlantis, *Criti.* 115c–118e). The traditional associations of Minoan Cnossos with bulls in Greek mythology were borne out by the images of bull leaping in wall paintings at Cnossos. It was also suggested that the bull catching depicted on the Minoan-style Vapheio cups was close to the ritual bull hunting by the kings of Atlantis (*Criti.* 119d–e). Crete, like Atlantis, is a mountainous island containing at least

---

[133] See Vitaliano 1978, 139; also Wright 1978, 174.

[134] For an overview of other types of recent Platonic scholarship on the Atlantis story, see the preface.

[135] This appendix is an updated version of pages ix–xii of the first edition of this book, which drew in turn on Gill 1976.

one large plain (*Criti.* 118a), and an island placed in an inland sea (which is how Plato describes the island of Atlantis, *Ti.* 24e–25a). Hence, it was proposed that Plato's account was based on (an exceptionally accurate) record of Minoan civilization, whose power and extent were not generally recognized in Plato's day.[136]

[47] A further parallel between Atlantis and Crete, it was also suggested, lay in the cause of the collapse of their power. The reason why Minoan civilization suffered disruption and decline in the mid-fifteenth century BC has long been a puzzle; but in the 1960s archaeologists put forward a new explanation. It had been known for some time that the island of Thera (or Santorini), 75 miles north of Crete, was torn apart in ancient times by a massive volcanic eruption. But it was only after 1967 that the excavations of the Greek archaeologist, Spiridon Marinatos, revealed a highly developed Minoan settlement at Akrotiri on Thera, buried beneath volcanic materials. The examinations of these remains made it possible to date the volcanic eruption approximately to the early fifteenth century. Since this is (approximately) the time of the disruptions in Crete, Marinatos thus found support for the hypothesis he had formed in the 1930s that the eruption of Thera was the cause of the cultural collapse in Minoan Crete. The eruption was extremely powerful, comparable with that at Krakatoa in 1883 rather than Vesuvius in AD 79. In 1965, analysis of cores from the seabed showed evidence of a wide dispersal of volcanic ash from the eruption in the Aegean, including the area around eastern Crete. This led some scholars in the late 1960s to accept Marinatos's theory that the various effects of the volcanic eruption (earthquake, airwaves, tidal waves and ash falls) disrupted Cretan civilization and caused its rapid decline.[137] This theory gave a special interest to Plato's account of the collapse of Atlantis: 'Later on, there were violent earthquakes and floods, and in the onset of a single terrible day and night, your whole fighting force sank below the earth all at once, and the island of Atlantis sank in the same way and disappeared below the sea' (*Ti.* 25c6–d3). If the Atlantis story was based on a genuine memory of

---

[136] See Luce 1970, 34–43, 135–47. The link between Minoan Crete and Atlantis was first made by K. T. Frost in *The Times* on 19 February 1909 and developed in Frost 1913.

[137] Luce 1970, 43–85. See also Marinatos 1939, 1968.

Minoan Crete, this was the only piece of ancient evidence that seemed to connect the collapse of Cretan civilization with the volcanic disruption of Thera.[138]

[48] But, if this view is correct, how did Plato come to have access to information about the extent of Minoan civilization, and the way it collapsed, which seems not to have been available to other Greeks at the time? And, if his island empire is really Cretan, why did he call it 'Atlantis' and place it in the Atlantic Ocean? Why did he make it so much larger than Crete and make it so remote in time (*c.* 9600)? Luce tried to answer these questions by taking at face value Plato's own account of the origin of his story.[139] Critias, the narrator, claimed that the story was transmitted to his family from Solon, and that Solon, in turn, gained his information from the Egyptian priests of Neïth at Saïs, whose records went back to a period of time about which the Greeks had little accurate information (*Ti.* 20d–23d). The divergences between Minoan Crete and Atlantis crept in, Luce argued, through certain misunderstandings that occurred between Solon and his Egyptian sources. The Egyptian name for Crete was (probably) Keftiu, and, when the priests mentioned it, Solon would have asked where it was. The Egyptian worldview, at that time, was based on the eastern Mediterranean, and the priests probably replied that it was in the 'far west'. Solon, who had a more accurate knowledge of the Mediterranean than they did, would have imagined it in *his* far west, that is, beyond the Pillars of Heracles (Straits of Gibraltar). He may have identified it with the island described by Homer (*Odyssey* 1.48–54) as occupied by the daughter of Atlas, and so named it 'Atlantis'.[140] The size of the island, and its remoteness in time, were expanded (deliberately or mistakenly) by the priests or by Solon. Plato may have added his own embellishments, but Luce believes he preserved 'the hard core of the legend … the tradition of a great and highly civilized island empire which had once menaced the autonomy of Greece in general and Athens

[138] Luce 1970, 148–59. See also 98–134 for Luce's review of other Greek myths which may recall the eruption at Thera (though without linking it with the end of Minoan Crete).

[139] Luce 1970, 38–43, 137–47.

[140] Luce 1970, 41–43.

in particular, and which came to an end as the result of a natural catastrophe'.[141]

[49] How sound are these arguments? There are a number of problems. There are chronological problems in accepting Marinatos's theory that the eruption of Thera was the direct cause of the collapse of Minoan civilization. When Luce wrote his book, the evidence of datable pottery suggested that the eruption occurred about 1500, whereas the widespread destruction of palaces in Crete took place about 1450. Supporters of Marinatos's theory, such as Luce, tried to close this 50-year gap, either by imagining the Thera eruption as a two-stage process, lasting several decades in all, or by redating both waves of destruction to 1470 or thereabouts.[142] The findings of geologists and archaeologists, presented at three major international congresses about Thera (in 1969, 1978 and 1989), have tended not to confirm these suggestions.[143] It is now widely supposed that the eruption at Thera took place in the late seventeenth or early sixteenth century, and that the large-scale burning of palaces in Crete occurred significantly later.[144] It is still quite possible that the eruption at Thera played a role in the decline of Minoan culture. For instance, Driessen and Macdonald maintain that 'the archaeological evidence suggests a severe economic dislocation, triggered by the Santorini eruption and gradually building up' in the period leading up to the burning of palaces.[145] However, the view that the destructive effects of the eruption reached as far as Crete and constituted the direct cause of the collapse of Minoan culture is no longer seen as tenable.[146] This shift in scholarly opinion does not directly affect the identification of Atlantis with Crete (after all, Plato may still have associated the eruption of Thera with the Minoan collapse, even if the two events were not causally

---

[141] Luce 1970, 20.

[142] Luce 1970, 53–60, 1976.

[143] See Popham 1979, reviewing the proceedings of the second congress and Sherratt 1991, reviewing the proceedings of the third congress. See also Naddaf 1994, 192–93, esp. n. 18. The link with Atlantis has not figured in recent archaeological debate.

[144] See the summary of current scholarly opinion in Driessen and Macdonald 1997, 5, though they themselves are inclined to date the eruption slightly later, to 1550–30 (23).

[145] Driessen and Macdonald 1997, 117.

[146] See Driessen and Macdonald 1997, 85–115, reviewing the evidence and debate on the relationship between the two events.

related); but it does lessen the motivation for making the identification. It was the fact that Plato seemed to provide unique documentary support for the theory of volcanic destruction of Crete that had made his story suddenly seem so important to archaeologists.

[50] There are, in any case, independent reasons for doubting that Plato's Atlantis is based on Minoan Crete.[147] The resemblance between the two locations is, really, very slight, and much special pleading is needed to show how Atlantis could have been based on Crete. Cnossos (in northern Crete) has to be resited in the plain of Messara (in southern Crete) before its topography is even roughly similar to that of Atlantis. Plato's measurements of the capital city of Atlantis need to be retained (to fit Cnossos), but his measurements of the plain of Atlantis need to be divided by ten (to fit the plan of Messara).[148] There is no basis for matching the political institutions of Atlantis with anything we can reconstruct in Minoan Crete. Even the bull motif is less striking than it seems initially. In Plato's Atlantis, the kings hunt and kill a bull with wooden clubs and nooses (*Critias* 119d–e). This may remind us of the actions shown on the (Minoan-style) cups found at Vapheio near Sparta; but the catching and sacrifice of bulls was not unique to Minoan Crete. What was distinctive about Minoan practice was the acrobatic bull leaping which we find so often represented in Cretan art; and there is no hint of this in Plato's text. In short, there are so few points of contact between the two cultures that it is hard to see how an account of Minoan Crete could have ended up as the Atlantis story.

[51] There are also considerable difficulties in accepting that Plato (or Solon) could have received detailed information about Crete from the Egyptians. Luce assembled the evidence available to us from fifteenth-century Egypt, and considered it similar to that which would have been available to Solon.[149] Can we find there the story of Atlantis, under the name of Keftiu? In fact, the Egyptian records have rather little to say about Keftiu at all, and contain nothing which would suggest it was a threatening maritime power. The sum total of the evidence Luce cites

---

[147] For defence of this claim and relevant details, see Luce 1970, 140–44.

[148] Luce 1970, 140, acknowledges the need for these adjustments.

[149] Luce 1970, 38–43, 144–46.

gives no *description* of Keftiu at all; there is nothing which would have enabled Plato to delineate the engineering, architecture and topography of Minoan Crete, with measurements accurate to the nearest stade. There is no evidence that the Egyptians knew about the eruption at Thera, or that they connected it with any decline in the culture of Minoan Crete.

[52] One can also question Luce's assumption that Solon (or Plato) could have received from the Egyptians an account of Minoan civilization and not recognized it for what it was, because of his ignorance of Minoan culture.[150] In fact, the Athenians of the classical period had a much clearer picture of Minoan Crete (including the features most relevant to the Atlantis story) than the Egyptians seem to have had. One of the most famous Athenian legends, that of Theseus and the Minotaur, presents, in mythical form, the themes of Minoan maritime power, conflict between Crete and Athens, Cretan technology (Daedalus and the labyrinth) and even the bull motif (the Minotaur). It was on the basis of such legends that Greek historians such as Herodotus (7.170-1) and Thucydides (1.4), as well as Plato himself (*Laws* 706a-b), produced their picture of Minoan Crete as a great naval power, dominating the Mediterranean. Indeed, it is quite possible that this traditional view of Minoan Crete was one of the models Plato used to create his fictitious Atlantis.[151] But, if so, he was drawing on well-known Greek traditions and not on a garbled version of (alleged) Egyptian records.

[53] There are, therefore, considerable problems with the theory that Plato derived his story primarily from an authentic Egyptian account of Minoan Crete and its destruction. Luce probably overstated the credibility of this idea in his book. He himself subsequently gave a more cautious statement of the theory, and expressed doubt about whether Solon transmitted the story to Plato, and whether Egyptian records conveyed to Solon detailed information about Minoan Crete.[152] Suggestive though it seemed at one point, this hypothesis, like so many other attempts to 'find' Atlantis, ultimately fails to convince.

---

[150] Luce 1970, 156-57.

[151] As Forsyth points out (1980, ch. 10), there is no reason to think that, in using historical material to flesh out the Atlantis story, Plato had a single source in mind.

[152] Luce 1978, 64-67.

Bibliography

Annas, J. and Rowe, C. (eds) (2002), *New Perspectives on Plato, Modern and Ancient* (Cambridge, MA: Center for Hellenic Studies and Harvard University Press).

Archer-Hind, R. D. (ed.) (1888), *The Timaeus of Plato* (London: Macmillan).

Boys-Stones, G., El Murr, D. and Gill, C. (eds) (2013), *The Platonic Art of Philosophy* (Cambridge: Cambridge University Press).

Brisson, L. (1970), 'De la philosophie à l'épopée: le *Critias* de Platon', *Revue de Métaphysique et de Morale* 75: 402–38.

Brisson, L. (1982), *Platon: les mots et les mythes* (Paris: Maspero).

Brisson, L. (1992), *Platon: Timée-Critias*, translated with introduction and notes (Paris: Flammarion).

Broadie, S. (2001), 'Theodicy and Pseudo-history in the *Timaeus*', *Oxford Studies in Ancient Philosophy* 21: 1–28.

Broadie, S. (2012), *Nature and Divinity in Plato's Timaeus* (Cambridge: Cambridge University Press).

Broadie, S. (2013), 'Truth and Story in the *Timaeus-Critias*', in G. Boys-Stones, D. El Murr and C. Gill (eds), *The Platonic Art of Philosophy* (Cambridge: Cambridge University Press), 249–68.

Burnet, J. (ed.) (1902), *Platonis Opera*, Vol. 4 (Oxford: Oxford University Press).

Clay, D. (1999), 'Plato's Atlantis: The Anatomy of a Fiction', in J. J. Cleary and G. M. Gurtler (eds), *Proceedings of the Boston Area Colloquium in Ancient Philosophy*, Vol. 15 (Leiden: Brill), 1–21.

Cornford, F. M. (1937), *Plato's Cosmology: The Timaeus of Plato Translated with a Running Commentary* (London: Routledge and Kegan Paul).

Davies, J. K. (1971), *Athenian Propertied Families* (Oxford: Oxford University Press).

Driessen, J. and Macdonald, C. F. (1997), *The Troubled Island: Minoan Crete before and after the Santorini Eruption* (Aegaeum 17) (Brussels: University of Liège/Austin: University of Austin at Texas).

Ferrari, G. R. F. (1989), 'Plato and Poetry', in G. Kennedy (ed.), *Cambridge History of Literary Criticism* (Cambridge: Cambridge University Press), 92–148.

Finley, M. I. (1971), *The Ancestral Constitution* (Cambridge: Cambridge University Press).

Forsyth, P. Y. (1980), *Atlantis, The Making of Myth* (Toronto: University of Toronto Press).

Fredericks, S. C. (1978), 'Plato's Atlantis: A Mythologist Look at Myth', in E. S. Ramage (ed.), *Atlantis: Fact or Fiction?* (Bloomington: Indiana University Press), 64–78.

Friedländer, P. (1958), *Plato: An Introduction*, trans. H. Meyerhoff (London: Routledge and Kegan Paul).

Frost, K. T. (1913), 'The *Critias* and Minoan Crete', *Journal of Hellenic Studies* 33: 186–206.

Gill, C. (1976), 'The Origin of the Atlantis Myth', *Trivium* 11: 1–11.

Gill, C. (1977), 'The Genre of the Atlantis Story', *Classical Philology* 72: 287–304.

Gill, C. (1979a), 'Plato and Politics: The Critias and the Politicus', *Phronesis* 24: 148–167.

Gill, C. (1979b), 'Plato's Atlantis Story and the Birth of Fiction', *Philosophy and Literature* 3: 64–78.

Gill, C. (1995), 'Rethinking Constitutionalism in *Statesman* 291–303', in C. Rowe (ed.), *Reading the Statesman* (Sankt Augustin: Academia Verlag), 292–305.

Gill, C. (1996a), 'Afterword: Dialectic and the Dialogue Form in Late Plato', in C. Gill and M. M. McCabe (eds), *Form and Argument in Late Plato* (Oxford: Oxford University Press), 283–311.

Gill, C. (1996b), *Personality in Greek Epic, Tragedy, and Philosophy: The Self in Dialogue*, (Oxford: Oxford University Press).

Gill, C. (2002), 'Dialectic and the Dialogue Form', in J. Annas and C. Rowe (eds), *New Perspectives on Plato, Modern and Ancient* (Cambridge, MA: Center for Hellenic Studies and Harvard University Press), 145–71.

Gill, C. (2003), 'The *Laws* – is it a Real Dialogue?', in S. Scolnicov and L. Brisson (eds), *Plato's Laws: From Theory into Practice* (Sankt Augustin: Academia Verlag), 42–47.

Gill (2006), 'The Platonic Dialogue', in M. L. Gill and P. Pellegrin (eds), *A Companion to Ancient Philosophy* (Oxford: Blackwell), 136–50.

Bibliography

Gill, C. and McCabe, M. M. (eds) (1996), *Form and Argument in Late Plato* (Oxford: Oxford University Press).

Hackforth, R. (1944), 'The Story of Atlantis: Its Purpose and Moral', *Classical Review* 58: 7–9.

Jacoby, F. (ed.) (1923), *Fragmente der Griechischen Historiker*, Berlin: Weidmann.

Johansen, T. K. (2004), *Plato's Natural Philosophy: A Study of the Timaeus-Critias* (Cambridge: Cambridge University Press).

Kahn, C. (2002), 'On Platonic Chronology', in J. Annas and C. Rowe (eds), *New Perspectives on Plato, Modern and Ancient* (Cambridge, MA: Center for Hellenic Studies and Harvard University Press), 93–127.

Klosko, G. (1986), *The Development of Plato's Political Theory* (Oxford: Oxford University Press).

Loraux, N. (1986), *The Invention of Athens*, trans. A. Sheridan (Cambridge, MA: Harvard University Press).

Luce, J. V. (1970), *The End of Atlantis* (St. Albans: Paladin).

Luce, J. V. (1976), 'Thera and the Devastation of Minoan Crete: A New Interpretation of the Evidence', *American Journal of Archaeology* 80: 9–16.

Luce, J. V. (1978), 'The Sources and Literary Form of Plato's Atlantis Narrative', in E. S. Ramage (ed.), *Atlantis: Fact or Fiction?* (Bloomington: Indiana University Press), 49–78.

Marinatos, S. (1939), 'The Volcanic Destruction of Minoan Crete', *Antiquity* 13: 425–39.

Marinatos, S. (1968), *Excavations at Thera* (Athens: Archaiologikē Hetaireia).

Marr, J. L. and Rhodes, P. J. (2008), *The Old Oligarch: The Constitution of the Athenians Attributed to Xenophon*, edited with a translation and commentary (Oxford: Oxbow).

Morgan, K. A. (1998), 'Designer History: Plato's Atlantis Story and Fourth-century Ideology', *Journal of Hellenic Studies* 118: 101–18.

Morgan, K. A. (2000), *Myth and Philosophy from the Presocratics to Plato* (Cambridge: Cambridge University Press).

Naddaf, G. (1994), 'The Atlantis Myth: An Introduction to Plato's Later Philosophy of History', *Phoenix* 48: 189–209.

Nesselrath, H.-G. (2006), *Platon: Kritias*, with translation and commentary (Göttingen: Vandenhoeck and Ruprecht).

Osborne, C (1996), 'Creative Discourse in the *Timaeus*', in C. Gill and

M. M. McCabe (eds), *Form and Argument in Late Plato* (Oxford: Oxford University Press), 179–211.

Otto, I.-D. (1997), 'Der Kritias vor dem Hintergrund des *Menexenus*', in T. Calvo and L. Brisson (eds), *Interpreting the Timaeus-Critias* (Sankt Augustin: Academia Verlag), 65–81.

Pollitt, J. J. (1974), *The Ancient View of Greek Art* (New Haven: Yale University Press).

Popham, M. (1979), 'Thera and the Aegean', *Antiquity* 53: 57–70.

Popper, K. (1961), *The Open Society and its Enemies, Vol. 1: The Spell of Plato* (London: Routledge and Kegan Paul).

Pradeau, J.-F. (1997), *Le Monde de la politique: sur le récit Atlante de Platon, Timée (17–27) et Critias* (Sankt Augustin: Academia Verlag).

Pradeau, J.-F. (2002), *Plato and the City: A New Introduction to Plato's Political Thought*, trans. J. Lloyd (Exeter: University of Exeter Press).

Ramage, E. S. (ed.) (1978a), *Atlantis: Fact or Fiction?* (Bloomington: Indiana University Press).

Ramage, E. S. (1978b), 'Perspectives Ancient and Modern', in *Atlantis: Fact or Fiction?* (Bloomington: Indiana University Press), 3–45.

Rivaud, A. (ed.) (1925), *Platon: œuvres complètes tome 10, Timée-Critias*, with French translation, introduction and notes (Paris: Les Belles Lettres).

Rowe, C. (1995), *Plato's Statesman*, with translation and commentary (Warminster: Aris and Phillips).

Rowe, C. (1996), 'The *Politicus*: Structure and Form', in C. Gill and M. M. McCabe (eds), *Form and Argument in Late Plato* (Oxford: Oxford University Press), 153–78.

Rowe, C. (1997), 'Why is the Ideal Athens of the *Timaeus-Critias* Not Ruled by Philosophers?', *Méthexis* 10: 51–7.

Rowe, C. (1999), 'Myth, History and Dialectic in Plato's *Republic* and *Timaeus-Critias*', in R. G. A. Buxton (ed.), *From Myth to Reason? Studies in the Development of Greek Thought* (Cambridge: Cambridge University Press), 263–78.

Rowe, C. (2004), 'The Case of the Missing Philosophers in Plato's *Timaeus-Critias*', *Würzburger Jahrbücher für die Altertumswissenschaft* 28(b), 57–70.

Rowe, C. (forthcoming), 'Plato on Equality and Democracy', in G. Anagnostopoulos and J. Santas (eds), *Democracy, Justice, and Equality in Ancient Greece: Historical and Philosophical Perspectives* (Proceedings of the 2015 San Diego Conference on 'Greek

Democracy, Equalities, and Inequalities: Historical and Philosophical Perspectives').

Ruben, T. (2016), *Le Discours Comme Image: Énonciation, Récit et Connaisssance dans le Timée-Critias de Platon* (Paris: Les Belles Lettres).

Schofield, M. (1997), 'The Disappearance of the Philosopher King', in J. J. Cleary and G. M. Gurtler (eds), *Proceedings of the Boston Area Colloquium, Vol. 13* (Leiden: Brill), 213–41.

Schofield, M. (2006), *Plato* (Oxford: Oxford University Press).

Schofield, M. (2013), 'Friendship and Justice in the *Laws*', in G. Boys-Stones, D. El Murr and C. Gill (eds), *The Platonic Art of Philosophy* (Cambridge: Cambridge University Press), 283–97.

Sedley, D. (2007), *Creationism and its Critics in Antiquity* (Berkeley: University of California Press).

Sherratt, S. (1991), 'Review of D. A. Hardy and A. C. Renfrew (eds), *Thera and the Aegean World*, London 1989–91', *Antiquity* 62: 998–1001.

Taylor, A. E. (1928), *A Commentary on Plato's Timaeus* (Oxford: Oxford University Press).

Tulli, M. (2013), 'The Atlantis Poem in the *Timaeus-Critias*', in G. Boys-Stones, D. El Murr and C. Gill (eds), *The Platonic Art of Philosophy* (Cambridge: Cambridge University Press), 269–82.

Vidal-Naquet, P. (1964), 'Athènes et l'Atlantide', *Revue des Études Grecques* 77: 420–44; reprinted in P. Vidal-Naquet, *Le Chasseur noir: formes de pensée et formes de société dans le monde grec* (Paris: Maspero), 335–60.

Vidal-Naquet, P. (2007), *The Atlantis Story: A Short History of Plato's Myth*, trans. J. Lloyd (Exeter: University of Exeter Press).

Vitaliano, D. B. (1978), 'Atlantis from the Geological Point of View', in E. S. Ramage (ed.), *Atlantis: Fact or Fiction?* (Bloomington: Indiana University Press), 137–60.

Vlastos, G. (1981), *Platonic Studies*, 2nd ed. (Princeton: Princeton University Press).

Weil, R. (1959), *L'Archéologie de Platon* (Paris: Klincksieck).

Welliver, W. (1977), *Character, Plot and Thought in Plato's Timaeus-Critias* (Leiden: Brill).

Wright, H. E. (1978), 'Glacial Fluctuations, Sea-level Changes, and Catastrophic Floods', in E. S. Ramage (ed.), *Atlantis: Fact or Fiction?* (Bloomington: Indiana University Press), 161–74.

TRANSLATION:
PLATO *TIMAEUS* 17a–27b, *CRITIAS*

Timaeus 17a–27b

17a–19b:
Socrates's summary of the Republic's ideal state

SOCRATES: One, two, three – but where, my dear Timaeus, is our 17a
fourth member, of those who were my guests yesterday and who are
going to provide the feast today?
TIMAEUS: He must have been taken ill in some way, Socrates; he
wouldn't miss this meeting voluntarily.
SOCRATES: Then surely it's up to you and these others to provide
the portion that the absent person would have done?
TIMAEUS: Certainly, and as far as we can, we won't fall short. It b
would be unfair, since we were entertained by you with such fitting
hospitality, for those of us who remain not to feast you in return,
and with enthusiasm.
SOCRATES: So, do you remember the topics I assigned for you to
speak on and their scope?
TIMAEUS: We remember some, and, since you are here, you will
remind us of what we don't. Better still, if it's not too much trouble
for you, briefly run through them again from the start, so that they
become more firmly fixed in our minds.
SOCRATES: I'll do that. Of what I said yesterday, the chief topic c
was what kind of state seemed to me the best and of what kind of
men it would consist.
TIMAEUS: Yes indeed, Socrates, and we all agreed with what was
said.
SOCRATES: Then didn't we separate the class of farmers and the
other craftsmen from the class of those fighting on their behalf?

TIMAEUS: Yes.

SOCRATES: And assigning to each person only the one job which

d   was naturally suited to him individually, one craft for each person, we said that those whose duty it was to fight on everyone's behalf should be guardians of the city and nothing else. If someone from outside or indeed from inside the city planned to do harm, they would be gentle in passing judgement on their own subjects, who

18a   are naturally their friends, but would be harsh on those enemies they encountered in battle.

TIMAEUS: Absolutely.

SOCRATES: And I think we said that there was a certain character which the guardians should have, an exceptional combination of spirited and philosophical qualities, to enable them to be gentle and harsh in the correct way towards each type of person.

TIMAEUS: Yes.

SOCRATES: What about their upbringing? Didn't we say that they should have been trained in athletics and culture and all the branches of learning appropriate for them?

TIMAEUS: Absolutely.

b   SOCRATES: We also said, I think, that those brought up in this way should not regard gold or silver or anything else as their private possession. Like mercenaries, they should receive from those protected by them a wage for their guardianship which is as much as is reasonable for people of moderate habits. They should share their expenses, and live and spend their time with each other, devoting their attention entirely to excellence, having leisure from all other occupations.

TIMAEUS: We said that too.

c   SOCRATES: We also made special mention of women, saying that those whose nature was similar to the male guardians should be brought into harmony with them, and that all these women should be given occupations, both in war and the rest of their way of life, which are wholly shared with the men.

TIMAEUS: This too was said.

SOCRATES: What about the production of children? Or is this easy to remember because of the unusual character of what was said? We

58

laid it down that all their marriages and children should be held in common by all of them; and that the guardians should arrange it so that no one should ever recognize any of those born as his own   d child. Everyone should regard everyone else as his relative, treating as brothers and sisters everyone falling within an appropriate age group, and those born before and of an earlier age group as their parents and grandparents, and those of a later age group as their children and grandchildren.

TIMAEUS: Yes, and these points are easy to remember, as you say.

SOCRATES: To ensure that their natures should be the best possible from the start, do you remember that we said that the rulers, male and female, should secretly, by use of lots, arrange the contraction of marriages so that bad and good men would each as a group be   e joined up with women of the same kind; and there would not be any resulting animosity among them, because they would think that the allocation was due to chance.

TIMAEUS: We remember that.

SOCRATES: In addition, we said that the children of the good   19a parents should be brought up, while those of the bad parents should be secretly handed over to the rest of the city. The rulers must keep them under continuous observation as they grow up and, noting the ones who deserve it, transfer them back again, and exchange those returning with the ones in the guardian group who do not deserve to be there.

TIMAEUS: We did say so.

SOCRATES: So, have we now covered everything from yesterday, at least as far as giving an overall review is concerned, my dear Timaeus, or do we still miss anything from the discussion that has been left out?

TIMAEUS: Nothing at all; this is just what was said, Socrates.   b

19b–20c:
Socrates's request – a story about the ideal state in action

SOCRATES: Following on from this, you might now like to hear how I feel about the constitution we have described. My feeling is like that of someone who has been looking at beautiful animals, either in a picture or even actually alive but standing still, and

c   is filled with the desire to see them moving and competing in a contest in any of the ways that seems appropriate for their bodily form. That's just what I feel about the city we have described. I would like to hear someone describing in a story the kind of competitions that cities compete in, and this city engaging in these contests with other cities, going to war and fighting in a fitting way and expressing qualities that reflect its education and upbringing in achievements in action and negotiations in words with each of the other cities.

As far as these things are concerned, Critias and Hermocrates,

d   my judgement on myself is that I would never be capable of providing an adequate eulogy of the city and its men. In my case, this fact is in no way surprising. But I have also formed the same view about the poets, both those of the distant past and those living now. It is not that I have no respect for poets as a group but it is clear to everyone that imitators as a class will imitate most easily and best the surroundings in which they have been brought up; what falls outside their upbringing in each case is difficult to imitate

e   in actions and yet more difficult in words. As for the sophists as a group, I've always thought that they are very skilful in making many speeches and other fine things; but I fear perhaps that, because they wander from city to city and haven't maintained their own home anywhere, they would miss the target of representing men who are both philosophers and statesmen. They would fail to bring out the scale and quality of their actions and speeches, both as regards what they actually do in war and battle and how they negotiate in words in each of their encounters.

So that leaves people of your type, who are equally equipped by

20a   nature and training to take part in both philosophy and politics.

Timaeus here is from Locris in Italy, a city with excellent laws, and is the equal of anyone there in property and family background. He has occupied the most important offices and held the highest honours in the city, and in addition he has, in my opinion, reached the summit in philosophy as a whole. As for Critias, all of us here know that he is no layman in any of these areas. As regards the natural ability and training of Hermocrates, since many people give witness that they are equal to all these topics, we must believe b them. I was already aware of this yesterday and so, when you asked me to discuss the subject of the state, I agreed with enthusiasm, knowing that, if you were willing, no one would provide a more effective sequel. You alone of your contemporaries would launch our city in an appropriate war and provide an account that matches the character of this city in every way. So, after speaking on the topic set for me, I've set a topic for you in turn: the one I've just described. You agreed that, after consulting with each other, you would reciprocate in providing the feast of words for me today, and c here I am dressed up for that and readier than anyone to receive it.

20c–27b:
Critias's response to Socrates's request

HERMOCRATES: Yes indeed, as Timaeus here said, Socrates, we will not be at all lacking in enthusiasm nor do we have any excuse for not doing this. Why, even yesterday, as soon as we got back to the guest quarters in Critias's house where we are staying, and even before, on the way, we were thinking about this. He told us a story d based on an ancient report; tell Socrates the story too, Critias, so that he can judge, as well as us, whether or not it is suitable for the required task.
CRITIAS: That's what we should do if our third partner, Timaeus, also agrees with us.
TIMAEUS: I certainly agree.
CRITIAS: Then, listen to a story which is very strange, Socrates, but entirely true, as Solon once claimed, the wisest of the Seven e

Wise Men. He was a relative and a very good friend of my great-grandfather Dropides, as he himself said in many places in his poems. Dropides told the story to my grandfather Critias, and, when he was old he in turn used to tell it to us from memory. He said that there were great and wonderful achievements of our city in ancient times which had been obliterated by time and the destruction of human life, and one achievement that was the 21a   greatest of all. Retelling this achievement would be a fitting way to repay our debt to you and at the same time to offer a hymn, as it were, of just and true praise to the goddess on her festival.

SOCRATES: Well said. What was this ancient achievement that Critias described which, though unreported, was actually performed by our city, according to what Solon said.

CRITIAS: I'll tell you, having heard it as an ancient story from a b   man who was far from young himself. In fact, at that time, Critias was nearly ninety years old and I was about ten. It happened to be the third day – the Koureotis – of the Apatouria festival. The normal programme for children at the festival took place on that occasion too: our fathers offered prizes for recitation. Many compositions by many poets were recited; and many of the children sang those of Solon, because they were new at that time. One of the members of our civic group, either because it was his real opinion or because he c   was doing a favour to Critias, said that he thought that Solon had been the wisest of all people in other respects, and that in poetry he was the most independent-minded of all the poets. The old man – indeed, I remember it very well – was very pleased and said, with a smile, 'Yes, Amynandrus, if Solon hadn't treated poetry as a side activity but had put all his efforts into it, like other poets, and if he had completed the story he brought back from Egypt, and had not been forced to neglect it because of the political conflicts and all the other problems he found when he came back, in my opinion neither d   Hesiod nor Homer nor any other poet would ever have become more famous than him'. 'What was the story, Critias?', he asked. 'It was', he said, 'a story about the greatest exploit and what fully deserves to be the most famous of all that our city has achieved, but because of the length of time and the destruction of those who performed it the story has not lasted down to our time'. 'Tell us from the beginning', he said. 'What was the story which Solon told, and how, and from whom, did he acquire is as one that is true?'

'In Egypt', Critias said, 'at the apex of the Delta, where the flow   e
of the Nile divides, there is a district called the Saïtic. The most important city there is Saïs, and this is also the city from which King Amasis came. This city was founded by a god whose name in Egyptian is Neïth and, according to the people there, Athena in Greek. They are very friendly towards the Athenians and claim that they are somehow related to them. Solon said that when he travelled there, he was treated by them with great respect. When he enquired   22a
about ancient times from those of the priests who were most expert in these subjects, he discovered that he, like other Greeks, knew virtually nothing about such matters. One day, wanting to draw them into a discussion about antiquity, he set about talking about the things regarded as most ancient here. He told the story about Phoroneus, said to be the first human being, and Niobe, and how   b
Deucalion and Pyrrha survived the flood. He then traced their descendants and, by recording the years since the events he was speaking about, tried to calculate their dates.

Then one of the priests, a very old man, said: 'Ah, Solon, Solon, you Greeks are always children, and in Greece there is no one who is old.' Hearing this, Solon asked, 'What do you mean by this?' 'You are all young in your minds', he said. 'You have in your minds no belief about antiquity based on ancient tradition nor any learning that is grey with age. The reason for that is this. There have been   c
and will be many events destructive of human life in many ways, the greatest of these by fire and water, and other lesser ones with countless other causes. Take, for instance, the story told by your people of how Phaethon, son of the Sun, on one occasion harnessed his father's chariot but, because he couldn't drive it along his father's route, he burnt things on the surface of the earth and was himself destroyed by a thunderbolt. This story has the form of a myth but the truth is that there is a deviation in the movement of   d
heavenly bodies around the earth, which recurs with long intervals in between, and which causes destruction of things on the surface

of the earth by huge fires. On these occasions, those who live on mountains or in high and dry places suffer greater destruction than those living close to rivers and the sea. In our case, the Nile, our saviour in other ways too, is released and saves us from this disaster as well. On the other hand, whenever the gods deluge the earth with water and purify it, the cowherds and shepherds living on

e   the mountains are saved, but those of you living in cities are swept by the rivers into the sea. But in this region water does not flow from above on to the fields, then or at other times; on the contrary, everything naturally rises from below. This is the reason why the records preserved here are said to be the most ancient. The truth is that in all places where excessive cold or heat does not prevent

23a   it, the human race always exists in greater or smaller numbers at different times.

'Of the events we hear about in your region, or here or anywhere else, if there are any which are excellent or great actions or distinguished in some other way, they have all been inscribed here in our temples and preserved from antiquity onwards. But in your case and those of others, just as you have been equipped at any one time with writing and the other requirements of urban life, then again, after the usual number of years, the flood from heaven

b   comes like a plague borne down upon you, and spares only those among you who are lacking in literacy and culture, so that you become children, as it were, all over again, knowing nothing of what happened in ancient times either here or in your own region. In any case, the genealogies of your own people that you just recounted, Solon, are little different from children's stories. First of all, you only remember one flood, although there were many earlier ones. Further, you do not know that the finest and best race

c   in all humankind lived in your land, from which you and the whole of the city which is now yours are derived because a small seed remained; you are unaware of this because for many generations those who survived died without expressing themselves in writing. There was a time, Solon, before the biggest of the destructive floods, when the city which is now Athens was the best in warfare and was also distinguished by the excellence of its laws in every respect.

This city is said to have had the finest achievements and political   d
institutions in the world which have been reported to us'.

Solon said that he was astonished when he heard this and that
he enthusiastically begged the priests to give him all the detailed
information about those ancient citizens. The priest replied,
'Willingly, Solon, I'll tell you both for your own sake and your
city's, but most of all for the goddess who was allocated, and who
nurtured and educated, both your city and ours – yours first, when
she received your seed from Earth and Hephaestus, and ours a   e
thousand years later. The date of the establishment of our organization is recorded in our sacred writings as eight thousand years
ago. As regards your citizens of nine thousand years ago, I'll briefly
describe their laws and the finest of their achievements. We will go   24a
through the details about everything on another occasion at our
leisure, and consult the writings themselves.

'Consider your ancient laws in relation to those here. You will
find here now among us many parallels to yours at that time. First,
the class of priests is distinct and separate from the other classes;
next, in the case of the class of craftsmen, each group (herdsmen,
hunters and farmers) practises its craft as a separate unit, without   b
being mixed up with others. Surely you have also noticed that our
warrior class is separate from all others, and that they are required
by law to concern themselves with nothing by warfare. Further,
their style of armament consists of shields and spears, which we
were the first in Asia to use to arm ourselves, under the guidance
of the goddess – just as, in your region, you were the first to do so.
Again, as far as intellectual activity is concerned, surely you see   c
what care the law has devoted from the beginning to cosmology.
From these divine principles, it has derived all the arts bearing
on human affairs, including divination and medicine directed at
producing health, and it has acquired all the other studies that
are connected with these. All this organization and system was
established and put in order by the goddess at that time; and
she did so first in your case, choosing the place you were born,
recognizing that the harmoniousness of its climate would produce   d
the most intelligent men. Because she is a lover of warfare and

wisdom, the goddess chose the location that was likely to produce men most like herself and established this first. You lived there employing laws such as these and even better ones, and so you were superior in excellence to all human beings, as one might expect in the case of those engendered and educated by gods.

e
'Many of your city's great achievements are recorded here and arouse our admiration, but one stands out from them all in scale and excellence. Our records tell us how your city once brought to a halt a great power as it advanced with unprovoked violence against the whole of Europe and Asia combined, launching its invasion from outside, from the Atlantic Ocean. At that time, the ocean there was navigable, since there was an island in front of the strait which, as you say, you call the Pillars of Heracles. The island was bigger than Libya and Asia combined, and it provided passage at

25a
that time for those travelling to the other islands, and from there to the whole continent opposite which surrounds the sea which truly deserves that name. In fact, everything inside the strait we are talking about is evidently just a harbour with a narrow entrance, whereas that is the real ocean, and the land which completely surrounds it could truly be called 'the continent'. On this island of Atlantis there established itself a great and remarkable power, ruled by kings, which governed the whole island as well as many other islands and parts of the continent. What's more, within the strait,

b
they governed Libya as far as Egypt, and Europe as far as Tyrrhenia. This whole power, concentrating all its forces into one, tried with a single assault to enslave your region and ours and the whole region inside the strait. Then it was, Solon, that the power of your city shone out clearly for everyone to see in its excellence and might. She stood out from all the others in her brave spirit and military

c
skill; first she led the Greeks, and then, deserted by the others, she was forced to stand alone and arrived at a point of intense danger. Even so, she defeated the invaders and celebrated her victory; she prevented those not yet enslaved from being enslaved, and she generously liberated all the rest of us who live inside the Pillars of Heracles. Later on, there were violent earthquakes and floods, and

d
in the onset of a single terrible day and night, your whole fighting

force sank below the earth all at once, and the island of Atlantis sank in the same way and disappeared below the sea. That is why the sea in this area is to this day impassable and impenetrable, since it is obstructed by mud a little way down, which the island left as it settled down'.

You have now heard, Socrates, in broad outline, what we were told by old Critias, based on Solon's report. So, when you spoke yesterday about the constitution and the men whom you described, I was amazed, remembering what I've just told you, and realizing that by some divine chance much of what you said corresponded with Solon's report and was not off-target. But I did not want to speak about this right away; because of the length of time, I didn't remember it well enough. I considered that I should first go over it properly in my mind and then tell it to you. So I was quick to agree with the demands you made on us yesterday, thinking that we would be pretty well equipped to offer a story suitable for your plans, which is the most important task in all such situations. So yesterday, as Hermocrates said, as soon as we left here, I started telling them the story as it came back to me, and after leaving them I concentrated on it during the night and recovered almost all of it. How true it is – as is commonly said – that what we learn in childhood has an amazing hold on our memory. In my case, I am not sure whether I could recall everything I heard yesterday, but I would be quite amazed if any of these things that I heard so long ago has escaped my memory. I listened to the story then with much childish pleasure, and the old man was eager to teach it to me as I kept asking one question after another, so that the story has stayed with me like the indelible markings of a picture with the colours burnt into it. What's more, I told these things to them first thing this morning, so that they too, along with me, would be well supplied for our speeches.

Now, to come to the point of these preliminaries, I am ready to tell the story, Socrates, not just in its main points but with the details as I heard it. The citizens and the city you described yesterday in mythical fashion, we shall now translate into actual fact, placing it here and regarding it as that real city; and the citizens you

e

26a

b

c

d

conceived, we shall say are those true ancestors of ours whom the priest described. They will fit in every way, and we will not strike a false note in saying that they are the ones who existed at that time. Dividing up the task between us, we shall all try to do our best to provide what is appropriate for your assignment. So you must consider, Socrates, whether this story matches our intention, or whether we still need to search for another in its place.

SOCRATES: What story, Critias, could we prefer to this one? It would be most appropriate for the present festival of the goddess, because of the connection with her; and the fact that it is not a made-up story but a true account is all-important, I suppose. How and from where shall we find others if we let them go? It is impossible; it's for you to speak – and good luck to you! – and for me to sit back and listen in return for my discussion yesterday.

CRITIAS: Consider then, Socrates, the arrangement we have made between us for your entertainment. We thought that Timaeus, because he is the astronomical expert among us, and has made understanding the nature of the universe his special job, should speak first, beginning with the origin of the universe, and ending with the nature of human beings. I'll go next, receiving from him the human beings brought to birth in his speech, some of them educated in a distinctive way by you. I'll proceed, on the basis of Solon's account and his law code, to lead them into this courtroom, as it were, and to make them citizens of this city, treating them as being the Athenians of that time, whom the report of the sacred writings has rescued from oblivion, and from now on to talk about them as actual Athenian citizens.

SOCRATES: It seems likely that I shall be receiving a complete and splendid banquet of speeches in return for mine. It seems to be your job, Timaeus, to speak next, after invoking the gods in the customary way.

Critias

106a–108d:
Critias's introduction to his story

TIMAEUS: How glad I am, Socrates, like someone who has found   106a
rest after taking a long road, that I have now happily brought to
an end the journey of my exposition. I pray to the god who came
into being long ago in fact, but who did so just now in words, to
preserve those parts of our account which were spoken in good
measure and, if we have inadvertently struck a false note, to impose   b
the appropriate penalty. The correct penalty for someone who plays
out of tune is to make him play in tune. So, to enable us in future
to speak correctly about the origin of the gods, we pray that he will
give us the most perfect and best of remedies, that is, knowledge.
With this prayer, I hand on to Critias the job of giving the next
speech in the sequence, in line with our agreement.

CRITIAS: Well, Timaeus, I accept this. But I also make the same
plea that you used at the start of your speech, when you asked for   c
understanding on the grounds that you were about to speak about
a great subject. Indeed, I think I have a still stronger claim for   107a
obtaining it and to a greater extent, given the nature of my subject.
Although I am all too well aware that the request I am about to
make is highly assertive and more uncivil than it should be, even
so I must make it. Nobody in their right mind would claim that
your speech was not an excellent one; what I must somehow try to
show is that the subject of the speech I am about to give is more
difficult and deserves more understanding. It is easier, Timaeus, to
give the impression of providing an adequate account of gods when

b   speaking to human beings than it is when speaking to us about mortals. The combination of inexperience and sheer ignorance in one's audience on subjects of which they are not informed provides a great opportunity to someone speaking about them; and about the gods, of course, we know how we are placed.

So that I can explain more clearly what I mean, please follow me in this line of thought. Everything that we all say must in some sense be representation and likeness. In the case of visual representation of divine and human bodies by artists, let us consider how

c   things stand regarding the relative ease or difficulty of seeming to spectators to have given an adequate representation. We shall observe first that we are satisfied if anyone is capable of producing even a slight likeness of the earth, mountains, rivers and woods, the sky as a whole and the things that are found there and move around it. In addition to this, because we do not have exact knowledge about such things, we do not examine paintings closely or criticize

d   them, but are content in their case with an imprecise and deceptive sketch. But whenever anyone tries to produce a likeness of our bodies, we are quick to notice faults because of our intimate and life-long observation and so we are harsh critics of anyone who fails to provide a complete likeness in every detail. We should recognize that the same is true of words. In the case of heavenly and divine subjects, we are content with accounts that even slightly resemble their subject matter, but we examine closely those of mortal and

e   human subjects. In the case of the present account, which is after all an improvisation, if I fail to provide what is appropriate in every respect, you must excuse me. You must realize that it is not easy but difficult to produce a likeness which corresponds to people's

108a   expectations. I have said all this, Socrates, wanting to remind you of these points, and asking for more, rather than less, understanding, as regards the speech I am about to give. If I seem to be justified in asking for this favour, grant it with good will.

SOCRATES: Why should we not grant it, Critias? And what is more, let us grant the same favour to Hermocrates, the third

b   speaker. Obviously, a little later, when he needs to make his speech, he will make the same request as you. So, to enable him to devise another introduction and not be forced to say the same thing as you, let him speak when the time comes, with this understanding available to him. But I must say in advance what the attitude of the audience is towards you. The poet who preceded you made an amazingly good impression, so that you will need a great deal of understanding, if you are going to be able to take over from him.

HERMOCRATES: The same recommendation, Socrates, applies to me as much as to him. But even so, Critias, faint-hearted men have never yet celebrated a victory. You must advance bravely towards your speech, calling on Apollo Paean and the Muses to help you bring out the excellence of those ancient citizens and sing their praises.

CRITIAS: My dear Hermocrates, because you are positioned in the rear, and have someone else in front of you, you are still confident. But what it is like to be at the front like this, experience itself will soon show you. But I must take note of your urging and encouragement, and as well as the gods you have mentioned, call on the others, above all, Mnemosune. Virtually everything that is most important in my speech depends on this goddess. If I can remember adequately and report what was told by the Egyptian priests and brought here by Solon, I am virtually certain that I will seem to our audience to have completed our task in due measure. So then, this is what must now be done, and there must be no delay.

108e–113b:
Critias's account of primaeval Athens

First of all, let us remember the chief point: it was recorded that, nine thousand years ago, a war occurred between those living outside and beyond the Pillars of Heracles and all those living inside them. We need now to finish the narrative of this war. We are told that, on one side, this city of ours took the lead and fought the whole war through to its completion, and on the other, the kings of the island of Atlantis. As we said, the island was once bigger than Libya and Asia combined, but now it has been submerged by

earthquakes and creates a mass of impenetrable mud, which is an
109a   obstacle to those sailing from here to the open sea, so that they
can no longer make voyages there. As regards the many barbarian
nations and those Greek peoples that existed then, the course of the
story, being unrolled, so to speak, will bring out the relevant fact
on each occasion, point by point. But first, at the beginning, I must
describe the condition of the Athenians at that time and of the
opponents with which they carried through the war, the resources
of each side and their constitutions. Of these topics, we must give
preference to describing the situation here.

b   At one point, the gods divided up the whole earth, region by
region – but without dispute. It would not be right to say that gods
do not know what properly belongs to each of them, or again that
they do know what belongs rather to others but try to secure this
for themselves through disputes. Receiving what was naturally
their own by the allocations of justice, the gods established
communities in their lands. After setting them up, they took
care of us, as herdsmen look after flocks, as their possessions and
livestock – but with one difference. They did not exert physical
c   force on our bodies, as herdsmen drive their flocks to pasture
by hitting them, but where a creature is most manageable, they
steered it from the stern. They directed its mind by persuasion as
they thought best, like someone using a rudder, and in this way
steered the human being as a whole.

So, different gods were allocated different regions and began to
put them in order. But Hephaestus and Athena shared a common
nature, both because they were brother and sister from the same
father and because they pursued the same ends in their love of
wisdom and craft. So they both received this land as a single
allocation, because it was congenial to their character and naturally
d   suited to them in their excellence and intelligence, and, producing
good men from the earth, they put into their minds the organization of the constitution. Their names have been preserved, but
their actions have been lost because of the disasters affecting their
successors and the length of time. Those of their race who survived
at any one time, as was said earlier, were left as illiterate mountain

dwellers, who had heard only the names of those who were rulers in the land and, besides, a few of their actions. It pleased them to   e
give the names to their children, but they knew nothing of the good qualities and laws of their ancestors, except for some hazy rumours about each of them. For many generations, they and their children were short of basic necessities, and they gave their attention to the things they needed and limited their discussion to these, and   110a
failed to think about what had happened in earlier times and long ago. Study of myths and enquiry into the distant past make their entrance into cities at the same time as leisure, whenever they see that some people are now equipped with the necessities of life, but not before. That is how the names of those in the distant past but not their actions have been preserved. I say this using as evidence the fact that the names of Cecrops, Erechtheus, Erichthonius, Erysichthon, and most of the things which are recorded about each of the names of the others too prior to Theseus – the majority of   b
these names, according to Solon, were given by those priests, in their narrative of the war of that time, and the names of the women in the same way. Consider too the appearance of the statue of the goddess. Since at that time military practices were common to women and men, in line with that custom the people of that time set up the image of the goddess in armour. This is evidence that, in the case of animals which are gregarious, male and female alike,   c
the whole kind is naturally capable, as a group, of practising the excellence appropriate to each kind.

At that time in this country there were different classes of citizens, some concerned with manufacture and agriculture, while the military class had been separated off from the beginning by god-like men and lived apart. They had everything that was required for their training and education, but none of them had any private property, and they regarded everything as being held in common with all of them. They did not expect to receive from   d
the other citizens more than was needed for basic maintenance, and they carried out all those practices that were spoken about yesterday, which we ascribed to the guardians we proposed in our theory.

Moreover, the long-standing claims about our territory are reliable and true: first of all, the borders at that time were drawn at the Isthmus and, on the mainland to the north, they reached as far

e   as the heights of Cithaeron and Parnes; coming down from these heights the borders included the region of Oropus on the right and stopped at the River Aesopus on the left, facing the sea. In addition, every other country was inferior to this one in fertility, so that the land was capable at that time of supporting a great army that was released from the work of agriculture. Here is strong evidence of its fertility: the present remnant of the land can compete with any

111a   other in the variety and quality of its crops and in the rich pasture it provides for all kinds of animals. But at that time, apart from its quality, our land produced all this in great quantity. How is this credible? and what justifies us in saying that it is a mere remnant of the land at that time?

The whole land, extending from the rest of the mainland far into the sea, lies outstretched like a headland; also, as it happens, the basin of the sea all around is deep close to the shore. There have been many great floods in nine thousand years – which is the

b   number of years from that time to the present. During this time and because of these events, the topsoil washed down from the high ground did not, as in other places, create any alluvial deposit of any significance but, continuously rolling over and over, it vanished into the depths of the sea. As in the case of small islands, if you compare what is there now to what was there then, what remains is like the skeleton of a sick body now that the rich soft soil has been eroded, and only the thin body of the land is left. At that time the

c   land was untouched and it had as mountains lofty mounds, and what is now called the plains of Phelleus were full of rich soil. In the mountains there were dense forests, of which there are still clear indications. Although some of the mountains provide only enough food for bees, it is not long since trees were cut down from those parts as roof-timbers for the biggest buildings, and the roofs still survive. There were also many different kinds of tall cultivated

d   trees, and they provided remarkable fodder for beasts. In addition, every year the land took the benefit of rain from Zeus, and it was not lost, as it is now, flowing from the bare earth into the sea. The land absorbed a great deal of water and stored it away, protecting it with non-porous clay, and drawing the water from all sort of high places into its hollows, it provided an abundant flow of water to feed streams and rivers throughout all its regions. Even today shrines at what were springs in earlier times remain as evidence of the truth of what I am claiming now about the land. This was the nature of the countryside; and it was cultivated as you might expect of those who were truly farmers, and who just did that one thing, who wanted to create fine crops and were naturally suited for their role, and who also had the best land and the most abundant supply of water, and, besides the land, a climate that was most moderately blended.

    The city, on the other hand, was laid out at that time in this way. First, the condition of the Acropolis was very different from what it is now. A single night of torrential rain stripped it of earth and left it bare as it is now, at the same time as earthquakes and a violent flood, which was the third such disaster before that of Deucalion. Before this, in a different era, in its size it reached as far as the rivers Eridanus and Ilissos, and held the Pnyx within its circuit, and had Mount Lycabettus as its border on the side opposite the Pnyx, as well as being covered with deep soil and almost entirely flat. The area outside the Acropolis and just beneath its slopes was occupied by craftsmen and the farmers who worked the neighbouring land. But the military class alone, by itself, had occupied the upper parts around the sanctuary of Athena and Hephaestus, which they had also surrounded with a single enclosing wall as though it were the garden of a single house. On the northern side of it, they lived in shared dwellings and provided themselves with dining halls for winter use and had everything which was needed for their common way of life in the form of housing for themselves and their priests, with the exception of gold and silver – they made no use of these for any purpose. Rather, following a middle course between extravagance and servility, they built for themselves tasteful houses, where they and their grandchildren grew old, and they always handed them down to others like themselves. As for the southern

e

112a

b

c

d   side, when they abandoned their gardens, gymnasia and dining halls, as is natural in summer, they used this area for these purposes. There was a single spring in the location of the present Acropolis, which was choked by the earthquakes, so that now all that remains are small rivulets flowing in a circle, although for all those living at that time, it provided an abundant supply and was the same in temperature in both summer and winter.

This was their form of life; and they were guardians of their own citizens, leaders of the other Greeks who willingly followed their lead, and they kept, on a permanent basis, the same number of men e   and women who were already or still of military age, about twenty thousand. So, because they had this character and always led their city and Greece in the same way, with justice, they were famous throughout Europe and Asia for the beauty of their bodies and for their excellence in different kinds of mental qualities and were the most renowned of all people at that time.

As for the condition of their opponents, what sort it was and how it became so from the beginning, unless I have lost the memory of what I heard when I was still a child, I shall now publicly hand over these things to be common property with you, my friends. One 113a   brief explanation must still be given before I give my account, so that you are not amazed when hearing Greek names often used for non-Greeks. Here is the reason for that: when Solon was planning to use the story as the basis for his poem and enquired about the significance of the names, he found out that the Egyptians who first wrote them down translated them into their own language. Solon, b   in turn, recovered the meaning of each of the names and wrote it down as he translated them into our language. These very writings were in the possession of my grandfather and are still now in my possession, and were studied by me as a child. So, if you hear me saying names like those used here, do not be surprised at this, since you know the reason. What follows was a sort of introduction to the long story I heard then.

113b–119b:
Critias's description of the physical features of Atlantis

As was said earlier, the gods divided up the whole earth into portions, bigger in some places and smaller in others, as they c established sanctuaries and sacrifices for themselves. So Poseidon was allocated the island of Atlantis, and settled there children whom he fathered from a mortal woman in a place on the island that I will describe. On the coast, in the middle of the whole island, was a plain, which is said to have been the most beautiful of all plains and adequate too in its fertility. And, in turn, near the plain and in the middle of it, fifty stades inland, was a mountain, not very high at any point. Here lived one of the men from there who was originally born from the earth; his name was Evenor and d he lived there with his wife Leucippe, and their only child was a daughter called Cleito. The girl was just coming to marriageable age when her mother and father both died. Poseidon was attracted to her and made love to her; and he fortified the mound where she had been settled by enclosing it all around, making rings of sea and land alternately, of increasing size, one around the other, two of land and three of sea, at all points equidistant from each other, like a man using a turning-lathe from the centre of the island, to e make it inaccessible to human beings, since there were no ships or navigation at that time. He himself put in order the central island, easily, as is natural for a god; he drew up twin springs of water from under the ground, one warm and one cold, and each one flowing from a fountain, and he produced from the ground varied and sufficient foodstuffs. He fathered five pairs of male twins and brought them up, and he divided up the whole island of Atlantis into ten parts. To the first-born of the oldest set of twins, he allocated as his portion his mother's home and the area that 114a encircled it, since that was the largest and best. Poseidon also set him up as king of the rest, with the others as governors, and gave to them each rule over many people and a very large territory. He gave names to all of them, and to the oldest, their king, the one from which the whole island and sea acquired its designation; it was b called Atlantic, because the name of the first king at that time was Atlas. To his twin brother, born after him, he who took as his share the edge of the island on the side of the Pillars of Heracles, facing the region which is now called Gadiran after that place, he gave the name Eumelus in Greek but Gadirus in the language of that country, the very name which must have provided this designation. To the twins born second, he gave one the name Ampheres and the other Evaemon. To the twins born third, he gave the name

c Mneseus to the elder and Autochthon to the younger. To those born fourth, he gave the name Elasippus to the elder and Mestor to the younger. In the case of the fifth set, the first-born received the name Azäes and the second-born Diaprepes. All these and their descendants occupied these regions for many generations; they were not only rulers of many other islands in the ocean, but also, as mentioned before, extended their rule over the people within the Pillars of Heracles in our direction as far as Egypt and Tyrrhenia.

d The race of Atlas became great and respected in general, and the oldest king handed down the kingdom to his oldest son for many generations and thus maintained it. They acquired wealth on a scale that no previous king in any royal line has ever done and that nobody in the future could ever easily do. They were provided with everything they needed in the city and the rest of

e the country. Because of their empire, many things were brought to them from outside, but the island itself provided most of what was needed for their livelihood. First of all, there was whatever could be dug up by mining, solid and fusible materials, including something that is now only a name – but at that time orichalch was more than a name and was a type of metal mined in many places on the island and more valuable than everything then except gold. Also, whatever woods can provide for the work of craftsmen, the island produced in abundance; as regards animals, it produced enough to feed both tame and wild animals, and in particular the

115a species of elephants was numerous there. There was ample pasture for all the other animals which feed by marshes, lakes and rivers, or again on mountains or the plains, and similarly for this animal [the elephant], which is by nature the biggest and most voracious.

In addition, whatever fragrant plants the earth bears today – roots, shoots, wood of trees, or gums exuded by flowers or fruit – the island produced them and maintained them well. It also bore cultivated crops, both the dry type which we use as our basic source of nutrition, and the things we use in addition as foodstuff — we call them, as a whole, pulses. Further, it bore the fruit of trees which provides drinks, foods and oils, and the fruit from treetops, which is hard to store and which is used for amusement and pleasure, and what we offer as welcome dessert to someone who is suffering to soothe his fullness. All these things were produced by the sacred island then, when it was still under the sun, and they were beautiful, amazing and limitless in number. Taking all these things from the earth, they constructed temples, royal palaces, harbours and dockyards, and organized the whole land with the arrangement I will now describe.

b

c

First of all, they placed bridges over the rings of sea around their mother's ancient city, and made a road out of and into the palace. They constructed the palace right away from the beginning in the place where the god and their ancestors had lived. Each king took over from another and, improving what was already improved, produced something superior to his predecessor as far as he could, until they made their residence an object of astonishment to look at in its size and the beauty of its construction. Also, starting from the sea, they dug a canal three hundred feet wide, one hundred feet deep and fifty stades long, to the outermost ring, and in this way created access to it from the sea, like a harbour, opening up an entrance that was large enough for the biggest ships to sail in through. In addition, in the rings of land that separated the rings of water, at the bridges, they made gaps big enough to allow one trireme at a time to sail through from one ring of water to the next, and roofed the gaps over above to make an underground naval passage; the sides of the rings of land were high enough above the sea to enable this. The largest of the rings, into which a channel from the sea had been dug, was three stades in breadth, and the adjacent ring of land was equal to that. Of the second pair, the land ring was two stades in breadth, and the ring of land was equal to

d

e

116a   the preceding ring of water. The ring running around the island in
the centre was one stade in breadth.

The island on which the palace was located was five stades
in diameter. They surrounded this island and the rings and the
bridge, which was a hundred feet wide, on both sides, with a stone
wall all around, and they placed guard houses and gates on the
bridges, at the access points from the sea and on each side. They
quarried the stone from under the central island, all around it,
and from the two rings of land, both outside and inside each ring;

b   some stone was white, some black, some red. As they quarried, they
hollowed out interior double dockyards, roofed over by the rock
itself. Some of their buildings were uniform in colour, while they
made others varied by combining different types of stone for the
sake of amusement, giving the buildings an inherent attractiveness.
They also covered the whole circuit of the wall of the outermost

c   ring with bronze, as though applying varnish, and covered that of
the inner ring with tin, and the wall around the citadel itself with
orichalch, which gleamed like fire.

The layout of the palace buildings inside the citadel was as
follows. In the very middle was a shrine sacred to Cleito and
Poseidon, which was kept consecrated and which nobody could
enter, surrounded by a wall of gold. This was the place where,
at the beginning, they conceived and gave birth to the family of
the ten kings. Also here each year seasonal offerings from all ten
provinces were made to each of the original kings. The temple of

d   Poseidon was also here; it was one stade long, three hundred feet
wide and was proportionate in its height to look at, though there
was something barbaric about its appearance. They overlaid the
whole exterior of the temple with silver, except for the pediment
sculptures, which were overlaid with gold. As for the interior, they
overlaid it with a complete surface of ivory, decorated with gold,

e   silver and orichalch. They placed gold statues inside, one of the god,
standing on a chariot as the charioteer of six winged horses, which
was so tall that the head touched the roof, and a hundred Nereids
riding dolphins in a circle around him – which is how many people
thought there were then – and there were many other statues inside

which were the offerings of private individuals. Around the temple on the outside stood gold statues of all the wives and descendants of the ten kings, and many other important votive offerings of the kings or private individuals from the city of Atlantis itself or from the people outside that they ruled. There was an altar too, 117a which corresponded to this set-up in its size and the quality of its workmanship; and the palace buildings in the same way matched the greatness of the empire and elaborateness of the temples.

They drew their water from springs, one of cold running water and one of hot, which were abundant in quantity, and each of which was wonderfully suited by nature, in the flavour and the quality of its waters, for the use to which it was put. They put around them buildings and plantations of trees which were suitable b for the waters; and they also constructed around them pools, some open to the air, and others roofed over for winter use as warm baths; they kept separate the pools for the kings, and for private individuals, with different ones again for women and for horses and other beasts of burden, and they assigned the type of decoration appropriate to each group. They channelled the overflow into the grove of Poseidon, and to trees of all kinds which were of remarkable beauty and height because of the fertility of the soil, and also to the outer rings of land through pipes which ran along c the bridges.

Here too numerous shrines to numerous gods, and numerous gardens and areas for exercise had been built, separately, for men and horses on each of the two islands formed by the rings, and in particular a racecourse was reserved in the middle of the larger island. It was a stade in width; as for its length, a space was left free around the whole circuit of the land for horse-racing. Located around it on either side were guard houses for the majority of the d royal bodyguards. For those who were more trustworthy, a garrison was set up on the smaller island and nearer the citadel, while those who were exceptionally trustworthy were given quarters inside the citadel around the kings themselves. The dockyards were full of triremes and the equipment that triremes need, and all of this was in good working order.

This was the layout of buildings around the dwelling of the kings. But, as you went past the outer harbours, which were three in number, you saw a wall which began from the sea and went in
e   a circle, at a uniform distance of fifty stades from the largest ring of water and the great harbour, and completed its circuit at the mouth of the canal by the sea. This whole area was occupied by many closely packed houses, and the canal and the biggest harbour was full of ships and merchants arriving from all over the world, whose numbers created shouting, commotion and every kind of din day and night.

I have now given a pretty full report of what was recorded then
118a   about the city and the area around the ancient dwelling of the kings. But now I must try to recall the nature of the rest of the country and the form of its organization. First of all, the whole region was said to be very high and rose sheer from the sea; the area around the city, which surrounded it, consisted entirely of a plain, which was completely surrounded by mountains sloping down to the sea. The plain was smooth and level, and oblong as a whole, measuring
b   three thousand stades on each side and two thousand stades across at its midpoint from the sea. This region, out of the whole island, faced south and was sheltered from the northern winds. The surrounding mountains of that time were praised for their number, size and beauty, and were said to go beyond all those which exist today. They contained many villages with large populations, and also rivers, lakes and meadows that provided sufficient pasture for all tame and wild beasts, and wood that was, in its quantity and the variety of its types, abundant both for all kinds of work and for each individual requirement.

c   This is how the plain was by nature and how it was when modified by many kings over a long period. It was originally, as I said, quadrilateral, with mostly straight sides, and oblong in shape. Where it fell short of this, they made it straight by digging a canal around it. As for its depth, width and length, what was claimed is incredible for a work of human hands – that it should be so great in comparison with the other building works; but we must in any case report what we have been told. The canal was dug to a depth of a hundred feet, the width was a stade at each point and, as it was dug around the whole plain, the length turned out to be ten thousand stades. The canal received the flow of water that came off the mountains, formed a complete circuit round the plain and reached the city on both sides, and there released it to flow out into the sea. Further inland, channels about a hundred feet wide were cut in straight lines from the canal across the plain and they discharged their waters back into the main canal on the seaward side. These channels were spaced a hundred stades apart. They also cut cross-channels at right angles linking the channels with each other and the city; in that way they brought down wood from the mountains to the city, and transported seasonal produce by boat. They harvested the land twice a year, using the rain sent by Zeus in the winter and in summer what the land provided, extracting a flow of water from the channels.

As for the number of men on the plain fit to serve in war, it had been laid down that each district should provide one leader; the size of the district was ten square stades, and the total number of districts was sixty thousand. The number of people from the mountains and the rest of the country was said to be incalculable; but they were all allocated by region and village to these districts and to serve under their leaders. In time of war, each leader was required to provide a sixth part of the equipment of a war chariot, as a contribution to a total of ten thousand chariots; two horses and riders, and, besides, a pair of horses without a chariot but equipped with a foot soldier with a small shield, and a charioteer for both horses who stands behind the chariot fighter; two hoplites; archers and slingers, two of each; lightly armed stone-throwers and javelin-throwers, three of each; also four sailors contributing to the complement of twelve thousand ships. This was the military organization of the royal city; each of the nine other cities had their own different arrangements and it would take a long time to describe them.

d

e

119a

b

119c–121c:
the political structure of Atlantis and its moral decline

c   Powers and positions of honour were organized in the following way from the beginning. In his own individual region and as regards his own city, each of the ten kings had authority over men and most of the laws, punishing and killing whomever he wanted. But the distribution of authority between them and their mutual relationships were regulated by the commands of Poseidon, as was laid down for them by law and by an inscription written by the first

d   rulers on a column of orichalch, which was situated in the middle of the island in the temple of Poseidon. They came together there every fifth or sixth year, alternately, giving an equal share to the even and the odd; and when they came together, they considered matters of common concern and enquired closely if any of them was doing something wrong, and passed judgement on them. Whenever they were about to pass judgement, they gave each other pledges first in the following way.

 Some bulls were allowed to run free in the sanctuary of Poseidon;

e   when the ten kings were on their own, they prayed to the god to let them capture the victim which would please him. They hunted the bulls using wooden clubs and nooses, but no iron weapon; and they led the bull they caught to the column and cut its throat over the top so that the blood ran down over the inscription. On the column, in addition to the laws, there was an oath calling down terrible curses

120a upon anyone who disobeyed the laws. When they had sacrificed the bull according to their own laws, they consecrated all its limbs. They mixed a bowl of wine and threw in a clot of the bull's blood on behalf of each of them; then they put the rest of the blood into the fire and purified the column. After this, they drew off the blood from the mixing bowl into golden bowls, and poured libations down into the fire. They swore that they would pass judgement according to the laws on the column and punish anyone who had committed any offence in the past, and that in the future they would not willingly break any of the terms of the inscription and

b   would neither exercise rule or obey anyone else's rule unless they were doing so in line with their father's laws. Each of them swore this oath on his own behalf and that of his descendants, and then they drank and dedicated their bowl to the temple of the god. Then they gave attention to their meal and other things they needed to do. When it was dark and the fire around the sacrificial offerings had cooled down, they all put on dark blue robes which were of the very greatest beauty, and sat on the ground by the embers of the sacrificial fire made in support of their oath. Then, when it was c night, and they had put out all the fires throughout the sanctuary, they were judged and passed judgement if anyone accused anyone else of committing an offence. After they had passed judgement, when it was light, they wrote the judgements on a golden tablet, which they dedicated as a memorial offering along with the robes. There were many other specific laws about the privileges of each of the kings, but the most important points were that they should not make war against each other, and that they should all help if anyone in any of their cities tried to overthrow the royal family, and d that, as in the past, they should reach decisions in common about war and other actions, while granting the leading role to the house of Atlas. It was also specified that the king of this house should not have the right to kill any of his relatives, unless it was approved by more than half of the ten kings.

This was the scale and character of the power that existed at that time in those regions, and which the god assembled and brought against our regions, and did so, as the story went, for the following reason. For many generations, as long as the nature of e the god was sufficiently strong in them, they were obedient to the laws and well-disposed towards their innate divinity. They formed judgements that were true and great in every way, and they reacted with a combination of mildness and good sense towards their fortunes as they happened to be at any one time and towards each other. They looked down on everything but virtue and regarded their current prosperity as being unimportant. They bore without 121a difficulty the bulk of their gold and other possessions, as though they were a burden; and they were not intoxicated by luxury, because of their wealth. Nor did they lose control of themselves and trip up but, remaining sober, they saw clearly that all these things are increased by reciprocal friendship combined with virtue, but that if you take them seriously and overvalue them they are themselves destroyed, and so is virtue. By reasoning of this kind and because of the divine nature that remained in them, the prosperity we described before increased for them.

b
But when the portion of god in them became weakened through frequent admixture with a large mortal element, and the human character became predominant, then they were unable to bear their current good fortune and started to disgrace themselves. To someone who could see clearly, they were obviously shameful since they had lost the finest of what had been the most valuable of their possessions; but to those unable to see the life that truly leads to happiness, they were regarded as being most splendid and blessed, though they were activated by unjust greed for possessions and power.

c
Zeus, god of the gods, who rules by laws, and is able to discern such things, realized that this noble race was in a terrible state; he wanted to punish them to render them self-controlled and more harmonious. He summoned all the gods to their most honoured dwelling, which stands in the middle of the whole universe and looks down on everything that has a share in becoming, and after drawing them together he said ...

The Atlantis Story:

Greek Text and Commentary

(Plato *Timaeus* 17a–27b, *Critias*)

The text printed here is the Oxford Classical Text, vol. 4, ed. J. Burnet (Oxford: Oxford University Press, first ed. 1902, often reprinted). The format of the Greek text is that of the Thesaurus Linguae Graecae, which supplied a digital file of the two Platonic dialogues.

The translation provided earlier in the book assumes a different reading from Burnet's in a small number of places, which are discussed in the notes, though the text itself is unchanged. The relevant passages are: *Timaeus* 25d5, 26c1; *Critias* 106a1, 111c1, 114b5, 118c2, 118e3. As explained in the preface, the text is interleaved with headings, summary and notes, in order to give the reader the fullest possible help in understanding the meaning of the Greek. Anyone preferring to read the Greek text without interruption can do so by using Burnet's text in the Oxford Classical text format; the translation provided in the present book also runs continuously.

The introduction is referred to by paragraph numbers in square brackets (e.g. 'see [24]'). For scholarly works cited, see the bibliography. Combinations of numbers and letters in the form '17d2' or '20a' refer to the Stephanus pages and divisions of the *Timaeus* and *Critias* (abbreviated as *Ti.* and *Criti.*). All dates are BC unless otherwise indicated. The translations suggested here (in inverted commas) are the same as those given earlier, sometimes explained further by more literal versions (indicated by lit. = literally).

In the notes, readers are referred to the following works for grammatical guidance:

RG   Joint Association of Classical Teachers' Greek Course, *Reading Greek: Grammar and Exercises*, 2nd ed. (Cambridge: Cambridge University Press, 2007); references are to sections.

AM   Abbot and Mansfield, *A Primer of Greek Grammar* (London: Duckworth, 1977, reprint of 1893 ed.); references are to paragraph numbers of 'Syntax'.

G   W. W. Goodwin, *A Greek Grammar* (London: Macmillan, 1959); references are to paragraph numbers.

Goodwin *SMT*   W. W. Goodwin, *Syntax of the Moods and Tenses of the Greek Verb* (London: Macmillan, 1897).

LSJ   H. G. Liddell and R. Scott (revised by H. S. Jones and R. MacKenzie), *A Greek-English Lexicon*, 9th ed. (Oxford: Oxford University Press, 1996).

Timaeus 17a–27b

17a–19b:
Socrates's summary of the *Republic*'s ideal state

Plato begins the *Timaeus* by marking a connection with the theory of the *Republic*, but also indicating that this theory will be treated selectively. He makes Socrates summarize the 'ideal state' of *Republic* Books II to V, of which the basic institution was that of a guardian class in charge of government and defence, and living as a cohesive group without private property or family life. Socrates includes reference to the elementary education of the guardian class (*Republic* Books II and III), but excludes from his summary the intellectual education given to a small élite of 'philosopher-rulers' in *Republic* Books VI and VII. This is an indication that this story, like Timaeus's cosmology, will focus on putting an ideal structure into concrete, embodied form, not on progress towards knowledge of the ideal (see [15, 24] and the note on 17d2). Plato also makes it plain that the imaginary conversation in which the ideal state was described was not the same as the discussion that made up the *Republic*. The imaginary conversation took place 'yesterday', on the festival of Athena (*Timaeus* 21a, 26e), not of Bendis (*Republic* 327a, 354a), and the participants are different people. Plato thus maintains the convention followed throughout his dialogues that one dialogue does not refer explicitly to another unless they form part of a connected series of discussions (e.g. *Theaetetus*, *Sophist* and *Statesman*; see Gill 2002, 153–61).

Plato's Atlantis Story

17a1   {ΣΩ.} Εἷς, δύο, τρεῖς· ὁ δὲ δὴ τέταρτος ἡμῖν, ὦ φίλε Τίμαιε, ποῦ τῶν χθὲς μὲν δαιτυμόνων, τὰ νῦν δὲ ἑστια-
τόρων;
{ΤΙ.} Ἀσθένειά τις αὐτῷ συνέπεσεν, ὦ Σώκρατες· οὐ γὰρ
5   ἂν ἑκὼν τῆσδε ἀπελείπετο τῆς συνουσίας.
{ΣΩ.} Οὐκοῦν σὸν τῶνδέ τε ἔργον καὶ τὸ ὑπὲρ τοῦ ἀπόντος
ἀναπληροῦν μέρος;

17a1   We do not know the identity of the missing member of
'yesterday's' group, or why Plato has included a missing person
in his imaginary group.

17a2–3   Yesterday's account of the ideal state is described as a feast, or
entertainment (17b, also 27b), and thus suitable for a festival
(26e). For the image of an intellectual 'feast', see *Gorgias* 447a;
Republic 352b, 354a.

17a4   ἀσθένειά τις implies vagueness on Timaeus's part: translate
'he must have been taken ill in some way' (συνέπεσεν is
aor). οὐ γὰρ ἂν ἑκὼν … ἀπελείπετο, pass. impf. with ἄν =
present unfulfilled condition, 'he wouldn't miss this meeting
voluntarily', RG 402, AM 179 ii.

17b1   {ΤΙ.} Πάνυ μὲν οὖν, καὶ κατὰ δύναμίν γε οὐδὲν ἐλλεί-
ψομεν· οὐδὲ γὰρ ἂν εἴη δίκαιον, χθὲς ὑπὸ σοῦ ξενισθέντας
οἷς ἦν πρέπον ξενίοις, μὴ οὐ προθύμως σὲ τοὺς λοιποὺς ἡμῶν
ἀνταφεστιᾶν.
5   {ΣΩ.} Ἆρ' οὖν μέμνησθε ὅσα ὑμῖν καὶ περὶ ὧν ἐπέταξα
εἰπεῖν;
{ΤΙ.} Τὰ μὲν μεμνήμεθα, ὅσα δὲ μή, σὺ παρὼν ὑπομνήσεις·
μᾶλλον δέ, εἰ μή τί σοι χαλεπόν, ἐξ ἀρχῆς διὰ βραχέων πάλιν
ἐπάνελθε αὐτά, ἵνα βεβαιωθῇ μᾶλλον παρ' ἡμῖν.

17b2–4   'It would be unfair' (potential opt., RG 401) 'since we were
entertained by you [ξενισθέντας agrees with τοὺς λοιποὺς
ἡμῶν] … for those of us who remain not to feast you in return
and with enthusiasm'. The double negative (μὴ οὐ) follows the

negative main clause (RG 428, G 1616). οἷς ξενίοις, contraction of τοῖς ξενίοις οἷς: 'with such fitting hospitality'. The image of a 'return feast' may indicate that the *Timaeus-Critias* will constitute an unusual combination of disciplines, including cosmology and (quasi-)history, and going beyond Socrates's normal focus on ethical and political philosophy (Broadie 2013, 120–21.)

17b9   'so that they become more firmly fixed in our minds'. The aor. subj. βεβαιωθῇ has no time significance; it differs from the pres. only in signifying a single event rather than a continuing process (AM 72, RG 417).

17c1   {ΣΩ.} Ταῦτ' ἔσται. χθές που τῶν ὑπ' ἐμοῦ ῥηθέντων
λόγων περὶ πολιτείας ἦν τὸ κεφάλαιον οἷά τε καὶ ἐξ οἵων
ἀνδρῶν ἀρίστη κατεφαίνετ' ἄν μοι γενέσθαι.
{ΤΙ.} Καὶ μάλα γε ἡμῖν, ὦ Σώκρατες, ῥηθεῖσα πᾶσιν κατὰ
5   νοῦν.
{ΣΩ.} Ἆρ' οὖν οὐ τὸ τῶν γεωργῶν ὅσαι τε ἄλλαι τέχναι
πρῶτον ἐν αὐτῇ χωρὶς διειλόμεθα ἀπὸ τοῦ γένους τοῦ τῶν
προπολεμησόντων;
{ΤΙ.} Ναί.

17c2–3   The clause beginning οἷα develops the idea in περὶ πολιτείας: 'the chief topic was, I think [που], what kind of state seemed to me the best, and of what kind of men it would consist'. ἄν … γενέσθαι (virtual indirect speech after verb of thinking, κατεφαίνετο μοι) represents ἄν γένοιτο in direct speech.

17c6–8   ὅσαι τε ἄλλαι τέχναι, understand 'the practitioners' (of all the other crafts), i.e. 'the other craftsmen'; for the kind of crafts meant here, see *Republic* 370c–371e.

10   {ΣΩ.} Καὶ κατὰ φύσιν δὴ δόντες τὸ καθ' αὑτὸν ἑκάστῳ
17d1   πρόσφορον ἓν μόνον ἐπιτήδευμα, μίαν ἑκάστῳ τέχνην, τούτους οὓς πρὸ πάντων ἔδει πολεμεῖν, εἴπομεν ὡς ἄρ' αὐτοὺς

δέοι φύλακας εἶναι μόνον τῆς πόλεως, εἴτε τις ἔξωθεν ἢ καὶ
τῶν ἔνδοθεν ἴοι κακουργήσων, δικάζοντας μὲν πρᾴως τοῖς
18a1 ἀρχομένοις ὑπ' αὐτῶν καὶ φύσει φίλοις οὖσιν, χαλεποὺς δὲ
ἐν ταῖς μάχαις τοῖς ἐντυγχάνουσιν τῶν ἐχθρῶν γιγνομένους.

17c10–18a2 'and assigning to each person only the one job which was
naturally [κατὰ φύσιν] suited to him individually [καθ'αὑτὸν],
one craft for each person, we said that those whose duty it was
to fight on everyone's behalf should be guardians of the city
and nothing else [μόνον]'. It is a basic principle of the *Republic*'s
ideal state that each person should be placed in the class for
which his nature suits him, and that each class should do the
job for which its nature suits it. The job of the guardian class
is to be 'harsh' (χαλεποὺς) in the defence of the state against
external or internal enemies, but to deal 'gently' (πρᾴως) in
their judgements on their subjects, and so the members of
the guardian class must be naturally disposed to do this (see
18a4–7 and *Republic* 374a–376d). Socrates maintains that such
a state, based on natural principles, would create harmony and
friendship between ruler and subject (*Republic* 431e–432b, also
590d–e): hence here the subjects are said to be 'naturally friends'
with the rulers (18a1).

17d2–18a7 See *Republic* 375c. The wording of d2–3 also echoes *Republic*
414b, in which Plato introduces the distinction between the
inner élite of guardians and their assistants or 'auxiliaries'
(ἐπίκουροι), but we find no hint of that distinction here.

17d4 κακουργήσων, fut. part. expressing purpose, 'to do harm' (RG
393(v), AM 97).

{ΤΙ.} Παντάπασι μὲν οὖν.
{ΣΩ.} Φύσιν γὰρ οἶμαί τινα τῶν φυλάκων τῆς ψυχῆς
5 ἐλέγομεν ἅμα μὲν θυμοειδῆ, ἅμα δὲ φιλόσοφον δεῖν εἶναι
διαφερόντως, ἵνα πρὸς ἑκατέρους δύναιντο ὀρθῶς πρᾶοι καὶ
χαλεποὶ γίγνεσθαι.
{ΤΙ.} Ναί.

10 {ΣΩ.} Τί δὲ τροφήν; ἆρ’ οὐ γυμναστικῇ καὶ μουσικῇ μαθήμασίν τε ὅσα προσήκει τούτοις, ἐν ἅπασι τεθράφθαι;
{ΤΙ.} Πάνυ μὲν οὖν.

18a4–6 ‘I think we said that there was a certain character [φύσιν
… τινα … τῆς ψυχῆς], which the guardians must have, an
exceptional combination of spirited and philosophical qualities’.
διαφερόντως, adverb, should be taken with both adjectives.
φιλόσοφον, fem.; like most compound adjectives, φιλόσοφος
has two terminations (RG 226, AM, Accidence, 68). See also
Republic 375e–376d.

18a9–10 Supply ἐλέγομεν from the previous sentence with the second
question. τούτοις, masc., refers to φύλακες: ‘the branches of
learning appropriate to them’. ἐν ἅπασι agrees with μαθήμασίν
and is placed at the end of the sentence for emphasis.
τεθράφθαι, perf. pass. infin. of τρέφω; the adult guardians
should *have been* educated in all these branches of education.

18b1 {ΣΩ.} Τοὺς δέ γε οὕτω τραφέντας ἐλέχθη που μήτε χρυσὸν
μήτε ἄργυρον μήτε ἄλλο ποτὲ μηδὲν κτῆμα ἑαυτῶν ἴδιον
νομίζειν δεῖν, ἀλλ’ ὡς ἐπικούρους μισθὸν λαμβάνοντας τῆς
φυλακῆς παρὰ τῶν σῳζομένων ὑπ’ αὐτῶν, ὅσος σώφροσιν
5 μέτριος, ἀναλίσκειν τε δὴ κοινῇ καὶ συνδιαιτωμένους μετὰ
ἀλλήλων ζῆν, ἐπιμέλειαν ἔχοντας ἀρετῆς διὰ παντός, τῶν
ἄλλων ἐπιτηδευμάτων ἄγοντας σχολήν.
{ΤΙ.} Ἐλέχθη καὶ ταῦτα ταύτῃ.

18b3–7 In the *Republic*, the word ἐπίκουροι signified the larger class
of secondary guardians or auxiliaries (414b); but here the
word is used in its regular sense of ‘mercenaries’, emphasizing
that *all* the guardians have a fixed wage and no private
wealth (compare *Republic* 416c–417b). b4: ὅσος κ.τ.λ., the
wage is ‘as much as (no more than) is reasonable for people
of moderate habits’. b6: ἀρετῆς, governed by ἐπιμέλειαν,
signifies ‘excellence’ in the execution of their special job, that

of guarding. τῶν ἄλλων κ.τ.λ., 'having leisure from other occupations', that is, being relieved of them; gen. of separation (AM 21) with σχολήν.

18c1   {ΣΩ.} Καὶ μὲν δὴ καὶ περὶ γυναικῶν ἐπεμνήσθημεν, ὡς τὰς φύσεις τοῖς ἀνδράσιν παραπλησίας εἴη συναρμοστέον, καὶ τὰ ἐπιτηδεύματα πάντα κοινὰ κατά τε πόλεμον καὶ κατὰ τὴν ἄλλην δίαιταν δοτέον πάσαις.
5   {ΤΙ.} Ταύτῃ καὶ ταῦτα ἐλέγετο.

18c1–4 In this compressed statement, Plato suggests two of his proposals in the *Republic*: that women who are similar in character to the male guardians (τὰς φύσεις τοῖς ἀνδράσιν παραπλησίας) should be educated alongside them and should share their way of life, and that their natures should be adapted (ξυναρμοστέον) so that they come to resemble the male guardians and can play the same roles as effectively as their male counterparts (*Republic* 455d–457b); for education as 'harmonization' of the character, see *Republic* 412a, 443d–e. Translate 'that those [i.e. those women] whose nature was similar to the male [guardians] should be brought into harmony with them'. εἴη is opt. in indirect speech in secondary sequence (RG 299, AM 80). ξυναρμοστέον, δοτέον are verbal adjectives, conveying obligation, used impersonally; see also θρεπτέον, διαδοτέον (19a1–2), RG 294, AM 111.

        {ΣΩ.} Τί δὲ δὴ τὸ περὶ τῆς παιδοποιίας; ἢ τοῦτο μὲν διὰ τὴν ἀήθειαν τῶν λεχθέντων εὐμνημόνευτον, ὅτι κοινὰ τὰ τῶν γάμων καὶ τὰ τῶν παίδων πᾶσιν ἁπάντων ἐτίθεμεν, μηχανω-μένους ὅπως μηδείς ποτε τὸ γεγενημένον αὐτῶν ἰδίᾳ γνώ-
18d1   σοιτο, νομιοῦσιν δὲ πάντες πάντας αὐτοὺς ὁμογενεῖς, ἀδελφὰς μὲν καὶ ἀδελφοὺς ὅσοιπερ ἂν τῆς πρεπούσης ἐντὸς ἡλικίας γίγνωνται, τοὺς δ᾽ ἔμπροσθεν καὶ ἄνωθεν γονέας τε καὶ

γονέων προγόνους, τοὺς δ᾽ εἰς τὸ κάτωθεν ἐκγόνους παῖδάς
5   τε ἐκγόνων;
{ΤΙ.} Ναί, καὶ ταῦτα εὐμνημόνευτα ἢ λέγεις.

18c6–d6   In the *Republic* Plato forbids his guardians to have family life
in the ordinary sense: the whole guardian class is to regard
itself as one extended family, and they are to be bred without
the formation of family units (*Republic* 460–463). τὰ τῶν
γάμων, 'the matters concerning marriage': translate as 'the
rights of marriage' or simply 'marriages'. μηχανώμενους (c8–9),
understand φύλακας (or the ἄρχοντας and ἄρχουσας mentioned
in d8–9), acc. loosely governed by indirect command: 'we laid
it down [ἐτίθεμεν] that their marriages and children should be
in common … and that they [the guardians] should arrange
…'. ὅπως μηδείς γνώσοιτο (fut. opt. act. with mid. form of
γιγνώσκω) and (ὅπως) νομιοῦσι δὲ πάντες (fut. indic.) are
both clauses signifying the object aimed at (AM 168, compare
purpose clause, RG 399). Fut. indic. and opt. are both found in
such clauses in secondary sequence (G 1372); Plato uses both for
variety.

{ΣΩ.} Ὅπως δὲ δὴ κατὰ δύναμιν εὐθὺς γίγνοιντο ὡς ἄριστοι
τὰς φύσεις, ἆρ᾽ οὐ μεμνήμεθα ὡς τοὺς ἄρχοντας ἔφαμεν καὶ
τὰς ἀρχούσας δεῖν εἰς τὴν τῶν γάμων σύνερξιν λάθρα
18e1   μηχανᾶσθαι κλήροις τισὶν ὅπως οἱ κακοὶ χωρὶς οἵ τ᾽ ἀγαθοὶ
ταῖς ὁμοίαις ἑκάτεροι συλλήξονται, καὶ μή τις αὐτοῖς ἔχθρα διὰ
ταῦτα γίγνηται, τύχην ἡγουμένοις αἰτίαν τῆς συλλήξεως;
{ΤΙ.} Μεμνήμεθα.

18d7–e3   In the *Republic*, the breeding of the guardians is organized
on eugenic principles: it is arranged for the best guardians to
mate with each other (at special festivals) to generate the best
children. But the mating is made to seem a matter of chance by
the use of manipulated lots allocating sexual partners (*Republic*
459c–460b). εἰς τὴν τῶν γάμων σύνερξιν, lit. 'with respect to the

contraction of marriages', μηχανᾶσθαι ... ὅπως as in 18c8-9.
καὶ μὴ ... γίγνηται is then written as if the context were that of
an ordinary purpose clause introduced by ἵνα or ὅπως (as in
d7 - except that e3 has the subjunctive instead of the optative,
because συλλήξονται (e2) has, in effect, made a transition into
primary sequence).

19a1 {ΣΩ.} Καὶ μὴν ὅτι γε τὰ μὲν τῶν ἀγαθῶν θρεπτέον ἔφαμεν
εἶναι, τὰ δὲ τῶν κακῶν εἰς τὴν ἄλλην λάθρᾳ διαδοτέον πόλιν·
ἐπαυξανομένων δὲ σκοποῦντας ἀεὶ τοὺς ἀξίους πάλιν ἀνάγειν
δεῖν, τοὺς δὲ παρὰ σφίσιν ἀναξίους εἰς τὴν τῶν ἐπανιόντων
5   χώραν μεταλλάττειν;
{ΤΙ.} Οὕτως.

19a1-5 Understand τέκνα with τὰ δὲ ... τὰ δὲ. εἰς τὴν ἄλλην πόλιν
signifies the transference of the children produced by inferior
guardians to the lower craftsmen's class. Grammatically,
σκοποῦντας only governs τοὺς ἀξίους but it must apply also
to ἐπαυξανομένων; 'but [the rulers] must keep them under
continuous observation as they grow up and, noting the ones
who deserve it, transfer them back again' to the guardian class.
τοὺς δὲ παρὰ σφίσιν ἀναξίους: those children who turn out not
to deserve their place in the guardian class. See *Republic* 415c,
423c-d, 460c.

{ΣΩ.} Ἆρ' οὖν δὴ διεληλύθαμεν ἤδη καθάπερ χθές, ὡς
ἐν κεφαλαίοις πάλιν ἐπανελθεῖν, ἢ ποθοῦμεν ἔτι τι τῶν
ῥηθέντων, ὦ φίλε Τίμαιε, ὡς ἀπολειπόμενον;
19b1 {ΤΙ.} Οὐδαμῶς, ἀλλὰ αὐτὰ ταῦτ' ἦν τὰ λεχθέντα, ὦ
Σώκρατες.

19a7-9 ὡς ... ἐπανελθεῖν + infin. construction used to limit a previous
assertion (LSJ, ὡς, B I 3): 'at least as far as giving an overall
review is concerned'. ὡς ἀπολειπόμενον, ὡς + participle, causal

(LSJ, ὡς, C I): 'or do we still miss anything from the discussion that has [lit. 'as being'] left out?'

19b1–2   Timaeus's positive response on the scope of this summary, which only covers Books II–V of the *Republic*, and omits Books VI–VII on the education of the philosopher-rulers, underlines that 'yesterday's' discussion is not the same as that of the *Republic* as a whole.

19b–20c:
Socrates's request – a story about the ideal state in action

Socrates asks his interlocutors to tell a story which will illustrate the nature of the ideal state in some great action, such as that of war. He seems to have in mind an imaginary story, and describes the task as a 'poetic' or literary one. But he wants the story to be told by narrators who (unlike most poets) genuinely understand the nature of their subject, and who combine knowledge of philosophy and politics; he claims his interlocutors are such people. Plato seems to be preparing his readers to receive a philosophical myth or allegory, which will illustrate the qualities of the ideal state in narrative form.

    {ΣΩ.} Ἀκούοιτ᾽ ἂν ἤδη τὰ μετὰ ταῦτα περὶ τῆς πολιτείας
    ἣν διήλθομεν, οἷόν τι πρὸς αὐτὴν πεπονθὼς τυγχάνω. προσ-
5   έοικεν δὲ δή τινί μοι τοιῷδε τὸ πάθος, οἷον εἴ τις ζῷα καλά
    που θεασάμενος, εἴτε ὑπὸ γραφῆς εἰργασμένα εἴτε καὶ ζῶντα
    ἀληθινῶς ἡσυχίαν δὲ ἄγοντα, εἰς ἐπιθυμίαν ἀφίκοιτο θεά-
    σασθαι κινούμενά τε αὐτὰ καί τι τῶν τοῖς σώμασιν δοκούντων
19c1   προσήκειν κατὰ τὴν ἀγωνίαν ἀθλοῦντα· ταὐτὸν καὶ ἐγὼ
    πέπονθα πρὸς τὴν πόλιν ἣν διήλθομεν.

19b3–4   ἀκούοιτ᾽ἄν, pres. opt., polite command (RG 421 (ii)). The word order is un-English; rephrase: 'you might now like to hear how I feel about the state we've described'.

19b4–6   προσέοικεν κ.τ.λ., rearrange order in English: 'My feeling is like that of someone who has been looking at beautiful animals

... and is filled with the desire ...'. The imaginary situation is put in the form of a future remote conditional clause (RG 402, AM 181 iv). At *Republic* 472d–e, Socrates had also compared the ideal state to a pattern produced by an artist for people to use as a standard (see also *Republic* 592a–b). However, Socrates does not refer to a question that appears in those passages in the *Republic* (and 499a–e), whether or not the ideal state could really exist in practice. Here, Socrates only asks to see the character of the ideal state illustrated by appropriate actions and words (19e6–8, 20b4–6), and leaves the question of feasibility to one side; see also [38].

19b8–c1   Translate 'competing in a contest in any of the ways [τι] that seems appropriate for their bodily form'.

ἡδέως γὰρ ἄν του
λόγῳ διεξιόντος ἀκούσαιμ' ἂν ἄθλους οὓς πόλις ἀθλεῖ, τούτους
αὐτὴν ἀγωνιζομένην πρὸς πόλεις ἄλλας, πρεπόντως εἴς τε

5   πόλεμον ἀφικομένην καὶ ἐν τῷ πολεμεῖν τὰ προσήκοντα
ἀποδιδοῦσαν τῇ παιδείᾳ καὶ τροφῇ κατά τε τὰς ἐν τοῖς
ἔργοις πράξεις καὶ κατὰ τὰς ἐν τοῖς λόγοις διερμηνεύσεις
πρὸς ἑκάστας τῶν πόλεων.

19c2–8   ἡδέως ... ἀκούσαιμ'ἄν, aor. opt. expressing wish for future (RG 244, AM 148); polite request. του (gen. of τις) governed by ἀκούσαιμ', 'I would like to hear someone describing in a story the kind of competitions that cities [lit. 'a city'] compete in, and this city [αὐτὴν] engaging in these contests with other cities'. οὓς (ἄθλους) ... ἀθλεῖ, τούτους ... ἀγωνιζομένην, internal or 'cognate' accusatives (G 1051). πρεπόντως ... προσήκοντα, the way in which the citizens enter, and carry out, this imagined war must be both 'fitting' (i.e. honourable) and also 'appropriate' to the character and education of the ideal state.

The literary project Socrates has in mind closely recalls his criteria for good artistic creation in the *Republic*: an accurate representation of a good subject by someone with knowledge of its real nature (377b–379a, 401b–c, 500b–501c). The complaint that poets, as a class, are mere imitators of appearance (*Timaeus* 19d) is developed at length in *Republic* 596d–598c. The claim that poets (like sophists) lack the required combination of philosophical understanding and practical experiences of politics and warfare (*Timaeus* 19d–e) matches similar criticism of poets in *Republic* 600a–e. See also [37–38] and Gill 1979b, 72–73, 1993, 47–51.

ταῦτ' οὖν, ὦ Κριτία καὶ Ἑρμό-

19d1 κρατες, ἐμαυτοῦ μὲν αὐτὸς κατέγνωκα μή ποτ' ἂν δυνατὸς
γενέσθαι τοὺς ἄνδρας καὶ τὴν πόλιν ἱκανῶς ἐγκωμιάσαι. καὶ
τὸ μὲν ἐμὸν οὐδὲν θαυμαστόν· ἀλλὰ τὴν αὐτὴν δόξαν εἴληφα
καὶ περὶ τῶν πάλαι γεγονότων καὶ περὶ τῶν νῦν ὄντων
5 ποιητῶν, οὔτι τὸ ποιητικὸν ἀτιμάζων γένος, ἀλλὰ παντὶ
δῆλον ὡς τὸ μιμητικὸν ἔθνος, οἷς ἂν ἐντραφῇ, ταῦτα μιμή-
σεται ῥᾷστα καὶ ἄριστα, τὸ δ' ἐκτὸς τῆς τροφῆς ἑκάστοις
19e1 γιγνόμενον χαλεπὸν μὲν ἔργοις, ἔτι δὲ χαλεπώτερον λόγοις
εὖ μιμεῖσθαι.

19c8–d2   ταῦτ'οὖν κ.τ.λ., 'As far as these things are concerned' (acc. of respect) ... 'my judgement on myself is that I would never be capable ...'. κατέγνωκα, perf. with pres. meaning (γιγνώσκω); ἂν γενέσθαι (ind. statement) represents ἂν γένοιτο (potential) in direct statement. The negative in indirect statement is normally οὐ (RG 397 (iv, note), AM 114), but καταγιγνώσκω regularly takes μή + infin. in such contexts (LSJ, καταγιγνώσκω, I).

19d3   τὸ ἐμὸν κ.τ.λ., 'In my own case [LSJ, ἐμός, 3] [this fact] is in no way [οὐδὲν, neut. as adverb] surprising'. Presumably, Socrates considers himself neither an imaginative writer (*Phaedo* 61a–b) nor a politician in the conventional sense (*Apology* 32a–b; *Gorgias* 473e). Nothing is more characteristic of the Platonic Socrates than his profession of ignorance (see e.g. *Apology* 21b–22e).

19d6 οἷς ἂν ἐντραφῇ, ταῦτα; indef. rel. clause (RG 282–83, AM 166 ii), 'the surroundings in which they [= the ἔθνος] are brought up'.

19e1–2 ἔργοις might be taken to mean 'works of art' (cf. ὑπὸ γραφῆς εἰργασμένα, b6), but more probably means 'actions' (see c7–8, where Socrates refers both to actions and words (i.e. negotiations with other cities). The remark is perhaps surprising (and runs counter to a related comment in *Republic* 473a). However, Proclus (Neoplatonist commentator, see [42]) suggests that representation of actions can be merely external, whereas representation of words requires an engaged understanding of the character of the person speaking (*Commentary on Timaeus*, 1.65.4–66.8); and this suggestion matches the stress on poets' lack of understanding of this subject matter in 19d4–7.

τὸ δὲ τῶν σοφιστῶν γένος αὖ πολλῶν μὲν
λόγων καὶ καλῶν ἄλλων μάλ' ἔμπειρον ἥγημαι, φοβοῦμαι
δὲ μή πως, ἅτε πλανητὸν ὂν κατὰ πόλεις οἰκήσεις τε ἰδίας
5   οὐδαμῇ διῳκηκός, ἄστοχον ἅμα φιλοσόφων ἀνδρῶν ἢ καὶ
πολιτικῶν, ὅσ' ἂν οἷά τε ἐν πολέμῳ καὶ μάχαις πράττοντες
ἔργῳ καὶ λόγῳ προσομιλοῦντες ἑκάστοις πράττοιεν καὶ
λέγοιεν. καταλέλειπται δὴ τὸ τῆς ὑμετέρας ἕξεως γένος,
ἅμα ἀμφοτέρων φύσει καὶ τροφῇ μετέχον.

19e2–8 The comment reflects Plato's typically low estimation of sophists (e.g. *Sophist* 224a–226a). ἥγημαι (pf. ἡγέομαι), 'I have always thought', see also εἴληφα (d3). φοβοῦμαι δὲ μή πως … ἤ, 'I fear that they may perhaps [πως] be …', fear for future (RG 293, AM 169). ὅσ'ἂν οἷα τε … πράττοιεν καὶ λέγοιεν, 'the scale [lit. 'how great'] and quality of their actions and speeches'; potential opt. with ἂν for imaginary situation. The latter part of this sentence (e6–8) is rather awkwardly phrased, with the idea of 'words' and actions' repeated three times (see also c7–8). The point seems to be to stress both sides of what Socrates wants to see represented (the combination of words and actions, as well as the combination of warfare and negotiation) to underline how challenging this would be for sophists. ἕκαστοις (e7) seems to mean 'each of their encounters' with others (in both warfare and negotiation).

19e8–20a1 καταλέλειπται, 'that leaves' (lit. 'is left') by elimination. ἅμα, 'equally' (lit. 'at the same time'). ἀμφοτέρων, i.e. 'both philosophy and politics'.

20a1   Τίμαιός τε γὰρ
ὅδε, εὐνομωτάτης ὢν πόλεως τῆς ἐν Ἰταλίᾳ Λοκρίδος, οὐσίᾳ
καὶ γένει οὐδενὸς ὕστερος ὢν τῶν ἐκεῖ, τὰς μεγίστας μὲν
ἀρχάς τε καὶ τιμὰς τῶν ἐν τῇ πόλει μετακεχείρισται, φιλο-
5 σοφίας δ' αὖ κατ' ἐμὴν δόξαν ἐπ' ἄκρον ἁπάσης ἐλήλυθεν·
Κριτίαν δέ που πάντες οἱ τῇδε ἴσμεν οὐδενὸς ἰδιώτην ὄντα ὧν
λέγομεν. τῆς δὲ Ἑρμοκράτους αὖ περὶ φύσεως καὶ τροφῆς,
πρὸς ἅπαντα ταῦτ' εἶναι ἱκανὴν πολλῶν μαρτυρούντων
πιστευτέον.

20a   Timaeus is totally unknown and is probably a fictional mouthpiece for the cosmological theories that occupy most of the *Timaeus* (27c–92c). The other two men bear the name of well-known politicians of the late fifth century, both linked in different ways with anti-democratic politics and with Athens's defeat in the Peloponnesian War. Hermocrates, a Syracusan, helped to organize the defeat of Athens on the Sicilian expedition of 415–413, but later came into conflict with the Syracusan democracy. Critias (*c.* 460–403) was one of the '30 tyrants' set up in 404–403 by the Spartans to replace Athenian democracy after Athens's defeat in the Peloponnesian War. He also had intellectual interests (he was at one point an associate of Socrates), and poetic works are ascribed to him. However, chronological difficulties may mean that the 'Critias' named here must be the grandfather of the tyrant. Even so, since the grandfather is unknown to us and was probably unknown to Plato's contemporary readers, the connotations of the tyrant may be meant to colour the impression that we form about this figure. See also the note on 20e1–4 and [9].

20a7–9 With ἱκανὴν understand φύσιν and τροφήν; μαρτυρούντων, 'since many people give witness that they are equal to all these topics (gen. absolute, RG 222–23, AM 19) we must believe them [πιστευτέον]'.

20b1 διὸ καὶ χθὲς ἐγὼ διανοούμενος, ὑμῶν δεομένων
τὰ περὶ τῆς πολιτείας διελθεῖν, προθύμως ἐχαριζόμην, εἰδὼς
ὅτι τὸν ἑξῆς λόγον οὐδένες ἂν ὑμῶν ἐθελόντων ἱκανώτερον
ἀποδοῖεν – εἰς γὰρ πόλεμον πρέποντα καταστήσαντες τὴν
5   πόλιν ἅπαντ' αὐτῇ τὰ προσήκοντα ἀποδοῖτ' ἂν μόνοι τῶν
νῦν – εἰπὼν δὴ τἀπιταχθέντα ἀντεπέταξα ὑμῖν ἃ καὶ νῦν
λέγω. συνωμολογήσατ' οὖν κοινῇ σκεψάμενοι πρὸς ὑμᾶς
20c1 αὐτοὺς εἰς νῦν ἀνταποδώσειν μοι τὰ τῶν λόγων ξένια, πάρειμί
τε οὖν δὴ κεκοσμημένος ἐπ' αὐτὰ καὶ πάντων ἑτοιμότατος ὢν
δέχεσθαι.

20b1–5 'I was already aware of this yesterday and so … I agreed with enthusiasm, knowing …'. The εἰδὼς clause expresses the content of his thoughts. τὸν ἑξῆς λόγον, the speech that comes next in the series, 'the sequel'. ἄν... ἀποδοῖεν, ἀποδοῖτ'ἄν, potential opt., 'would provide'. καταστήσαντες, 'launch' or set the city in war.

20b7–c2 σκεψάμενοι is probably part of the indirect statement, nom. in agreement with the subject (RG 236, AM 157a): 'You agreed that, after consulting with each other, you would'. Socrates is 'dressed up' (κεκοσμημένος) for the intellectual 'feast' (τὰ τῶν λόγων ξένια), see also 17a–b.

20c–27b:
Critias's response to Socrates's request

Critias undertakes to fulfil Socrates's request with a narrative he says came from Solon; Solon, in turn, is said to have obtained it from the Egyptian priests of Neïth at Saïs. It is the account of a war fought over 9,000 years earlier between primaeval Athens and a powerful civilization that has now disappeared, that of Atlantis. Critias claims that his narrative is a factual account of a historical event. However, the remoteness of the period of the war and the slender and unsupported line of transmission, among other factors, make this claim difficult to accept. Critias says that the character and institutions of primaeval Athens were similar to those of Socrates's ideal state; and so the account of the war can serve as the illustrative parable Socrates requires. However, he himself seems more preoccupied with the glory that this story confers on Athens and the privileged role of his own family in preserving it than with the philosophical ideas he is supposed to be illustrating. In this respect, as in his emphasis on the historical truth of his story, Critias seems to have a rather different mindset and priorities from Socrates, despite their apparent agreement on the value of Critias's story (see [17–20, 23]).

{EP.} Καὶ μὲν δή, καθάπερ εἶπεν Τίμαιος ὅδε, ὦ Σώκρατες,
5   οὔτε ἐλλείψομεν προθυμίας οὐδὲν οὔτε ἔστιν οὐδεμία πρόφασις ἡμῖν τοῦ μὴ δρᾶν ταῦτα· ὥστε καὶ χθές, εὐθὺς ἐνθένδε
ἐπειδὴ παρὰ Κριτίαν πρὸς τὸν ξενῶνα οὗ καὶ καταλύομεν
ἀφικόμεθα, καὶ ἔτι πρότερον καθ' ὁδὸν αὐτὰ ταῦτ' ἐσκοποῦμεν.
20d1   ὅδε οὖν ἡμῖν λόγον εἰσηγήσατο ἐκ παλαιᾶς ἀκοῆς· ὃν καὶ
νῦν λέγε, ὦ Κριτία, τῷδε, ἵνα συνδοκιμάσῃ πρὸς τὴν ἐπίταξιν
εἴτ' ἐπιτήδειος εἴτε ἀνεπιτήδειός ἐστι.
{ΚΡ.} Ταῦτα χρὴ δρᾶν, εἰ καὶ τῷ τρίτῳ κοινωνῷ Τιμαίῳ
5   συνδοκεῖ.
{ΤΙ.} Δοκεῖ μήν.

20c4   καὶ μὲν δή, Hermocrates's entry into the dialogue (and his only
         speech in the *Timaeus*) is marked by an emphatic group of
         particles: 'Yes indeed'.

20c5–6   πρόφασις κ.τ.λ., 'excuse for not doing this'. εὐθὺς ... ἐπειδὴ, 'as
         soon as'. οὗ, gen of ὅς, gen. of place (G 1138), 'where'.
20d1–2   ὅδε = Critias. ἐκ παλαιᾶς ἀκοῆς, 'based on an ancient report'.
         ἵνα συνδοκιμάσῃ, 'so that he [Socrates] can judge, as well as
         [συν-] us'.

{ΚΡ.} Ἄκουε δή, ὦ Σώκρατες, λόγου μάλα μὲν ἀτόπου,
         παντάπασί γε μὴν ἀληθοῦς, ὡς ὁ τῶν ἑπτὰ σοφώτατος
20e1   Σόλων ποτ' ἔφη. ἦν μὲν οὖν οἰκεῖος καὶ σφόδρα φίλος ἡμῖν
         Δρωπίδου τοῦ προπάππου, καθάπερ λέγει πολλαχοῦ καὶ
         αὐτὸς ἐν τῇ ποιήσει· πρὸς δὲ Κριτίαν τὸν ἡμέτερον πάππον
         εἶπεν, ὡς ἀπεμνημόνευεν αὖ πρὸς ἡμᾶς ὁ γέρων, ὅτι μεγάλα
5   καὶ θαυμαστὰ τῆσδ' εἴη παλαιὰ ἔργα τῆς πόλεως ὑπὸ χρόνου
         καὶ φθορᾶς ἀνθρώπων ἠφανισμένα, πάντων δὲ ἓν μέγιστον,
21a1   οὗ νῦν ἐπιμνησθεῖσιν πρέπον ἂν ἡμῖν εἴη σοί τε ἀποδοῦναι
         χάριν καὶ τὴν θεὸν ἅμα ἐν τῇ πανηγύρει δικαίως τε καὶ
         ἀληθῶς οἷόνπερ ὑμνοῦντας ἐγκωμιάζειν.

20d6–7   On the 'truth' of the story, see [18–19, 23].
20d8–e1 The reasons for the choice of Solon as the 'source' for the story
         seem similar to the reasons for the choice of Socrates's three
         interlocutors (20a). He was a notable Athenian statesman who
         revised the constitution in the early sixth century (probably
         594/593). He was also famed for his wisdom (the only Athenian
         member of the traditional 'Seven Wise Men'); and, like Critias
         (the tyrant), he wrote poetry, on moral and political themes. His
         constitutional changes initiated Athens's development towards
         full democracy, but he was also claimed by oligarchs in the
         mid-fourth century as the author of the 'ancestral constitution'
         of Athens; see the introduction, text to nn. 50, 76, 82.
20e1–4   Scholarly reconstruction of Critias's family tree suggests
         that the speaker 'Critias' is more likely to be the grandfather
         of Critias the tyrant (also called 'Critias') than the tyrant.
         However, for various reasons, including the fact that he would
         have been much better known to Plato's readers, the younger

Critias (the tyrant) is a more plausible candidate for this role. It is possible that Plato has deliberately or mistakenly telescoped the generations of Critias's family referred to here (reducing five to three), thereby linking Critias the younger more closely to the source of the story. It is also possible that, although the speaker is presented as the grandfather, the connotations of Critias the tyrant colour our impression of the speaker (this is the view preferred here). See [8–9, 20–23].

20e4–6   See 24d6–e4, and Herodotus's opening statement in his *Histories*, that he wrote in order that ἔργα μεγάλα τε καὶ θωμαστά might not become τῷ χρόνῳ ἐξίτηλα. For the stress on the scale of the war, see also Thucydides 1.1. The clause ὅτι μεγάλα κ.τ.λ. is best translated by two English clauses: 'that there were [εἴη, opt. in ind. statement in secondary sequence] great and wonderful achievements … [which had been] obliterated'. For periodic natural disasters and discontinuity in civilization, see Plato, *Statesman* 270c–d; *Laws* 677a–679e; also *Ti.* 21d, 22c–23c, 25d; *Criti.* 109d, 111a–c.

21a1   οὐ νῦν κ.τ.λ., 'Retelling this achievement would be a fitting way to repay our debt to you and at the same time to offer a hymn, as it were, of just and true praise of the goddess on her festival'. Speeches celebrating heroic achievements of the Athenian past (such as the battle of Marathon), and hymns to Athena, formed part of the Panathenaic festival.

{ΣΩ.} Εὖ λέγεις. ἀλλὰ δὴ ποῖον ἔργον τοῦτο Κριτίας οὐ
5   λεγόμενον μέν, ὡς δὲ πραχθὲν ὄντως ὑπὸ τῆσδε τῆς πόλεως
     ἀρχαῖον διηγεῖτο κατὰ τὴν Σόλωνος ἀκοήν;
     {ΚΡ.} Ἐγὼ φράσω, παλαιὸν ἀκηκοὼς λόγον οὐ νέου ἀν-
     δρός. ἦν μὲν γὰρ δὴ τότε Κριτίας, ὡς ἔφη, σχεδὸν ἐγγὺς
21b1 ἤδη τῶν ἐνενήκοντα ἐτῶν, ἐγὼ δέ πη μάλιστα δεκέτης· ἡ
     δὲ Κουρεῶτις ἡμῖν οὖσα ἐτύγχανεν Ἀπατουρίων. τὸ δὴ τῆς
     ἑορτῆς σύνηθες ἑκάστοτε καὶ τότε συνέβη τοῖς παισίν· ἆθλα
     γὰρ ἡμῖν οἱ πατέρες ἔθεσαν ῥαψῳδίας. πολλῶν μὲν οὖν
5   δὴ καὶ πολλὰ ἐλέχθη ποιητῶν ποιήματα, ἄτε δὲ νέα κατ᾽

ἐκεῖνον τὸν χρόνον ὄντα τὰ Σόλωνος πολλοὶ τῶν παίδων
ᾔσαμεν.

21a7–b7   All the details seem designed to make the story seem to be
transmitted from the very remote past, while still establishing
Critias's direct connection with that past (see the note on
20e1–4). In fact, the poems of Solon (early sixth century) were
not 'new' in the childhood of Critias's grandfather (born *c.* 520),
and still less that of Critias the tyrant (born *c.* 460).

21b2   On the third day of the Apatouria Festival, the 'Koureotis', young
children's names were enrolled in the register of their phratries
(civic groups). Plato chooses this festival perhaps because its
name reminds us of deception (ἀπάτη). Certainly, casting his
account in the form of a story told by an old man to credulous
infants does nothing to make it more credible to Plato's readers.

εἶπεν οὖν τις τῶν φρατέρων, εἴτε δὴ δοκοῦν αὐτῷ
τότε εἴτε καὶ χάριν τινὰ τῷ Κριτίᾳ φέρων, δοκεῖν οἱ τά τε
21c1   ἄλλα σοφώτατον γεγονέναι Σόλωνα καὶ κατὰ τὴν ποίησιν
αὖ τῶν ποιητῶν πάντων ἐλευθεριώτατον. ὁ δὴ γέρων –
σφόδρα γὰρ οὖν μέμνημαι – μάλα τε ἥσθη καὶ διαμειδιάσας
εἶπεν· "Εἴ γε, ὦ Ἀμύνανδρε, μὴ παρέργῳ τῇ ποιήσει κατε-
5   χρήσατο, ἀλλ᾽ ἐσπουδάκει καθάπερ ἄλλοι, τόν τε λόγον ὃν
ἀπ᾽ Αἰγύπτου δεῦρο ἠνέγκατο ἀπετέλεσεν, καὶ μὴ διὰ τὰς
στάσεις ὑπὸ κακῶν τε ἄλλων ὅσα ηὗρεν ἐνθάδε ἥκων ἠναγ-
21d1   κάσθη καταμελῆσαι, κατά γε ἐμὴν δόξαν οὔτε Ἡσίοδος οὔτε
Ὅμηρος οὔτε ἄλλος οὐδεὶς ποιητὴς εὐδοκιμώτερος ἐγένετο
ἄν ποτε αὐτοῦ."

21c2   ἐλεθεριώτατον: 'independent minded [lit. 'most free']'; Solon,
who was a man of independent means and independent
judgement, expressed his views on the contemporary situation
with great frankness. Unlike many Greek poets (even Pindar),
he had no patron to please. σφόδρα κ.τ.λ., emphatic: 'indeed I
remember it very well [σφόδρα]'.

21c4–d2   Aorist and pluperfect tenses: past unfulfilled conditional sentence (RG 402 (iii), AM 179). On Solon, see the note on 20d8–e1. The 'political conflicts' (στάσεις) referred to are those which Solon tried to address in his role as archon (chief magistrate) in 594/593 by making changes to the constitution.

"Τίς δ' ἦν ὁ λόγος," ἦ δ' ὅς, "ὦ Κριτία;"
"Ἡ περὶ μεγίστης," ἔφη, "καὶ ὀνομαστοτάτης πασῶν δι-
5   καιότατ' ἂν πράξεως οὔσης, ἣν ἤδε ἡ πόλις ἔπραξε μέν, διὰ
δὲ χρόνον καὶ φθορὰν τῶν ἐργασαμένων οὐ διήρκεσε δεῦρο ὁ
λόγος." "Λέγε ἐξ ἀρχῆς," ἦ δ' ὅς, "τί τε καὶ πῶς καὶ
παρὰ τίνων ὡς ἀληθῆ διακηκοὼς ἔλεγεν ὁ Σόλων."

21d4–5   ἂν ... οὔσης stands for τῆς ἣ ἂν ἦν, 'It was a story about the greatest exploit – and what fully deserves [lit. 'would most rightly be'] the most famous of all ...'. Pres. part. with ἂν stands here for pres. unfulfilled condition (RG 402 (ii), AM 179, also G 1308); the clause beginning διὰ takes the place of an εἰ μή clause.

21d7–8   The claim of the (factual) truth of Solon's story is made, in the first instance, by Critias (the speaker) at 20d7; it is then restated in the reported conversation between the older Critias and Amynandrus (21d7–8, cf. d3–7).

21e1   "Ἔστιν τις κατ' Αἴγυπτον, " ἦ δ' ὅς, "ἐν τῷ Δέλτα, περὶ
ὃν κατὰ κορυφὴν σχίζεται τὸ τοῦ Νείλου ῥεῦμα Σαϊτικὸς
ἐπικαλούμενος νομός, τούτου δὲ τοῦ νομοῦ μεγίστη πόλις
Σάις – ὅθεν δὴ καὶ Ἄμασις ἦν ὁ βασιλεύς – οἷς τῆς πόλεως
5   θεὸς ἀρχηγός τίς ἐστιν, Αἰγυπτιστὶ μὲν τοὔνομα Νηίθ, Ἑλληνιστὶ δέ, ὡς ὁ ἐκείνων λόγος, Ἀθηνᾶ· μάλα δὲ φιλαθή-
ναιοι καί τινα τρόπον οἰκεῖοι τῶνδ' εἶναί φασιν. οἱ δὴ
Σόλων ἔφη πορευθεὶς σφόδρα τε γενέσθαι παρ' αὐτοῖς ἔντι-
22a1   μος, καὶ δὴ καὶ τὰ παλαιὰ ἀνερωτῶν ποτε τοὺς μάλιστα περὶ
ταῦτα τῶν ἱερέων ἐμπείρους, σχεδὸν οὔτε αὐτὸν οὔτε ἄλλον

Ἕλληνα οὐδένα οὐδὲν ὡς ἔπος εἰπεῖν εἰδότα περὶ τῶν τοιούτων ἀνευρεῖν.

21e2   κατὰ κορυφὴν, 'at its apex'.
21e4–5 The divine foundation of human cities is an important theme in
        the story: see also *Ti.* 23d–e, 24c–d; *Criti.* 109b–d, 113b–114c.
21e7   Solon's visit to Saïs is mentioned by Herodotus (1.30). However,
        the activities attributed to Solon here (investigation of the past
        by using Egyptian records which are vastly older than Greek
        traditions) closely resemble Herodotus's own enquiries (2.44–45,
        2.53–57, 2.100 and elsewhere). On the many echoes of Herodotus
        (esp. Book II) in the Atlantis story, see Pradeau 1997, 157–79.
        These echoes give the impression that the story is a pastiche
        of historiography, rather than an actual historical account, as
        Critias presents it (see [18–19]).

                καί ποτε προαγαγεῖν βουληθεὶς αὐτοὺς περὶ
5   τῶν ἀρχαίων εἰς λόγους, τῶν τῆδε τὰ ἀρχαιότατα λέγειν
        ἐπιχειρεῖν, περὶ Φορωνέως τε τοῦ πρώτου λεχθέντος καὶ
        Νιόβης, καὶ μετὰ τὸν κατακλυσμὸν αὖ περὶ Δευκαλίωνος
22b1   καὶ Πύρρας ὡς διεγένοντο μυθολογεῖν, καὶ τοὺς ἐξ αὐτῶν
        γενεαλογεῖν, καὶ τὰ τῶν ἐτῶν ὅσα ἦν οἷς ἔλεγεν πειρᾶσθαι
        διαμνημονεύων τοὺς χρόνους ἀριθμεῖν· καί τινα εἰπεῖν τῶν
        ἱερέων εὖ μάλα παλαιόν· Ὦ Σόλων, Σόλων, Ἕλληνες ἀεὶ
5   παῖδές ἐστε, γέρων δὲ Ἕλλην οὐκ ἔστιν.' Ἀκούσας οὖν,
        'Πῶς τί τοῦτο λέγεις; ' φάναι. 'Νέοι ἐστέ, ' εἰπεῖν, 'τὰς
        ψυχὰς πάντες· οὐδεμίαν γὰρ ἐν αὐταῖς ἔχετε δι' ἀρχαίαν
        ἀκοὴν παλαιὰν δόξαν οὐδὲ μάθημα χρόνῳ πολιὸν οὐδέν. τὸ
22c1   δὲ τούτων αἴτιον τόδε. πολλαὶ κατὰ πολλὰ φθοραὶ γεγό-
        νασιν ἀνθρώπων καὶ ἔσονται, πυρὶ μὲν καὶ ὕδατι μέγισται,
        μυρίοις δὲ ἄλλοις ἕτεραι βραχύτεραι.

22a4   Understand ἔφη with this and the following sentences.
22a5–b1 Hellanicus, a fifth-century contemporary of Herodotus,
         tried to systematize mythological genealogies (including

those derived from Phoronis, Deucalion and Atlantis = the daughter of Atlas). Plato's story may owe something here to Hellanicus's inspiration; see also *Criti.* 114a–c, and Luce 1978, 72.

22b2–3   'by recording the years since the events which he was speaking about, tried to calculate their dates'. οἷς stands for τοῖς ἅ; literally, it means 'the years which were *for* the events' (for this use of dat. to mean 'since', see G 1166).

22b4–c1   The phraseology echoes the earlier characterization of the story (as one told by an old man to children, see the note on 21b2), although the point here is different: the Greeks are 'young' because the discontinuity of civilization prevents knowledge of their own past.

τὸ γὰρ οὖν καὶ παρ᾽
ὑμῖν λεγόμενον, ὥς ποτε Φαέθων Ἡλίου παῖς τὸ τοῦ πατρὸς
5   ἅρμα ζεύξας διὰ τὸ μὴ δυνατὸς εἶναι κατὰ τὴν τοῦ πατρὸς
ὁδὸν ἐλαύνειν τά τ᾽ ἐπὶ γῆς συνέκαυσεν καὶ αὐτὸς κεραυ-
νωθεὶς διεφθάρη, τοῦτο μύθου μὲν σχῆμα ἔχον λέγεται, τὸ δὲ
22d1   ἀληθές ἐστι τῶν περὶ γῆν κατ᾽ οὐρανὸν ἰόντων παράλλαξις
καὶ διὰ μακρῶν χρόνων γιγνομένη τῶν ἐπὶ γῆς πυρὶ πολλῷ
φθορά. τότε οὖν ὅσοι κατ᾽ ὄρη καὶ ἐν ὑψηλοῖς τόποις καὶ
ἐν ξηροῖς οἰκοῦσιν μᾶλλον διόλλυνται τῶν ποταμοῖς καὶ θα-
5   λάττῃ προσοικούντων· ἡμῖν δὲ ὁ Νεῖλος εἴς τε τἆλλα σωτὴρ
καὶ τότε ἐκ ταύτης τῆς ἀπορίας σῴζει λυόμενος. ὅταν δ᾽
αὖ θεοὶ τὴν γῆν ὕδασιν καθαίροντες κατακλύζωσιν, οἱ μὲν
ἐν τοῖς ὄρεσιν διασῴζονται βουκόλοι νομῆς τε, οἱ δ᾽ ἐν ταῖς
22e1   παρ᾽ ὑμῖν πόλεσιν εἰς τὴν θάλατταν ὑπὸ τῶν ποταμῶν φέ-
ρονται· κατὰ δὲ τήνδε χώραν οὔτε τότε οὔτε ἄλλοτε ἄνωθεν
ἐπὶ τὰς ἀρούρας ὕδωρ ἐπιρρεῖ, τὸ δ᾽ ἐναντίον κάτωθεν πᾶν
ἐπανιέναι πέφυκεν.

22c7–d3   'This story has the form [or 'appearance'] of a myth'. τὸ δὲ ἀληθές κ.τ.λ., 'but the fact [or 'truth'] conveyed in mythical form 'is a deviation from' regular patterns in heaven and earth.

This deviation is itself a regular though infrequent occurrence (διὰ μακρῶν χρόνων); see also *Republic* 530a–b. This passage is reminiscent of *Statesman* 268e–270a, where traditional Greek myths are also explained by a periodic reversal of cosmic movement. However, in the *Statesman*, the explanation is also mythical in character; this passage is closer to *Laws* 676c–680a, where Plato examines in a more realistic way the fact of periodic natural calamity and its effect on the continuity of civilization (see [18]).

22d6   The Nile is 'released', either by the melting of the snow which constitutes its source or by the opening of dams and sluices in the irrigation system (see Cornford 1937, 365–66). In view of the emphasis on irrigation systems of Atlantis as a source of water in hot weather (*Criti.* 118e), the latter may be what Plato has in mind. See also e2–4: the water 'rises from below' because it comes from the Nile; but, controlled by irrigation, it does not devastate the land (as heavy rains do) and disrupt Egyptian civilization.

                ὅθεν καὶ δι' ἃς αἰτίας τἀνθάδε σῳζό-
5   μενα λέγεται παλαιότατα· τὸ δὲ ἀληθές, ἐν πᾶσιν τοῖς
τόποις ὅπου μὴ χειμὼν ἐξαίσιος ἢ καῦμα ἀπείργει, πλέον,
23a1 τοτὲ δὲ ἔλαττον ἀεὶ γένος ἐστὶν ἀνθρώπων. ὅσα δὲ ἢ παρ'
ὑμῖν ἢ τῇδε ἢ καὶ κατ' ἄλλον τόπον ὧν ἀκοῇ ἴσμεν, εἴ πού
τι καλὸν ἢ μέγα γέγονεν ἢ καί τινα διαφορὰν ἄλλην ἔχον,
πάντα γεγραμμένα ἐκ παλαιοῦ τῇδ' ἐστὶν ἐν τοῖς ἱεροῖς καὶ
σεσωσμένα·

22e4–5 There is no strong contrast between λέγεται and τὸ δὲ ἀληθές (whereas there is a contrast between λεγόμενον μέν and πραχθὲν ὄντως at 21a5); τὸ δὲ ἀληθές simply begins the priest's explanation of the reasons why Egyptian records are older than others. His main point is that, although in other places some of the population survives natural catastrophe, it is only in Egypt, with its special advantages of climate and irrigation, that the

instruments of higher civilization (records and literacy) also
survive for a considerable period.

22e6 ὅπου μὴ ... ἀπείργει, indef. rel. clause of place, hence μή negative
(AM 166). ὅπου, 'wherever', by itself conveys the general or
indefinite idea, and so we find indic. in place of ἄν + subj. (G
1432). Understand τοτὲ μὲν before πλέον: 'the human race always
exists in greater or smaller numbers at different times'.

5   τὰ δὲ παρ' ὑμῖν καὶ τοῖς ἄλλοις ἄρτι κατεσκευασμένα ἑκάστοτε τυγχάνει γράμμασι καὶ ἅπασιν ὁπόσων
πόλεις δέονται, καὶ πάλιν δι' εἰωθότων ἐτῶν ὥσπερ νόσημα
ἥκει φερόμενον αὐτοῖς ῥεῦμα οὐράνιον καὶ τοὺς ἀγραμμάτους
23b1 τε καὶ ἀμούσους ἔλιπεν ὑμῶν, ὥστε πάλιν ἐξ ἀρχῆς οἷον
νέοι γίγνεσθε, οὐδὲν εἰδότες οὔτε τῶν τῇδε οὔτε τῶν παρ'
ὑμῖν, ὅσα ἦν ἐν τοῖς παλαιοῖς χρόνοις.

23a7 δι'εἰωθότων ἐτῶν, 'after the usual number of years', compare
διὰ μακρῶν χρόνων, 22d2. On this usage of διά + gen., see LSJ,
διά A5.

23a8 ἥκει φερόμενον αὐτοῖς, 'comes, borne down on you'; αὐτοῖς
refers both to you and the others (apart from the Egyptians),
a5, and so is best translated as 'you' (not 'them').

23b1 ἔλιπεν, 'leaves' or 'spares'; the aor. is generalizing or gnomic
(AM 72, 4). πάλιν ... οἷον νέοι, 'children, as it were, ... again'.

                          τὰ γοῦν νυνδὴ
γενεαλογηθέντα, ὦ Σόλων, περὶ τῶν παρ' ὑμῖν ἃ διῆλθες,
5 παίδων βραχύ τι διαφέρει μύθων, οἳ πρῶτον μὲν ἕνα γῆς
κατακλυσμὸν μέμνησθε πολλῶν ἔμπροσθεν γεγονότων, ἔτι
δὲ τὸ κάλλιστον καὶ ἄριστον γένος ἐπ' ἀνθρώπους ἐν τῇ
χώρᾳ παρ' ὑμῖν οὐκ ἴστε γεγονός, ἐξ ὧν σύ τε καὶ πᾶσα ἡ
23c1 πόλις ἔστιν τὰ νῦν ὑμῶν, περιλειφθέντος ποτὲ σπέρματος
βραχέος, ἀλλ' ὑμᾶς λέληθεν διὰ τὸ τοὺς περιγενομένους ἐπὶ
πολλὰς γενεὰς γράμμασιν τελευτᾶν ἀφώνους.

23b3   τὰ γοῦν κ.τ.λ., 'In any case [qualifying or specifying the point
        made in the previous sentence], the genealogies of your own
        people that you just recounted'.

23b6   πολλῶν ἔμπροσθεν γεγονότων, gen. abs., 'although there were
        many earlier ones [lit. 'before it']'.

23b7   ἐπ' ἀνθρώπους the finest race 'in all humankind' (lit.
        'throughout or among humankind', LSJ ἐπί, C I 5).

23c2-3 ἐπὶ πολλὰς γενεὰς, 'for many generations', LSJ, ἐπί, C II,
        'time'. γράμμασιν κ.τ.λ., because they died 'without expressing
        themselves [lit. 'voiceless'] in writing'.

                                                              ἦν γὰρ δή
        ποτε, ὦ Σόλων, ὑπὲρ τὴν μεγίστην φθορὰν ὕδασιν ἡ νῦν
5   Ἀθηναίων οὖσα πόλις ἀρίστη πρός τε τὸν πόλεμον καὶ
        κατὰ πάντα εὐνομωτάτη διαφερόντως· ἧ κάλλιστα ἔργα καὶ
        πολιτεῖαι γενέσθαι λέγονται κάλλισται πασῶν ὁπόσων ὑπὸ
23d1   τὸν οὐρανὸν ἡμεῖς ἀκοὴν παρεδεξάμεθα.' Ἀκούσας οὖν ὁ
        Σόλων ἔφη θαυμάσαι καὶ πᾶσαν προθυμίαν σχεῖν δεόμενος
        τῶν ἱερέων πάντα δι' ἀκριβείας οἱ τὰ περὶ τῶν πάλαι πολι-
        τῶν ἐξῆς διελθεῖν.

23c4-6 Not, presumably, the 'recent' flood of Deucalion but the one
        which sank Atlantis (*Ti.* 25c–d, see also *Criti.* 112a). ἡ νῦν
        Ἀθηναίων οὖσα κ.τ.λ., 'the city which is now Athens' (lit.
        'of the Athenians'). For εὐνομία (i.e. having good laws and
        observing them faithfully) as a feature of primaeval Athens, see
        also 24d3–4 and, by implication, *Criti.* 112c, e. Atlantis is also
        presented as observing its laws (*Criti.* 119c) and maintaining
        virtue for many generations before the moral decline described
        in *Criti.* 121a–c.

23c7-d1 πολιτεῖαι here must mean political institutions: primaeval
        Athens, notably, had only *one* constitution. ὑπὸ τὸν οὐρανὸν,
        'in the world' (lit. 'under the heaven').

23d2   πᾶσαν προθυμίαν κ.τ.λ., recast 'that he enthusiastically
        begged'.

τὸν οὖν ἱερέα φάναι· ῾Φθόνος οὐδείς,
5   ὦ Σόλων, ἀλλὰ σοῦ τε ἕνεκα ἐρῶ καὶ τῆς πόλεως ὑμῶν,
μάλιστα δὲ τῆς θεοῦ χάριν, ἣ τήν τε ὑμετέραν καὶ τήνδε
ἔλαχεν καὶ ἔθρεψεν καὶ ἐπαίδευσεν, προτέραν μὲν τὴν παρ᾽
23e1   ὑμῖν ἔτεσιν χιλίοις, ἐκ Γῆς τε καὶ Ἡφαίστου τὸ σπέρμα
παραλαβοῦσα ὑμῶν, τήνδε δὲ ὑστέραν.

23d4   Φθόνος οὐδείς, 'I do not begrudge it', or 'willingly'.
23d7–e2 ἔλαχεν, 'was allocated'; on the allocation of different places to
         different patron gods, see *Criti.* 108d. ἐκ Γῆς κ.τ.λ. This is based
         on the tradition that the primaeval Athenian, Erichthonius,
         was created by the sperm of Hephaestus (aroused by lust for
         Athena) which fell on the earth and inseminated it (Euripides,
         Ion, 267–73). Autochthony (i.e. being born from one's
         native soil) is an important Athenian tradition (*Menexenus*
         237d–238a) and a recurrent theme in this story (e.g. *Criti.* 113c8–
         d1, 114c1). In the case of Atlantis, Poseidon's lust played a key
         role in setting up the state (*Criti.* 113d). However, in the case
         of primaeval Athens, Athena's role as patron takes the form of
         establishing a system of social order (*Ti.* 24c7–d4, also *Criti.*
         109c6–d2, where this role is shared with Hephaestus); see also
         Criti. 109b–c, and [26].

τῆς δὲ ἐνθάδε δια-
κοσμήσεως παρ᾽ ἡμῖν ἐν τοῖς ἱεροῖς γράμμασιν ὀκτακισχιλίων
ἐτῶν ἀριθμὸς γέγραπται. περὶ δὴ τῶν ἐνακισχίλια γεγονό-
5   των ἔτη πολιτῶν σοι δηλώσω διὰ βραχέων νόμους, καὶ τῶν
ἔργων αὐτοῖς ὃ κάλλιστον ἐπράχθη· τὸ δ᾽ ἀκριβὲς περὶ
24a1   πάντων ἐφεξῆς εἰς αὖθις κατὰ σχολὴν αὐτὰ τὰ γράμματα
λαβόντες διέξιμεν.

23e2–e4 The Egyptians were regarded as a very old, if not the oldest,
         civilization (Herodotus 2.2–4); in *Laws* 656e it is said to be at
         least 10,000 years old. So, to make primaeval Athens older still
         is to give it real antiquity. However, no explanation is offered

by the priests of how the Egyptians acquired knowledge of a culture which (according to 25d) had disappeared 1,000 years before Egypt was founded.

23e4–5 'As regards your citizens of nine thousand years ago': for this use of the acc. of extent of time, see G 1063. Note that at *Criti.* 108e1–4 it is the war that destroyed Athens which is said to be 9,000 years earlier, not Athens's foundation. Inconsistencies of the kind (see also the note on 26c2–5) tend to undermine confidence in the factual 'truth' of Critias's story (see [19], esp. n. 38).

23e6 ὃ κ.τ.λ. stands for τὸ κάλλιστον ὃ ἐπράχθη.

24a2 λαβόντες, 'and consult' (lit. 'taking up'). πρός, 'in relation to'. The comparison of Egyptian institutions with those of other cultures, notably Greek, is a feature of Herodotus Book II (e.g. 2.79–81): see the note on 21e7.

        τοὺς μὲν οὖν νόμους σκόπει πρὸς τοὺς
τῇδε· πολλὰ γὰρ παραδείγματα τῶν τότε παρ' ὑμῖν ὄντων
ἐνθάδε νῦν ἀνευρήσεις, πρῶτον μὲν τὸ τῶν ἱερέων γένος ἀπὸ
5   τῶν ἄλλων χωρὶς ἀφωρισμένον, μετὰ δὲ τοῦτο τὸ τῶν δημιουργῶν, ὅτι καθ' αὑτὸ ἕκαστον ἄλλῳ δὲ οὐκ ἐπιμειγνύμενον
δημιουργεῖ, τό τε τῶν νομέων καὶ τὸ τῶν θηρευτῶν τό τε
24b1   τῶν γεωργῶν. καὶ δὴ καὶ τὸ μάχιμον γένος ᾔσθησαί που
τῇδε ἀπὸ πάντων τῶν γενῶν κεχωρισμένον, οἷς οὐδὲν ἄλλο
πλὴν τὰ περὶ τὸν πόλεμον ὑπὸ τοῦ νόμου προσετάχθη μέλειν·
ἔτι δὲ ἡ τῆς ὁπλίσεως αὐτῶν σχέσις ἀσπίδων καὶ δοράτων,
5   οἷς ἡμεῖς πρῶτοι τῶν περὶ τὴν Ἀσίαν ὡπλίσμεθα, τῆς θεοῦ
καθάπερ ἐν ἐκείνοις τοῖς τόποις παρ' ὑμῖν πρώτοις ἐνδειξα-
μένης.

24a4–b3 On the class divisions in Egyptian society, see Herodotus 2.164. Isocrates (436–338) suggests in *Busiris* 15–16 that the principle of each person doing their own job (and sticking to it) was based on Egypt and that it was adopted by well-known philosophers (he seems to have Plato's *Republic* in mind). Also, we learn from Proclus (fifth century AD), *Commentary on Timaeus*

1.76.1–9, that Plato was criticized in his own day for basing the institutions in the *Republic* on the social structure of Egypt. So the links between Egypt and Plato's ideal state which form part of the Atlantis story were also noted in antiquity; see Morgan 1998, 110; Tarrant 2007, 168–69.

24b4   'Their style of armaments consists of (lit. is of) shields and spears'.

τὸ δ' αὖ περὶ τῆς φρονήσεως, ὁρᾷς που τὸν νόμον
τῇδε ὅσην ἐπιμέλειαν ἐποιήσατο εὐθὺς κατ' ἀρχὰς περί τε
24c1   τὸν κόσμον, ἅπαντα μέχρι μαντικῆς καὶ ἰατρικῆς πρὸς
ὑγίειαν ἐκ τούτων θείων ὄντων εἰς τὰ ἀνθρώπινα ἀνευρών,
ὅσα τε ἄλλα τούτοις ἕπεται μαθήματα πάντα κτησάμενος.

24b7–c3   A difficult sentence, in which ὁ νόμος (the subject of all the verbs) stands for 'Egyptian culture'. The τε in b8 is coupled with the τε in c3 (both cosmology and the studies that are connected with it). τούτοις (c3) refers to τούτων θείων in c2 (these divine principles of cosmology) and so back to κόσμον in c1. 'Again, as far as intellectual activity is concerned, surely you see what care the law has devoted from the beginning to cosmology. From these divine principles [those of cosmology], it has derived all the arts bearing on human affairs, including [lit. 'as far as'] divination and medicine directed at producing health, and it has acquired all the other studies [e.g. astronomy and mathematics] that are connected with these [i.e. the divine principles of cosmology]'. According to Herodotus 2.83–84, there were certain central regulations in Egypt about the practice of divination and medicine. However, the idea that the order and regularity of the heavens can provide a model for the organization of human life is essentially Plato's own (*Timaeus* 90a–d; *Laws* 886a, 887b, also 893–899, 966c–967e) and one which partly explains the stress on the divine organization of society in this story.

ταύτην οὖν δὴ τότε σύμπασαν τὴν διακόσμησιν καὶ σύνταξιν
5   ἡ θεὸς προτέρους ὑμᾶς διακοσμήσασα κατῴκισεν, ἐκλεξαμένη
τὸν τόπον ἐν ᾧ γεγένησθε, τὴν εὐκρασίαν τῶν ὡρῶν ἐν αὐτῷ
κατιδοῦσα, ὅτι φρονιμωτάτους ἄνδρας οἴσοι· ἅτε οὖν φιλο-
24d1   πόλεμός τε καὶ φιλόσοφος ἡ θεὸς οὖσα τὸν προσφερεστάτους
αὐτῇ μέλλοντα οἴσειν τόπον ἄνδρας, τοῦτον ἐκλεξαμένη
πρῶτον κατῴκισεν. ᾠκεῖτε δὴ οὖν νόμοις τε τοιούτοις χρώμενοι καὶ ἔτι μᾶλλον εὐνομούμενοι πάσῃ τε παρὰ πάντας
5   ἀνθρώπους ὑπερβεβληκότες ἀρετῇ, καθάπερ εἰκὸς γεννήματα
καὶ παιδεύματα θεῶν ὄντας.

24c6–7   '... recognizing that the harmoniousness of its climate would
produce the most intelligent men'; the fut. opt. οἴσοι represents
the fut. indic. in indirect speech after a verb of thinking (RG
266, AM 160, G 1287), see also μέλλοντα οἴσειν, d1–2. The idea
that a harmonious climate produces 'well-blended' human
beings, who are physically healthy and intelligent, was a
common ancient notion; see Hippocrates *Airs, Waters, Places*,
12; on Athens's pure atmosphere as conducive to thought, see
Euripides, *Medea* 825–43. Critias here says 'men' (ἄνδρας),
rather than 'human beings', rather oddly, since Athena is a
female goddess, and her gender is presented in *Criti.* 110b–c (see
also *Ti.* 18c) as symbolizing that the qualities she represents are
gender-neutral. Perhaps here, though not in *Critias* (110b–c),
Critias overlooks this aspect of Socrates's ideal (on differences
between his approach in the two dialogues, see [25]); note also
ἄνδρας in 25e3, where Critias is referring to Socrates's summary
of the ideal state.
24d3   τοιούτοις, i.e. such as those described in Egypt, 24a–c.

πολλὰ μὲν οὖν ὑμῶν καὶ μεγάλα
ἔργα τῆς πόλεως τῇδε γεγραμμένα θαυμάζεται, πάντων μὴν
24e1   ἓν ὑπερέχει μεγέθει καὶ ἀρετῇ· λέγει γὰρ τὰ γεγραμμένα
ὅσην ἡ πόλις ὑμῶν ἔπαυσέν ποτε δύναμιν ὕβρει πορευομένην ἅμα ἐπὶ πᾶσαν Εὐρώπην καὶ Ἀσίαν, ἔξωθεν ὁρμη-

θεῖσαν ἐκ τοῦ Ἀτλαντικοῦ πελάγους. τότε γὰρ πορεύσιμον
5 ἦν τὸ ἐκεῖ πέλαγος· νῆσον γὰρ πρὸ τοῦ στόματος εἶχεν ὃ
καλεῖτε, ὥς φατε, ὑμεῖς Ἡρακλέους στήλας, ἡ δὲ νῆσος ἅμα
Λιβύης ἦν καὶ Ἀσίας μείζων, ἐξ ἧς ἐπιβατὸν ἐπὶ τὰς ἄλλας
νήσους τοῖς τότε ἐγίγνετο πορευομένοις, ἐκ δὲ τῶν νήσων
25a1 ἐπὶ τὴν καταντικρὺ πᾶσαν ἤπειρον τὴν περὶ τὸν ἀληθινὸν
ἐκεῖνον πόντον. τάδε μὲν γάρ, ὅσα ἐντὸς τοῦ στόματος οὗ
λέγομεν, φαίνεται λιμὴν στενόν τινα ἔχων εἴσπλουν· ἐκεῖνο
δὲ πέλαγος ὄντως ἥ τε περιέχουσα αὐτὸ γῆ παντελῶς ἀληθῶς
ὀρθότατ' ἂν λέγοιτο ἤπειρος.

24e4   The Atlantic was navigable then, it would seem (24e5–25a2),
because Atlantis and the other islands provided the frequent
resting place and harbours that ancient sailors needed. (Plato
may also have in mind the 'mud' mentioned as an obstacle to
navigation at 25d5.)

24e5   ὃ agrees with τοῦ στόματος, that is, the straits of Gibraltar. ἅμα
κ.τ.λ., Plato was not aware of the full extent of Africa (which
he calls Libya) and Asia; nonetheless, he imagines the island
as very large indeed. ἐπιβατὸν normally means 'accessible';
translate as '[the island] provided passage'.

25a1–5   Plato alters the traditional Greek world view in two respects.
He suggests that the 'real' sea (i.e. a sea of real size and
geographical significance) is not the Mediterranean, to which
Greek navigation was confined (which he describes as a mere
'harbour') but the Atlantic Ocean. And he suggests that the
(flat) world is bounded not by the Ocean (a belief going back to
Homer) but by an all-embracing continent (read παντελῶς in
25a4 as an adverb going with περιέχουσα). See Figures 1 and 2.
     These innovations appear to owe little to any actual
information from sailors. They seem to form part of Plato's
expansion of the normal horizons of space and time in his
story (see 22b–23a; for a comparable expansion, see also
Phaedo 109b–110a). The terms the 'real ocean' (πέλαγος ὄντως,
the ocean in a real sense) and the 'true continent' (ἀληθῶς
… ἤπειρος, the continent in a true sense) are very striking.

Along with 'the sea which truly deserves that name' (25a1–2), they refer to physical reality and truth, rather than marking the more typically Platonic contrast between ideal reality and truth and the physical world, conceived as being at a lower level of reality and truth (for the latter contrast, see *Timaeus* 27e–29d). Language similar to that of *Ti.* 25a1–5 is used in *Phaedo* 109e5–110a1. However, the *Phaedo*'s world view is more obviously idealized (110b–111c), and is linked with a more characteristically Platonic picture of the physical world as a prison from which the (immortal) psyche should try to escape (113d–114c).

5   ἐν δὲ δὴ τῇ Ἀτλαντίδι νήσῳ
ταύτῃ μεγάλη συνέστη καὶ θαυμαστὴ δύναμις βασιλέων,
κρατοῦσα μὲν ἁπάσης τῆς νήσου, πολλῶν δὲ ἄλλων νήσων
καὶ μερῶν τῆς ἠπείρου· πρὸς δὲ τούτοις ἔτι τῶν ἐντὸς τῇδε
25b1   Λιβύης μὲν ἦρχον μέχρι πρὸς Αἴγυπτον, τῆς δὲ Εὐρώπης
μέχρι Τυρρηνίας. αὕτη δὴ πᾶσα συναθροισθεῖσα εἰς ἓν ἡ
δύναμις τόν τε παρ' ὑμῖν καὶ τὸν παρ' ἡμῖν καὶ τὸν ἐντὸς τοῦ
στόματος πάντα τόπον μιᾷ ποτὲ ἐπεχείρησεν ὁρμῇ δουλοῦ-
σθαι.

25b2   Τυρρηνίας, Tyrrhenia (Etruria) here stands for Italy.
συναθροισθεῖσα εἰς ἕν, compare the war imagined at *Republic* 422d–e, in which the ideal state (which Socrates is beginning to describe) is imagined as capable, due to its unity and simplicity of lifestyle, of defeating any other city, even one in which the whole world's wealth is combined (εἰς μίαν ... πόλιν συναθροισθῇ, 422d8–e1).

5   τότε οὖν ὑμῶν, ὦ Σόλων, τῆς πόλεως ἡ δύναμις εἰς
ἅπαντας ἀνθρώπους διαφανὴς ἀρετῇ τε καὶ ῥώμῃ ἐγένετο·
πάντων γὰρ προστᾶσα εὐψυχίᾳ καὶ τέχναις ὅσαι κατὰ πόλε-
25c1   μον, τὰ μὲν τῶν Ἑλλήνων ἡγουμένη, τὰ δ' αὐτὴ μονωθεῖσα

ἐξ ἀνάγκης τῶν ἄλλων ἀποστάντων, ἐπὶ τοὺς ἐσχάτους
ἀφικομένη κινδύνους, κρατήσασα μὲν τῶν ἐπιόντων τρόπαιον ἔστησεν, τοὺς δὲ μήπω δεδουλωμένους διεκώλυσεν
5   δουλωθῆναι, τοὺς δ' ἄλλους, ὅσοι κατοικοῦμεν ἐντὸς ὅρων
Ἡρακλείων, ἀφθόνως ἅπαντας ἠλευθέρωσεν.

25b5–c6   τότε κ.τ.λ., this sentence evokes characterizations of the role
of Athens in the Persian Wars of the early fifth century, by
Herodotus (7.139.5–6), Plato (*Menexenus* 240d–e, referring
to Marathon) and Isocrates (*Panegyricus* 17, 52). The style is
eulogistic and typical of the funeral orations composed for dead
Athenians after battle (see [20], esp. n. 44) 'and celebrated their
victory', lit. 'set up a trophy'.

25c1–5   τὰ μὲν, τὰ δ' (lit. 'sometimes ... sometimes'); translate as 'first
... then'. c4: τοὺς μήπω δεδουλωμένους, μή with part. shows
that the phrase is general or indefinite (AM 166, G 1612).
διεκώλυσεν δουλωθῆαι, 'prevented ... from being enslaved':
aor. pass. infin. with verb of hindrance (the aor. has no time
significance here, G 1519, 1520).

                                      ὑστέρῳ δὲ
χρόνῳ σεισμῶν ἐξαισίων καὶ κατακλυσμῶν γενομένων, μιᾶς
25d1   ἡμέρας καὶ νυκτὸς χαλεπῆς ἐπελθούσης, τό τε παρ' ὑμῖν
μάχιμον πᾶν ἀθρόον ἔδυ κατὰ γῆς, ἥ τε Ἀτλαντὶς νῆσος
ὡσαύτως κατὰ τῆς θαλάττης δῦσα ἠφανίσθη· διὸ καὶ
νῦν ἄπορον καὶ ἀδιερεύνητον γέγονεν τοὐκεῖ πέλαγος,
5   πηλοῦ κάρτα βραχέος ἐμποδὼν ὄντος, ὃν ἡ νῆσος ἱζομένη
παρέσχετο.'"

25c6–d3   See also *Criti.* 112a1–4. A single natural disaster (or linked set
of disasters) removes from the scene both sets of participants:
the army/guardians of primaeval Athens and the entire island
of Atlantis. On ancient reception of this account see [45];
e.g. Aristotle reportedly said, 'He who invented it [Atlantis]
obliterated it'. On modern attempts to link this disaster with the

eruption at Thera (Santorini) in the second millennium BC, and on problems with this hypothesis, see [46–51, esp. 49].

25d5–6 Following Cornford 1937, 366–67, I prefer the reading found in a number of manuscripts, κατὰ βραχέος, meaning 'at a little depth', 'a little way down'. This 'mud' a little below the surface makes the sea shallow close to the coast (see Aristotle *Meteorologica* 354a22). This statement has some basis in the actual continental shelf off Gibraltar; but it is more plausibly interpreted as one of the ways (see also the note on 25c6–d3) in which Plato, rather arbitrarily, blocks off the new region and destroys the peoples he has created.

Τὰ μὲν δὴ ῥηθέντα, ὦ Σώκρατες, ὑπὸ τοῦ παλαιοῦ

25e1 Κριτίου κατ' ἀκοὴν τὴν Σόλωνος, ὡς συντόμως εἰπεῖν, ἀκήκοας· λέγοντος δὲ δὴ χθὲς σοῦ περὶ πολιτείας τε καὶ τῶν ἀνδρῶν οὓς ἔλεγες, ἐθαύμαζον ἀναμιμνῃσκόμενος αὐτὰ ἃ νῦν λέγω, κατανοῶν ὡς δαιμονίως ἔκ τινος τύχης οὐκ ἄπο

5 σκοποῦ συνηνέχθης τὰ πολλὰ οἷς Σόλων εἶπεν. οὐ μὴν

25a1 ἐβουλήθην παραχρῆμα εἰπεῖν· διὰ χρόνου γὰρ οὐχ ἱκανῶς ἐμεμνήμην. ἐνενόησα οὖν ὅτι χρεὼν εἴη με πρὸς ἐμαυτὸν πρῶτον ἱκανῶς πάντα ἀναλαβόντα λέγειν οὕτως. ὅθεν ταχὺ συνωμολόγησά σοι τὰ ἐπιταχθέντα χθές, ἡγούμενος, ὅπερ

5 ἐν ἅπασι τοῖς τοιοῖσδε μέγιστον ἔργον, λόγον τινὰ πρέποντα τοῖς βουλήμασιν ὑποθέσθαι, τούτου μετρίως ἡμᾶς εὐπορήσειν. οὕτω δή, καθάπερ ὅδ' εἶπεν, χθές τε εὐθὺς ἐνθένδε ἀπιὼν

26b1 πρὸς τούσδε ἀνέφερον αὐτὰ ἀναμιμνῃσκόμενος, ἀπελθών τε σχεδόν τι πάντα ἐπισκοπῶν τῆς νυκτὸς ἀνέλαβον.

25e4–5 ὡς δαιμονίως … οὐκ ἄπο σκοποῦ, 'how, by divine chance … not off-target'. Here, and in 26c7–d6, Critias shows complete confidence in the fit between this story and Socrates's specifications. However, his comment here seems to put the position the wrong way around: since it is his job to match Socrates's ideas, his story needs to be the one that is 'not off-target', not Socrates's ideas. See also the note on 26b4–7 and

[23]. The jarring effect is lessened if we take οὐκ ἄπο σκοποῦ to mean 'not deliberately' (i.e. Socrates did not intend this result), though even so the emphasis falls on how closely Socrates's ideas match the story, rather than the other way around.

26a1   διὰ χρόνου, 'after such an interval of time'.

26a2–3   εἴη, opt. for pres. indic. in virtual indirect speech in secondary sequence. οὕτως, '[after having made these preparations] *then* tell it to you'.

26a7   ὅδ'εἶπεν, i.e. Hermocrates at 20c6–d1.

ὡς δή
τοι, τὸ λεγόμενον, τὰ παίδων μαθήματα θαυμαστὸν ἔχει τι
μνημεῖον. ἐγὼ γὰρ ἃ μὲν χθὲς ἤκουσα, οὐκ ἂν οἶδ' εἰ
5   δυναίμην ἅπαντα ἐν μνήμῃ πάλιν λαβεῖν· ταῦτα δὲ ἃ πάμπολυν χρόνον διακήκοα, παντάπασι θαυμάσαιμ' ἂν εἴ τί με
αὐτῶν διαπέφευγεν. ἦν μὲν οὖν μετὰ πολλῆς ἡδονῆς καὶ
26c1   παιδιᾶς τότε ἀκουόμενα, καὶ τοῦ πρεσβύτου προθύμως με
διδάσκοντος, ἅτ' ἐμοῦ πολλάκις ἐπανερωτῶντος, ὥστε οἷον
ἐγκαύματα ἀνεκπλύτου γραφῆς ἔμμονά μοι γέγονεν· καὶ δὴ
καὶ τοῖσδε εὐθὺς ἔλεγον ἕωθεν αὐτὰ ταῦτα, ἵνα εὐποροῖεν
λόγων μετ' ἐμοῦ.

26b4–7   Read this as οὐκ οἶδ' εἰ (introducing ind. question) δυναίμην ἄν, potential opt. πάμπολυν χρόνον, 'a long time ago' (G 1063). θαυμάσαιμ' ἄν, potential opt.; εἰ ... διαπέφευγεν, past conditional clause, with no implications about its fulfilment (G 1390). The contrast between Critias's acknowledgement of his hazy memory of the discussion with Socrates about the ideal state ('yesterday', b4) and his confidence in his indelible memory of the story he heard in childhood (26b7–c3) is striking. Since his role in the discussion is to match Socrates's account of the ideal state (*Ti.* 17b–19b) with an appropriate story (imagined or real) (19b–20c), his firmer grasp of the childhood story than the philosophical theme it is designed to illustrate is rather troubling (see [23]).

26b7–c5 ἦν ... ἀκουόμενα, pass. part. + ἦν, alternative form of imperf. pass. The subject of ἦν and γέγονεν (c3) is ταῦτα (b5). The phrases μετὰ πολλῆς ἡδονῆς κ.τ.λ. and καὶ τοῦ πρεσβύτου κ.τ.λ. are descriptive phrases, attached to ἦν ... ἀκουόμενα and explaining why Critias found the story so memorable. τοῦ πρεσβύτου ... διδάσκοντος is gen. abs. (RG 222–23, AM 19), and so is ἅτ᾽ ἐμοῦ κ.τ.λ. In c1 I prefer to read παιδικῆς, 'with much childish pleasure' (found in two of the manuscripts) in place of the Oxford text's παιδιᾶς. c3: ἐγκαύματα, the marks burnt indelibly into a surface in 'encaustic' painting, see Pliny, *Natural History*, 35.149.

5 νῦν οὖν, οὗπερ ἕνεκα πάντα ταῦτα εἴρηται, λέγειν εἰμὶ ἕτοιμος, ὦ Σώκρατες, μὴ μόνον ἐν κεφαλαίοις ἀλλ᾽ ὥσπερ ἤκουσα καθ᾽ ἕκαστον· τοὺς δὲ πολίτας καὶ τὴν πόλιν ἣν χθὲς ἡμῖν ὡς ἐν μύθῳ διῄεισθα σύ, νῦν μετενεγ-
26d1 κόντες ἐπὶ τἀληθὲς δεῦρο θήσομεν ὡς ἐκείνην τήνδε οὖσαν, καὶ τοὺς πολίτας οὓς διενοοῦ φήσομεν ἐκείνους τοὺς ἀλη-θινοὺς εἶναι προγόνους ἡμῶν, οὓς ἔλεγεν ὁ ἱερεύς. πάντως ἁρμόσουσι καὶ οὐκ ἀπᾳσόμεθα λέγοντες αὐτοὺς εἶναι τοὺς ἐν
5 τῷ τότε ὄντας χρόνῳ. κοινῇ δὲ διαλαμβάνοντες ἅπαντες πειρασόμεθα τὸ πρέπον εἰς δύναμιν οἷς ἐπέταξας ἀποδοῦναι. σκοπεῖν οὖν δὴ χρή, ὦ Σώκρατες, εἰ κατὰ νοῦν ὁ λόγος ἡμῖν
26e1 οὗτος, ἤ τινα ἔτ᾽ ἄλλον ἀντ᾽ αὐτοῦ ζητητέον.

26c5 Paraphrase: 'to come to the point of these preliminaries'.
26c7–d3 'The citizens and the city you described yesterday in mythical fashion [ὡς ἐν μύθῳ], we shall now translate into actual fact [lit. 'truth', τἀληθὲς], placing it here and regarding it as that real [οὖσαν] city [i.e. primaeval Athens]; and the citizens you conceived, we shall say, are those true ancestors of ours, whom the priest described'. In δεῦρο θήσομεν (d1), Plato exploits two of the meanings of τίθημι: to 'place' (lit. 'bring *to* this place') and to 'regard' or 'suppose'. In a Platonic context, Critias's use of the contrast between 'myth' and 'truth' and 'real' is striking; typically (e.g. *Ti.* 27d–29b), philosophical ideas have the best

chance of achieving reality and truth, rather than empirical
facts. Also, despite Critias's presentation, we may well think that
his story is a myth (i.e. made up). See also the note on 25a1–5.

26d3–5 πάντως κ.τ.λ, 'They will fit in every way', that is, probably, fit
each other *and* fit the requirements of the story, 'and we shall
not strike a false note in saying that they [the ideal citizens] are
the [citizens] who existed at that time'.

26d6 τὸ πρέπον … οἷς = τὸ πρέπον τοῖς ἃ (ἡμῖν) ἐπέταξας.

{ΣΩ.} Καὶ τίν' ἄν, ὦ Κριτία, μᾶλλον ἀντὶ τούτου μεταλάβοιμεν, ὃς τῇ τε παρούσῃ τῆς θεοῦ θυσίᾳ διὰ τὴν οἰκειότητ'
ἂν πρέποι μάλιστα, τό τε μὴ πλασθέντα μῦθον ἀλλ' ἀληθινὸν
5   λόγον εἶναι πάμμεγά που. πῶς γὰρ καὶ πόθεν ἄλλους
ἀνευρήσομεν ἀφέμενοι τούτων; οὐκ ἔστιν, ἀλλ' ἀγαθῇ τύχῃ
χρὴ λέγειν μὲν ὑμᾶς, ἐμὲ δὲ ἀντὶ τῶν χθὲς λόγων νῦν
27a1   ἡσυχίαν ἄγοντα ἀντακούειν.

26e2–3 ἂν … μεταλάβοιμεν, ἂν πρέποι, potential optatives; ὃς refers to
τούτου (understand τοῦ λόγου). τό … εἶναι, noun clause (with
subject of infin. in acc., RG 258, G 895); understand ἐστί with
πάμμεγά. Although the two clauses in e3–4 are coupled by τε
… τε, there is a change of construction between clauses, from
a relative to an independent clause: 'It [lit. 'which'] would be
most appropriate … and the fact that it is not a made-up story
but a true account is all-important, I suppose.' The last phrase,
combining the rather exaggerated 'all-important' (πάμμεγά)
with the deflationary που ('perhaps' or 'I suppose'), suggests a
degree of irony or detachment on Socrates's part. Socrates may
be signalling scepticism about the story's truth or, more probably,
indicating that to him it is of no consequence whether the story is
factually true or not. What matters to him is consistency between
the story (imaginary or factually true) and the philosophical
theme it is meant to represent (*Ti.* 19b–20c); see also [23], esp. n. 55.

26e6 τούτων, 'them', that is, the citizens of primaeval Athens (see c7–
d3). οὐκ ἔστιν = οὐκ ἔξεστιν, 'it is impossible'.

{ΚΡ.} Σκόπει δὴ τὴν τῶν ξενίων σοι διάθεσιν, ὦ Σώκρατες,
ᾗ διέθεμεν. ἔδοξεν γὰρ ἡμῖν Τίμαιον μέν, ἅτε ὄντα ἀστρο-
νομικώτατον ἡμῶν καὶ περὶ φύσεως τοῦ παντὸς εἰδέναι
5 μάλιστα ἔργον πεποιημένον, πρῶτον λέγειν ἀρχόμενον ἀπὸ
τῆς τοῦ κόσμου γενέσεως, τελευτᾶν δὲ εἰς ἀνθρώπων φύσιν·

27a2-6 ξενίων, see also the note on 17a2-3, b2-4. a5: 'and has made
understanding the nature of the universe [περὶ φύσεως τοῦ
παντὸς εἰδέναι] his special job'. The introduction of Timaeus's
vast role (which occupies the rest of the *Timaeus*, 27-92) is
very unexpected. Even so, Socrates greets this addition with
much warmer and more enthusiastic language than he uses
in his response to Critias (27a7-8), and is still more positive
in the comment he makes in response to Timaeus's prelude
(29d4-6, responding to 27c-29d). This indicates that, despite
initial appearances, Timaeus's account of the origin of the
universe and humankind conveys a theme which matches
Socrates's original request. This theme (it is suggested in
the introduction) is that of seeking a concrete structure and
embodiment for the ideal, whether the ideal is the model for
the universe or the ideal political state. It is also suggested
there that, although Critias does not explicitly respond to
the presence of this theme in Timaeus' exposition, it informs
and influences the fuller version of the story he gives (or
starts to give) in *Critias*. This fuller version matches Socrates's
request more closely than the initial summary, and shows
how the social and material structures of primaeval Athens
and Atlantis bring out in concrete form salient differences
between the ideal state and its opponent. Another feature of
the fuller version is the location of the human (sociopolitical)
structures of the two states in the context of their natural
environments, which parallels the way that Timaeus shows
how humankind fits into the larger universe (a theme
indicated in 27a5-6). See [24-25].

ἐμὲ δὲ μετὰ τοῦτον, ὡς παρὰ μὲν τούτου δεδεγμένον ἀνθρώπους τῷ λόγῳ γεγονότας, παρὰ σοῦ δὲ πεπαιδευμένους δια-
27b1 φερόντως αὐτῶν τινας, κατὰ δὲ τὸν Σόλωνος λόγον τε καὶ
νόμον εἰσαγαγόντα αὐτοὺς ὡς εἰς δικαστὰς ἡμᾶς ποιῆσαι
πολίτας τῆς πόλεως τῆσδε ὡς ὄντας τοὺς τότε Ἀθηναίους,
οὓς ἐμήνυσεν ἀφανεῖς ὄντας ἡ τῶν ἱερῶν γραμμάτων φήμη,
5 τὰ λοιπὰ δὲ ὡς περὶ πολιτῶν καὶ Ἀθηναίων ὄντων ἤδη
ποιεῖσθαι τοὺς λόγους.
{ΣΩ.} Τελέως τε καὶ λαμπρῶς ἔοικα ἀνταπολήψεσθαι τὴν
τῶν λόγων ἑστίασιν. σὸν οὖν ἔργον λέγειν ἄν, ὦ Τίμαιε,
τὸ μετὰ τοῦτο, ὡς ἔοικεν, εἴη καλέσαντα κατὰ νόμον θεούς.

27a8–9 τῷ λόγῳ γεγονότας, 'brought to birth in his speech', that is,
human beings, whose creation is to be described by Timaeus as
part of his λόγος about the universe. παρὰ σοῦ κ.τ.λ., 'some of
them [i.e. human beings] educated in a distinctive way by you
[Socrates]', that is, the guardian class in the ideal state, whose
education is mentioned at 18a, also 19c6. Critias thus refers back
to Socrates's original request, that the guardian class of this idea
state should be represented in a narrative account of some great
exploit, 19b–c.

27b1–3 κατὰ δὲ κ.τ.λ., 'on the basis of Solon's account and his law code
to lead them into our courtroom, as it were [αὐτοὺς ὡς εἰς
δικαστὰς ἡμᾶς], and make them citizens of this city [Athens]'.
Critias describes their intellectual gathering as a law court set
up to test the right to Athenian citizenship of the type of men
described by his companions. He refers to Solon's historical role
as Athenian lawgiver (summarized by Aristotle, *Politics* 2.12.
1273.34–1274a23) as well as his role as the alleged source of the
story.

27b3–6 Critias says that he will take the guardian class of Socrates's
ideal state (see the note on 27a8–9) and treat them 'as being'
(or 'as if they were') (ὡς ὄντας in b3, see also ὡς ... ὄντων
in b5) the Athenian citizens of Solon's story. As elsewhere in
this section of the discussion, he stresses both the allegedly
factual nature of the story and the close link with Athens; he is

also very confident that his allegedly historical story matches Socrates's original request (note on 25e4–5 and [20, 23]).

27b7–8   For the idea of a 'banquet' or 'feast', see the notes on 17a2–3, b2–4. For Socrates's enthusiastic response, see the note on 27a2–6, first paragraph.

Critias 106–121

Critias 106a–108d:
Critias's introduction to his story

After Timaeus's vast, and intellectually impressive, account of the origin of the universe, Critias suggests that his task is more difficult because people are more searching critics of material they know well, and so it is harder to give a convincing picture of human action than of the nature of the universe. This is a surprising claim, given the very demanding nature of Timaeus's subject matter (which Critias ignores). Also, Critias's description of his task recalls features of poetic representation criticized in the *Republic*, namely its being simply an imitation of the external surface of human life which does not rest on genuine understanding of the subjects represented. This is a rather unpromising start to Critias's story and seems to echo the problematic aspects of his character, as presented in the *Timaeus*. See [26, 37–38].

106a1   {ΤΙ.} Ὡς ἄσμενος, ὦ Σώκρατες, οἷον ἐκ μακρᾶς ἀναπε-
         παυμένος ὁδοῦ, νῦν οὕτως ἐκ τῆς τοῦ λόγου διαπορείας
         ἀγαπητῶς ἀπήλλαγμαι. τῷ δὲ πρὶν μὲν πάλαι ποτ' ἔργῳ,
         νῦν δὲ λόγοις ἄρτι θεῷ γεγονότι προσεύχομαι, τῶν ῥηθέν-
5   των ὅσα μὲν ἐρρήθη μετρίως, σωτηρίαν ἡμῖν αὐτὸν αὐτῶν
106b1   διδόναι, παρὰ μέλος δὲ εἴ τι περὶ αὐτῶν ἄκοντες εἴπομεν,
         δίκην τὴν πρέπουσαν ἐπιτιθέναι.

106a1–3   Read ἄσμενος, rather than the ἄσμενος of Burnet 1902 in a1.
            Ὡς ... οἷον ... νῦν οὕτως, 'How glad ... like ... [so] now'.
106a3–b2   Timaeus began his speech with a prayer for the help of the gods
            (*Timaeus* 27c) and ends with another prayer. He prays to the

universe, whose creation he has just described (in the omitted section of the *Timaeus*): 'I pray to the god whose creation took place long ago in fact, but who did so just now in words'. The universe was commonly regarded by Greeks as divine (e.g. *Apology* 26d), and is described as θεὸς αἰσθητός at the end of the *Timaeus* (92c7).

τῶν ῥηθέντων (a4–5) is subdivided into ὅσα μὲν ἐρρήθη μετρίως ... παρὰ μέλος δὲ εἴ τι ... εἴπομεν ... The construction changes from a relative to a conditional sentence: 'I pray to the god ... to preserve [σωτηρίαν διδόναι is a more solemn version of σῴζειν] those parts of our account which were spoken in due measure and, if we have inadvertently [ἄκοντες] struck a false note, to impose the appropriate penalty'. For the significance of the musical metaphor in μετρίως ('in due measure') and παρὰ μέλος ('out of tune'), see the note on 106b2–3.

δίκη δὲ ὀρθὴ τὸν πλημ-
μελοῦντα ἐμμελῆ ποιεῖν· ἵν᾽ οὖν τὸ λοιπὸν τοὺς περὶ θεῶν
γενέσεως ὀρθῶς λέγωμεν λόγους, φάρμακον ἡμῖν αὐτὸν
5   τελεώτατον καὶ ἄριστον φαρμάκων ἐπιστήμην εὐχόμεθα
διδόναι, προσευξάμενοι δὲ παραδίδομεν κατὰ τὰς ὁμολογίας
Κριτίᾳ τὸν ἑξῆς λόγον.

106b2–3   δίκη δὲ ὀρθὴ κ.τ.λ., 'The correct penalty for someone who plays out of tune is to make him play in tune'. This image picks up παρὰ μέλος ('if we have inadvertently struck a false note') in b1 and μετρίως ('in due measure') in a5. The idea that justice is essentially corrective and has the aim or 'harmonizing' the criminal's moral character is a long-standing Platonic theme (*Protagoras* 324a–c, 326b; on virtue as psychic harmony see *Republic* 443d–e), and it recurs in *Critias*, 121c1–2. That wrongdoing is involuntary, and a product of ignorance, is a Socratic idea, retained by Plato even in his late works (*Ti.* 86d7–e2; *Laws* 860d–e).

106b6   κατὰ τὰς ὁμολογίας, see *Ti.* 27a–b.

{ΚΡΙ.} Ἀλλ᾽, ὦ Τίμαιε, δέχομαι μέν, ᾧ δὲ καὶ σὺ κατ᾽
106c1 ἀρχὰς ἐχρήσω, συγγνώμην αἰτούμενος ὡς περὶ μεγάλων
μέλλων λέγειν, ταὐτὸν καὶ νῦν ἐγὼ τοῦτο παραιτοῦμαι,
107a1 μειζόνως δὲ αὐτοῦ τυχεῖν ἔτι μᾶλλον ἀξιῶ περὶ τῶν μελλόντων ῥηθήσεσθαι. καίτοι σχεδὸν μὲν οἶδα παραίτησιν
εὖ μάλα φιλότιμον καὶ τοῦ δέοντος ἀγροικοτέραν μέλλων
παραιτεῖσθαι, ῥητέον δὲ ὅμως.

106b7–c1 ᾧ ... κατ᾽ ἀρχὰς ἐχρήσω: 'But I also make the same plea
[παραιτοῦμαι] that you used at the start of your speech, when
you asked for understanding on the grounds that you were
about to speak about a great subject. Indeed, I think I have a
still stronger claim [ἔτι μᾶλλον ἀξιῶ] for obtaining it [αὐτοῦ, cf.
ταὐτὸν], and to a greater extent [μειζόνως], given the nature of
my subject [lit. 'with regard to the things that are about to be
spoken of']'. Critias begins by referring to Timaeus's comments
at 27c–29d, esp. 29b–d. Timaeus is there making a substantive
philosophical point about the extent to which (on Platonic
principles of being and truth) an account of the physical world
can achieve truth. Timaeus claims that such an account can
only be, at best, 'likely' (see also [19], esp. n. 39, and Gill 1977,
290–91). Critias ignores the substance of Timaeus's point and
treats it as an appeal for indulgence or understanding.
107a2 σχεδὸν ... οἶδα, the adverb qualifies the assertiveness: 'I am all
too well aware' (lit. 'I rather know').

ὡς μὲν γὰρ οὐκ εὖ τὰ
5 παρὰ σοῦ λεχθέντα εἴρηται, τίς ἂν ἐπιχειρήσειεν ἔμφρων
λέγειν; ὅτι δὲ τὰ ῥηθησόμενα πλείονος συγγνώμης δεῖται
χαλεπώτερα ὄντα, τοῦτο πειρατέον πῃ διδάξαι. περὶ θεῶν
γάρ, ὦ Τίμαιε, λέγοντά τι πρὸς ἀνθρώπους δοκεῖν ἱκανῶς
107b1 λέγειν ῥᾷον ἢ περὶ θνητῶν πρὸς ἡμᾶς. ἡ γὰρ ἀπειρία καὶ
σφόδρα ἄγνοια τῶν ἀκουόντων περὶ ὧν ἂν οὕτως ἔχωσιν
πολλὴν εὐπορίαν παρέχεσθον τῷ μέλλοντι λέγειν τι περὶ
αὐτῶν· περὶ δὲ δὴ θεῶν ἴσμεν ὡς ἔχομεν.

107a4–6   ὡς … εἴρηται, ind. statement governed by λέγειν; ἐπιχειρήσειεν, potential aor. opt.; ὅτι κ.τ.λ., ind. statement, governed by διδάξαι.

107a7   περὶ θεῶν κ.τ.λ. Critias's remark here picks up Timaeus's description of the universe as a θεὸς αἰσθητός (Ti. 92c7, also 34b1–9). It also depends on the popular assumption that the heavenly bodies are gods (see the note on 106a3–b2).

107b1–3   ἡ γὰρ ἀπειρία καὶ σφόδρα ἄγνοια, 'the combination of inexperience and sheer [see σφόδρα in vocab.] ignorance in one's audience [lit. 'of those listening']'. παρέχεσθον is dual, governed by the two nouns. περὶ ὧν κ.τ.λ., in full this would be [περὶ τῶν] περὶ ὧν ἂν οὕτως ἔχειν, 'on subjects of which they are not informed [lit. 'about those things about which they happen to be', indef. rel. clause, RG 282] in this state'; for οὕτως ἔχειν (to be in such-and-such a state), see LSJ, ἔχω, B II 2.

107b4   περὶ κ.τ.λ., 'about the gods, of course [δὴ], we know how we are placed', i.e. in ignorance; on ὡς ἔχομεν, see the note on 107b1–3.

Critias discusses the difficulty of his task in terms that are strikingly different from those used by Socrates in his original request for the story. Socrates had emphasized the difficulty of finding a narrator with the right combination of philosophical and political knowledge (*Ti.* 19b–20a). He complained that most poets are simply imitators of what is familiar to them (19d), and this complaint echoes the description of poets in *Republic* Book X as mere imitators of the surface appearance of human life without any real knowledge of politics or morality (*Republic* 598–600, see also the note on *Ti.* 19c2–8 above).

Critias shows little concern with the question of his intellectual expertise; he emphasizes, rather, the difficulty of giving his narrative of human action a convincing surface realism, and in this respect he shares the concerns of the poets described in *Republic* Book X. Indeed, he goes so far as to describe the function of language as a whole as that of imitation and image-making (b5–7). Critias's description of his task seems to reflect features of his character also brought out in the *Timaeus*, namely his preoccupation with the importance of his own project and status, and a certain intellectual superficiality (see [23]). Also, his account of the two cities (especially Atlantis) does indeed offer a vivid and convincing picture of the two cities. This might make us think that the story is just an exercise in graphic representation (which is what Critias stresses here) or an early experiment in fiction by Plato. However, the story is, in fact, underpinned by important political themes, of the kind that match Socrates's original request (see [37–38, also 29], and Gill 1979b, 1993, 62–66).

ἵνα δὲ σαφέ-
5 στερον ὃ λέγω δηλώσω, τῇδέ μοι συνεπίσπεσθε. μίμησιν
μὲν γὰρ δὴ καὶ ἀπεικασίαν τὰ παρὰ πάντων ἡμῶν ῥηθέντα
χρεών που γενέσθαι· τὴν δὲ τῶν γραφέων εἰδωλοποιίαν
περὶ τὰ θεῖά τε καὶ τὰ ἀνθρώπινα σώματα γιγνομένην
107c1 ἴδωμεν ῥᾳστώνης τε πέρι καὶ χαλεπότητος πρὸς τὸ τοῖς
ὁρῶσιν δοκεῖν ἀποχρώντως μεμιμῆσθαι, καὶ κατοψόμεθα ὅτι
γῆν μὲν καὶ ὄρη καὶ ποταμοὺς καὶ ὕλην οὐρανόν τε σύμπαντα καὶ τὰ περὶ αὐτὸν ὄντα καὶ ἰόντα πρῶτον μὲν ἀγαπῶ-
5 μεν ἄν τίς τι καὶ βραχὺ πρὸς ὁμοιότητα αὐτῶν ἀπομιμεῖσθαι 5
δυνατὸς ᾖ, πρὸς δὲ τούτοις, ἅτε οὐδὲν εἰδότες ἀκριβὲς περὶ
τῶν τοιούτων, οὔτε ἐξετάζομεν οὔτε ἐλέγχομεν τὰ γεγραμ-
107d1 μένα, σκιαγραφίᾳ δὲ ἀσαφεῖ καὶ ἀπατηλῷ χρώμεθα περὶ
αὐτά·

107b7–d2   The structure of this complex sentence is as follows: ἴδωμεν ['let us consider'] … καὶ κατοψόμεθα ὅτι ['and we shall observe that'] … πρῶτον μὲν ἀγαπῶμεν ἄν τίς … δυνατὸς ᾖ, πρὸς δὲ τούτοις [this clause too governed by κατοψόμεθα] σκιαγραφίᾳ δὲ … χρώμθα.

107b8–c2   γιγνομένην κ.τ.λ., (as regards representation) 'let us consider how things stand [γιγνομένην] regarding the relative ease or difficulty of seeming to spectators to have given an adequate reproduction'.

107c4   καὶ τὰ περὶ αὐτὸν ὄντα καὶ ἰόντα, i.e. the heavenly bodies, sun, stars, etc.

107c5–6   πρὸς ὁμοιότητα αὐτῶν (lit. 'as regards their likeness'); πρὸς δὲ τούτοις, 'in addition to this'. See LSJ, πρός, acc. III 1; dat. III.

107d1   σκιαγραφίᾳ (lit. 'shadow-drawing'), a technique for producing
an impression of solidity by shading, esp. in scene painting;
translate as 'an imprecise and deceptive sketch'. At *Republic*
602d, Plato describes σκιαγραφία as typical of illusionistic
techniques of painting (see Pollitt 1974, 247–48). χρώμθα, 'we
are content with' (lit. 'we make use of').

τὰ δὲ ἡμέτερα ὁπόταν τις ἐπιχειρῇ σώματα ἀπεικάζειν, ὀξέως αἰσθανόμενοι τὸ παραλειπόμενον διὰ τὴν ἀεὶ
σύνοικον κατανόησιν χαλεποὶ κριταὶ γιγνόμεθα τῷ μὴ πάσας
5   πάντως τὰς ὁμοιότητας ἀποδιδόντι. ταὐτὸν δὴ καὶ κατὰ
τοὺς λόγους ἰδεῖν δεῖ γιγνόμενον, ὅτι τὰ μὲν οὐράνια καὶ
θεῖα ἀγαπῶμεν καὶ σμικρῶς εἰκότα λεγόμενα, τὰ δὲ θνητὰ
καὶ ἀνθρώπινα ἀκριβῶς ἐξετάζομεν.

107d4–5 κριταὶ ... τῷ μὴ ... ἀποδιδόντι: τῷ ... ἀποδιδόντι, dat. of
disadvantage (RG 440(ii), AM 32), indefinite: 'harsh critics of
anyone who fails to'.
107d6–7 ὅτι τὰ μὲν κ.τ.λ., 'in the case of heavenly and divine subjects,
we are content with accounts [lit. 'them being spoken of',
λεγόμενα] that even slightly resemble [καὶ σμικρῶς εἰκότα]
their subject matter'. On the contrast between this idea of
visible 'likeness' to the subject and Timaeus's characterization
of statements about the physical world as only 'likely' to be true
(29b–d), see Gill 1977, 290–91.

ἐκ δὴ τοῦ παραχρῆμα
107e1   νῦν λεγόμενα, τὸ πρέπον ἂν μὴ δυνώμεθα πάντως ἀποδιδό-
ναι, συγγιγνώσκειν χρεών· οὐ γὰρ ὡς ῥᾴδια τὰ θνητὰ ἀλλ'
ὡς χαλεπὰ πρὸς δόξαν ὄντα ἀπεικάζειν δεῖ διανοεῖσθαι.
108a1   ταῦτα δὴ βουλόμενος ὑμᾶς ὑπομνῆσαι, καὶ τὸ τῆς συγγνώμης
οὐκ ἔλαττον ἀλλὰ μεῖζον αἰτῶν περὶ τῶν μελλόντων ῥηθήσεσθαι, πάντα ταῦτα εἴρηκα, ὦ Σώκρατες. εἰ δὴ δικαίως
αἰτεῖν φαίνομαι τὴν δωρεάν, ἑκόντες δίδοτε.

107d8-e3 λεγόμενα may be taken as the direct object of συγγιγνώσκειν; or as an acc. of respect, thus: 'In the case of the present account [νῦν λεγόμενα], which is after all [δὴ] an improvisation, if I fail to provide what is appropriate in every respect [i.e., all the finishing touches – distinct fut. condition, AM 180, RG 402 (iii)], you must excuse me'. It is surprising to hear Critias describe his story as an 'improvisation' (ἐκ τοῦ παραχρῆμα), since at Timaeus 26b-c he said he had learnt it by heart (and at Critias 113b he refers to a written text he studied in his youth). However, it is perhaps the verbal 'finish' of the story (the touches that give artistic verisimilitude) that he must improvise, in the way orators regularly improvised on well-prepared set themes (Menexenus 235c-d).

107e3 πρὸς δόξαν ... ἀπεικάζειν, 'to produce a likeness which corresponds to people's expectations'.

108a1-2 καὶ τὸ τῆς συγγνώμης κ.τ.λ., lit: 'with respect to the matter of understanding [referred to above, 106c] I ask not for less but for more of it'; in more idiomatic English, 'asking for more, rather than less, understanding'.

5 {ΣΩ.} Τί δ' οὐ μέλλομεν, ὦ Κριτία, διδόναι; καὶ πρός
γε ἔτι τρίτῳ δεδόσθω ταὐτὸν τοῦτο Ἑρμοκράτει παρ' ἡμῶν.
δῆλον γὰρ ὡς ὀλίγον ὕστερον, ὅταν αὐτὸν δέῃ λέγειν,
108b1 παραιτήσεται καθάπερ ὑμεῖς· ἵν' οὖν ἑτέραν ἀρχὴν ἐκπορί-
ζηται καὶ μὴ τὴν αὐτὴν ἀναγκασθῇ λέγειν, ὡς ὑπαρχούσης
αὐτῷ συγγνώμης εἰς τότε οὕτω λεγέτω. προλέγω γε μήν,
ὦ φίλε Κριτία, σοὶ τὴν τοῦ θεάτρου διάνοιαν, ὅτι θαυμαστῶς
5 ὁ πρότερος ηὐδοκίμηκεν ἐν αὐτῷ ποιητής, ὥστε τῆς συγγνώμης δεήσει τινός σοι παμπόλλης, εἰ μέλλεις αὐτὰ
δυνατὸς γενέσθαι παραλαβεῖν.

108a5-b7 Critias's long prelude implied that he saw his role as like that of a poet or orator in a competition, aiming to make a good impression on his audience (see esp. 106b8-107a7, 107d8-108a4); orators typically preceded their speeches with carefully phrased

133

introductions (see Aristotle, *Rhetoric* 3.14). Socrates seems to echo this characterization, referring to Critias's role as a poet in a theatrical competition, like the one held at the Dionysiac Festival at Athens (θεάτρον … ποιητής, b4–5). However, as in *Ti.* 26e (see the note on 26e2–3), Socrates is unlikely to attach the same importance as Critias to the 'performance' side of his project, as opposed to communicating the underlying ideas, and thus satisfying the original request (*Ti.* 19b–20c)

108b3–5   εἰς τότε, 'then', that is, 'when the time comes'. προλέγω κ.τ.λ., 'But I must tell you in advance … what the state of mind of your audience will be towards you [σοὶ in emphatic position]. The poet who preceded you [ποιητής picks up the image of θεάτρου] made a wonderfully fine impression on it …'. Here, as also in *Ti.* 27b7–8, 29d4–6, Socrates's response to Timaeus's (more philosophically profound) contribution to the discussion is markedly warmer than to what Critias offers.

{ΕΡ.} Ταὐτὸν μήν, ὦ Σώκρατες, κἀμοὶ παραγγέλλεις ὅπερ
108c1   τῷδε. ἀλλὰ γὰρ ἀθυμοῦντες ἄνδρες οὔπω τρόπαιον ἔστησαν, ὦ Κριτία· προϊέναι τε οὖν ἐπὶ τὸν λόγον ἀνδρείως χρή, καὶ τὸν Παίωνά τε καὶ τὰς Μούσας ἐπικαλούμενον τοὺς παλαιοὺς πολίτας ἀγαθοὺς ὄντας ἀναφαίνειν τε καὶ ὑμνεῖν.

108c1–4   ἀλλὰ γάρ, 'But even so'. ἀθυμοῦντες κ.τ.λ., the phrase seems to be proverbial, compare 'faint heart never won fair lady', 'nothing ventured, nothing gained'. However, the military image suits Hermocrates's military and patriotic character (see also ἀνδρείως … τοὺς παλαιοὺς ἀγαθοὺς, and, on Hermocrates, see the note on *Ti.* 20a). Calling on Apollo Paean ('Healer') and the Muses for help is an appropriate precaution for a poet (see the note on 108a5–b2), although soldiers too sang paeans at the start of a campaign (Thucydides 7.75.7). c3–4, τοὺς παλαιοὺς πολίτας κ.τ.λ., 'bring out the excellence of those ancient citizens [of Athens] and sing their praises'; see also *Ti.* 26d.

5   {ΚΡ.} Ὦ φίλε Ἑρμόκρατες, τῆς ὑστέρας τεταγμένος, ἐπί-   5
     προσθεν ἔχων ἄλλον, ἔτι θαρρεῖς. τοῦτο μὲν οὖν οἷόν
     ἐστιν, αὐτό σοι τάχα δηλώσει· παραμυθουμένῳ δ᾽ οὖν καὶ
108d1 παραθαρρύνοντί σοι πειστέον, καὶ πρὸς οἷς θεοῖς εἶπες τούς
     τε ἄλλους κλητέον καὶ δὴ καὶ τὰ μάλιστα Μνημοσύνην.
     σχεδὸν γὰρ τὰ μέγιστα ἡμῖν τῶν λόγων ἐν ταύτῃ τῇ θεῷ
     πάντ᾽ ἐστίν· μνησθέντες γὰρ ἱκανῶς καὶ ἀπαγγείλαντες
5   τά ποτε ῥηθέντα ὑπὸ τῶν ἱερέων καὶ δεῦρο ὑπὸ Σόλωνος
     κομισθέντα σχεδὸν οἶδ᾽ ὅτι τῷδε τῷ θεάτρῳ δόξομεν τὰ
     προσήκοντα μετρίως ἀποτετελεκέναι. τοῦτ᾽ οὖν αὖτ᾽ ἤδη
     δραστέον, καὶ μελλητέον οὐδὲν ἔτι.

108c5-7   τῆς ὑστέρας [τάξεως] τεταγμένος, 'positioned at the rear';
           Critias takes up the military tone. τοῦτο μὲν κ.τ.λ., 'but what it
           is like to be at the front like this, experience itself [αὐτό] will soon
           show you'.

108d1   πρὸς οἷς θεοῖς, short for πρὸς τοῖς θεοῖς οὕς; Μνημοσύνη
           (Memory) is, traditionally, the mother of the Muses (c3). In
           calling on her, Critias reassumes the role of a historian, who
           has memorized a factual account (see also *Ti.* 26b–c), while still
           maintaining his role as a poet (see θεάτρῳ, d6).

Critias 108e-113b:
Critias's account of primaeval Athens

Critias prefaces his account of the great war (which is never actually given) with a description of the two opposing states, beginning with primaeval Athens. Although at a formal level this description simply offers in full the story outlined in the *Timaeus*, there are significant differences in emphasis and approach. These differences indicate that Critias, perhaps under the influence of Timaeus's more philosophically challenging account, is now responding more fully to the content and underlying message of Socrates's original request (see the note on *Timaeus* 27a2-6 and [25]). The description begins with features that also appeared in his summary, the divine organization of society and the use of evidence to study the distant past. However, both are treated in a more thoughtful and credible way than in the summary ([26]).

108e1   Πάντων δὴ πρῶτον μνησθῶμεν ὅτι τὸ κεφάλαιον ἦν
       ἐνακισχίλια ἔτη, ἀφ' οὗ γεγονὼς ἐμηνύθη πόλεμος τοῖς θ'
       ὑπὲρ Ἡρακλείας στήλας ἔξω κατοικοῦσιν καὶ τοῖς ἐντὸς
       πᾶσιν· ὃν δεῖ νῦν διαπεραίνειν. τῶν μὲν οὖν ἥδε ἡ πόλις
5   ἄρξασα καὶ πάντα τὸν πόλεμον διαπολεμήσασα ἐλέγετο,
       τῶν δ' οἱ τῆς Ἀτλαντίδος νήσου βασιλῆς, ἣν δὴ Λιβύης
       καὶ Ἀσίας μείζω νῆσον οὖσαν ἔφαμεν εἶναί ποτε, νῦν δὲ
       ὑπὸ σεισμῶν δῦσαν ἄπορον πηλὸν τοῖς ἐνθένδε ἐκπλέουσιν
109a1   ἐπὶ τὸ πᾶν πέλαγος, ὥστε μηκέτι πορεύεσθαι, κωλυτὴν παρα-
       σχεῖν.

108e2   ἐνακισχίλια ἔτη. At *Ti.* 23e4-5, ancient Athens was said to have been founded 9,000 years in the past; now this is the date of the war which destroyed that Athens. The slip indicates that Critias's claim about the factual 'truth' of this story (*Ti.* 20d8) should not be taken too seriously (see [19]).

108e4-6   Note the contrast between the *city* of Athens and the *kings* of Atlantis – a first sign of the political contrast drawn between the two states in Critias's story.

108e7   νῦν δε κ.τ.λ., 'but now the island has been submerged by

earthquakes and creates [a mass of] impenetrable mud which
is an obstacle to those sailing from here [the Mediterranean] to
the open sea, so that they can no longer make voyages there'.
See the note on *Ti.* 25d5–6.

τὰ μὲν δὴ πολλὰ ἔθνη βάρβαρα, καὶ ὅσα Ἑλλήνων
ἦν γένη τότε, καθ' ἕκαστα ἡ τοῦ λόγου διέξοδος οἷον ἀνειλ-
λομένη τὸ προστυχὸν ἑκασταχοῦ δηλώσει· τὸ δὲ Ἀθηναίων
τε τῶν τότε καὶ τῶν ἐναντίων, οἷς διεπολέμησαν, ἀνάγκη
κατ' ἀρχὰς διελθεῖν πρῶτα, τήν τε δύναμιν ἑκατέρων καὶ τὰς
πολιτείας. αὐτῶν δὲ τούτων τὰ τῇδε ἔμπροσθεν προτιμητέον
εἰπεῖν.

5

109a2–4   'As regards the many barbarian nations and those Greek peoples
            that existed then, the course of the story, being unrolled,
            so to speak [οἷον ἀνειλλομένη], will bring out the relevant
            fact [lit. 'that which meets us, that which comes to hand', τὸ
            προστυχὸν] on each occasion, point by point [καθ' ἕκαστα]'.
            The metaphor of 'unrolling' seems to allude to a papyrus roll
            being progressively unrolled and read.

109a4   A survey of the protagonist states is a feature of the histories
            of Thucydides (e.g. 1.89–90) and, especially, Herodotus, and
            adds to the sense that we are being offered a pastiche of
            historiography. There are strong echoes of Herodotus Book II
            (on Egypt), esp. in the description of Atlantis (Pradeau 1997,
            170–79).

109b1   Θεοὶ γὰρ ἅπασαν γῆν ποτε κατὰ τοὺς τόπους διελάγ-
            χανον – οὐ κατ' ἔριν· οὐ γὰρ ἂν ὀρθὸν ἔχοι λόγον θεοὺς
            ἀγνοεῖν τὰ πρέποντα ἑκάστοις αὐτῶν, οὐδ' αὖ γιγνώσκοντας
            τὸ μᾶλλον ἄλλοις προσῆκον τοῦτο ἑτέρους αὐτοῖς δι' ἐρίδων
5   ἐπιχειρεῖν κτᾶσθαι – δίκης δὴ κλήροις τὸ φίλον λαγχάνοντες
            κατῴκιζον τὰς χώρας,

109b1–5   This account of the division of the world between gods
           follows Greek tradition (e.g. Homer *Iliad* 15.187–93), except in
           the insistence on the absence of strife in the process (on the
           modification of traditional ideas of the gods as quarrelling and
           fighting with each other, see *Republic* 377e–378d). In particular,
           Critias denies the well-known legend of the contest between
           Athena and Poseidon for possession of Attica, and gives
           Poseidon no place in the cult of ancient Athens. Poseidon is the
           god of maritime Atlantis, not the land power, primaeval Athens
           (for the land-sea contrast, see [30]).

109b2   οὐ γὰρ ἂν ὀρθὸν ἔχοι λόγον, 'it would not be right to say that'.
109b5–6   δίκης δὴ κλήροις κ.τ.λ., 'Receiving what was naturally their own
           [lit. 'dear', φίλον] by the allocations of justice, the gods set up
           communities in their lands'. For the idea that different gods
           received the type of land that was naturally 'appropriate' for
           them (b3–4), see also c8–d2 and the note on *Timaeus* 24c6–7.
           κλῆρος here means allocation and not (random) lot (see LSJ,
           κλῆρος II). The allocation is presumably made by Zeus, whose
           supremacy, and whose concern with law and justice, is made
           clear at *Criti.* 121b7–c5.

                     καὶ κατοικίσαντες, οἷον νομῆς ποίμνια,
           κτήματα καὶ θρέμματα ἑαυτῶν ἡμᾶς ἔτρεφον, πλὴν οὐ σώμασι
109c1   σώματα βιαζόμενοι, καθάπερ ποιμένες κτήνη πληγῇ νέμοντες,
           ἀλλ’ ᾗ μάλιστα εὔστροφον ζῷον, ἐκ πρύμνης ἀπευθύνοντες,
           οἷον οἴακι πειθοῖ ψυχῆς ἐφαπτόμενοι κατὰ τὴν αὐτῶν διά-
           νοιαν, οὕτως ἄγοντες τὸ θνητὸν πᾶν ἐκυβέρνων.

109b7   πλὴν οὐ, 'but with one difference' (lit. 'except that ... not'). This
           qualifying phrase parallels οὐ κατ’ ἔριν (b2), marking the two
           modifications that are made in this account to traditional views
           of relations between gods and between gods and humans (see
           [26]).

109c2   ἀλλ’ ᾗ μάλιστα κ.τ.λ., 'but where a creature is most manageable,
           they steered it from the stern. They directed its mind by

persuasion as they thought best, like someone using a rudder,
and in this way steered the human being as a whole'. The
reference to persuasion evokes scenes such as that in *Iliad*
1.194–218, where Achilles is persuaded to restrain his anger
by Athena. However, as the story develops, it becomes clear
that what is involved is, rather, divine transmission of a social
structure in the case of Athens (109d) and, in Atlantis, a
divinely generated dynasty (113d–114c) and a law code governing
relations between its ten kings (119c, 120b1–2, 120c). The idea
of gods as divine 'shepherds' of human beings is a recurrent
one in Plato's late dialogues and one that carries a different
significance in each work (*Statesman* 271d–272a; *Laws* 713c–714a;
see also Gill 1979a).

>   ἄλλοι μὲν
> 5 οὖν κατ' ἄλλους τόπους κληρουχήσαντες θεῶν ἐκεῖνα ἐκό-
> σμουν, Ἥφαιστος δὲ κοινὴν καὶ Ἀθηνᾶ φύσιν ἔχοντες, ἅμα
> μὲν ἀδελφὴν ἐκ ταὐτοῦ πατρός, ἅμα δὲ φιλοσοφίᾳ φιλο-
> τεχνίᾳ τε ἐπὶ τὰ αὐτὰ ἐλθόντες, οὕτω μίαν ἄμφω λῆξιν
> τήνδε τὴν χώραν εἰλήχατον ὡς οἰκείαν καὶ πρόσφορον ἀρετῇ
> 109d1 καὶ φρονήσει πεφυκυῖαν, ἄνδρας δὲ ἀγαθοὺς ἐμποιήσαντες
> αὐτόχθονας ἐπὶ νοῦν ἔθεσαν τὴν τῆς πολιτείας τάξιν·

109c6–d1 Plato develops the idea that the two gods share a common
nature by explaining that they *both* share an inherited nature
(ἅμα μὲν ἀδελφὴν κ.τ.λ., 'both because they were brother
and sister from the same father [lit. 'having a nature that
was brotherly/sisterly from the same father', Zeus]') *and* have
common interests (ἅμα δὲ φιλοσοφίᾳ κ.τ.λ., 'and also pursuing
the same ends, in their love of wisdom and craft'). Athena and
Hephaestus were associated in historical times by their common
concern with the crafts and by their importance in Athenian
religion. But Plato's story heightens this association, perhaps
because he sees each god as the patron of one of the two classes
in his primaeval state (the intellectual warrior being the patron

of the guardians, and the craftsman god the patron of the
craftsmen), and the union of the patron gods accentuates the
unity of his state (see also 110b5–c1, 112b).

109c9–d1   καὶ πρόσφορον ἀρετῇ κ.τ.λ., see the note on *Timaeus* 24c6–7.

109d1–2   ἄνδρας δὲ ἀγαθοὺς κ.τ.λ., 'producing good men from the earth,
they put into their minds the organization of the constitution'.
These men are Erechtheus etc. (110a7–b1), who are also the
ἄνδρες θεῖοι of 110c5. For the female equivalents of these men,
see the note on 110b5. For the idea of the gods implanting a law
code, see the note on 109c2; and for the combination of divine
generation of humans and autochthony, see the note on *Ti*. 23e1.

ὧν

τὰ μὲν ὀνόματα σέσωται, τὰ δὲ ἔργα διὰ τὰς τῶν παραλαμ-
βανόντων φθορὰς καὶ τὰ μήκη τῶν χρόνων ἠφανίσθη. τὸ

5   γὰρ περιλειπόμενον ἀεὶ γένος, ὥσπερ καὶ πρόσθεν ἐρρήθη,
κατελείπετο ὄρειον καὶ ἀγράμματον, τῶν ἐν τῇ χώρᾳ δυνα-
στῶν τὰ ὀνόματα ἀκηκοὸς μόνον καὶ βραχέα πρὸς αὐτοῖς
τῶν ἔργων. τὰ μὲν οὖν ὀνόματα τοῖς ἐκγόνοις ἐτίθεντο

109e1   ἀγαπῶντες, τὰς δὲ ἀρετὰς καὶ τοὺς νόμους τῶν ἔμπροσθεν
οὐκ εἰδότες, εἰ μὴ σκοτεινὰς περὶ ἑκάστων τινὰς ἀκοάς, ἐν
ἀπορίᾳ δὲ τῶν ἀναγκαίων ἐπὶ πολλὰς γενεὰς ὄντες αὐτοὶ

110a1   καὶ παῖδες, πρὸς οἷς ἠπόρουν τὸν νοῦν ἔχοντες, τούτων πέρι
καὶ τοὺς λόγους ποιούμενοι, τῶν ἐν τοῖς πρόσθεν καὶ πάλαι
ποτὲ γεγονότων ἠμέλουν.

109d4–8   See also *Ti*. 22d–23b and *Laws* 677a–679e. d7, καὶ βραχέα κ.τ.λ.,
'and besides [lit. 'in addition to these', αὐτοις = τὰ ὀνόματα], a
few of their actions'.

109e1   ἀγαπῶντες, 'it pleased them to give the names [of these
legendary figures] to their children'.

110a1   πρὸς οἷς = πρὸς τοῖς ὧν ἠπόρουν, 'to the things they needed'.

μυθολογία γὰρ ἀναζήτησίς τε
τῶν παλαιῶν μετὰ σχολῆς ἅμ᾽ ἐπὶ τὰς πόλεις ἔρχεσθον,
5 ὅταν ἴδητόν τισιν ἤδη τοῦ βίου τἀναγκαῖα κατεσκευασμένα,
πρὶν δὲ οὔ. ταύτῃ δὴ τὰ τῶν παλαιῶν ὀνόματα ἄνευ τῶν
ἔργων διασέσωται.

110a3–5   ἔρχεσθον, dual, pres. act. indic.; ἴδητόν, dual, aor. subj. (after
ὅταν, RG 282, AM 173): '[they] make their entrance whenever
they see that some people are now equipped with the necessities
of life'. For the idea that intellectual enquiry only develops
once basic needs are fulfilled, see Aristotle, *Metaphysics*
981b19–24. Here Plato does not distinguish sharply between
μυθολογία (storytelling about the past) and methodical enquiry
(ἀναζήτησις) into the past; but in *Ti.* 22a–23d he distinguishes
between (Athenian) myth-making and (Egyptian) systematic
investigation of the past. In the sentence starting 110a7, Critias
seems to be trying to carry out systematic investigation of the
past on the basis of well-known Greek myths and legends.

λέγω δὲ αὐτὰ τεκμαιρόμενος ὅτι Κέ-
κροπός τε καὶ Ἐρεχθέως καὶ Ἐριχθονίου καὶ Ἐρυσίχθονος
110b1   τῶν τε ἄλλων τὰ πλεῖστα ὅσαπερ καὶ Θησέως τῶν ἄνω
περὶ τῶν ὀνομάτων ἑκάστων ἀπομνημονεύεται, τούτων ἐκείνους τὰ πολλὰ ἐπονομάζοντας τοὺς ἱερέας Σόλων ἔφη τὸν
τότε διηγεῖσθαι πόλεμον, καὶ τὰ τῶν γυναικῶν κατὰ τὰ
5 αὐτά. καὶ δὴ καὶ τὸ τῆς θεοῦ σχῆμα καὶ ἄγαλμα, ὡς κοινὰ
τότ᾽ ἦν τὰ ἐπιτηδεύματα ταῖς τε γυναιξὶ καὶ τοῖς ἀνδράσι
τὰ περὶ τὸν πόλεμον, οὕτω κατ᾽ ἐκεῖνον τὸν νόμον ὡπλι-
σμένην τὴν θεὸν ἀνάθημα εἶναι τοῖς τότε, ἔνδειγμα ὅτι πάνθ᾽
110c1   ὅσα σύννομα ζῷα θήλεα καὶ ὅσα ἄρρενα, τὴν προσήκουσαν
ἀρετὴν ἑκάστῳ γένει πᾶν κοινῇ δυνατὸν ἐπιτηδεύειν πέφυκεν.

110a7–b5   Critias uses Solon's story as evidence of his theory about the
gradual development of historical enquiry: in recently civilized
Athens (109d–e, also *Ti.* 22b–23c), people only remember the

names of their founding members, whereas in long-civilized Egypt (see *Ti.* 22d–e), the priests have records of the ancestors' achievements (especially the great war against Atlantis) as well as their names. 'I say this using as evidence the fact that [τεκμαιρόμενος ὅτι] [the names of] Cecrops, Erechtheus, Erichthonius, Erysichthon, and most of the things which are recorded [τὰ πλεῖστα ὅσαπερ ... ἀπομνημονεύεται] about each of the names [περὶ τῶν ἑκάστων] of the others too prior to Theseus [τῶν τε ἄλλων ... καὶ Θησέως τῶν ἄνω] – the majority of these names [τούτων ... τὰ πολλά], according to Solon, were given by those [ἐκείνους] priests, in their narrative of the war of that time, and the names of the women in the same way'. The sentence is awkwardly worded: in a7–8 ὀνόματα seems to be understood (from a6), but the idea of 'names' is then cumbersomely spelt out in b1–2; also τὰ πολλά in b3 repeats the idea of τὰ πλεῖστα in b1. (I am grateful to my former colleague, Rosemary Wright, for her help in elucidating this and other complex sentences.)

Plato's choice of pre-Theseus heroes seems designed to give prominence to the idea of autochthony (being born from the land) and of 'land' itself, a dominant theme in Plato's picture of primaeval Athens (see [30]). Erechtheus and Erichthonius are traditionally regarded as autochthonous, while the names Erichthonius and Erysichthon include the word χθών ('land'). See also Rivaud 1925, 234–7; Brisson 1970, 409–10.

110b4–c2   Critias supports his claim about the women of primaeval Athens (b4–5), and the underlying theory of female equality (see *Ti.* 18c1–4; *Republic* 453–457), by referring to the traditional representation of Athena as armed. 'Consider too the appearance of the statue [lit. 'appearance and statue'] of the goddess. Since at that time military practices were common to women and men, in line with that custom the people of that time set up the image of the goddess in armour [lit. 'the goddess in armour was a divine image for men at that time', but what seems to be meant is the setting-up or establishment of this type of image]'. 'This is evidence that, in the case of

animals which are gregarious, male and female alike [lit. 'all
female creatures which are gregarious and all male'], the whole
kind [understand γένος] is naturally capable, as a group [κοινῇ],
of practising the excellence appropriate to each kind'. τὸ …
σχῆμα (b5) and πανθ᾽ ὅσα (b8–c1) seem to be accusatives of
respect; the εἶναι clause beginning in b7 is ind. statement, ἔφη
being understood from b3.

Critias proceeds to give a more detailed account of the physical environment
and political institutions of primaeval Athens (110c–112e). The methodology
applied here and in 110a–b, using ancient names and physical observations
as indicators of the past, seems to imply a serious interest in reconstructing
the distant past, which anticipates *Laws* 676–679. A second prominent theme,
here and in the case of Atlantis, is that of locating human life in its physical
context, both natural and constructed. Both these themes indicate the implicit
influence of Timaeus's account of the nature and origin of the universe and of
human beings (seen as an integral part of the universe). A third theme is the
emphasis on key features of the social and political structure and character
of primaeval Athens, namely unity, stability and (stable) virtue, all of which
form a contrast with features later emphasized in the description of Atlantis.
See [26–29].

      Ὤικει δὲ δὴ τότ᾽ ἐν τῇδε τῇ χώρᾳ τὰ μὲν ἄλλα ἔθνη
      τῶν πολιτῶν περὶ τὰς δημιουργίας ὄντα καὶ τὴν ἐκ τῆς γῆς
5   τροφήν, τὸ δὲ μάχιμον ὑπ᾽ ἀνδρῶν θείων κατ᾽ ἀρχὰς ἀφο-
      ρισθὲν ᾤκει χωρίς, πάντα εἰς τροφὴν καὶ παίδευσιν τὰ
      προσήκοντα ἔχον, ἴδιον μὲν αὐτῶν οὐδεὶς οὐδὲν κεκτημένος,
110d1 ἅπαντα δὲ πάντων κοινὰ νομίζοντες αὐτῶν, πέρα δὲ ἱκανῆς
      τροφῆς οὐδὲν ἀξιοῦντες παρὰ τῶν ἄλλων δέχεσθαι πολιτῶν,
      καὶ πάντα δὴ τὰ χθὲς λεχθέντα ἐπιτηδεύματα ἐπιτηδεύοντες,
      ὅσα περὶ τῶν ὑποτεθέντων ἐρρήθη φυλάκων.

110c5–d4   See also *Ti.* 17c5–18a10, 24a–b3.

καὶ δὴ καὶ
5 τὸ περὶ τῆς χώρας ἡμῶν πιθανὸν καὶ ἀληθὲς ἐλέγετο, πρῶτον
μὲν τοὺς ὅρους αὐτὴν ἐν τῷ τότ' ἔχειν ἀφωρισμένους πρὸς
τὸν Ἰσθμὸν καὶ τὸ κατὰ τὴν ἄλλην ἤπειρον μέχρι τοῦ
110e1 Κιθαιρῶνος καὶ Πάρνηθος τῶν ἄκρων, καταβαίνειν δὲ τοὺς
ὅρους ἐν δεξιᾷ τὴν Ὠρωπίαν ἔχοντας, ἐν ἀριστερᾷ δὲ πρὸς
θαλάττης ἀφορίζοντας τὸν Ἀσωπόν·

110d4–e3 Primaeval Athens has more territory than Attica (the region
of Athens) in Plato's time, and more soil on that territory,
and in both respects it is more of a land power than fifth- or
fourth-century Athens (see [30]). καὶ δὴ καὶ κ.τ.λ., 'Moreover,
the long-standing claims [lit. 'what used to be said'] about our
territory are reliable and true'. Such claims were naturally made
about the Oropia (on the border between Attica and Boeotia,
and claimed by both states); but Megara was also believed to
have been part of Attica in ancient times, so that Attica reached
the Isthmus of Corinth.

ἀρετῇ δὲ πᾶσαν γῆν
ὑπὸ τῆς ἐνθάδε ὑπερβάλλεσθαι, διὸ καὶ δυνατὴν εἶναι τότε
5 τρέφειν τὴν χώραν στρατόπεδον πολὺ τῶν περὶ γῆν ἀργὸν
ἔργων. μέγα δὲ τεκμήριον ἀρετῆς· τὸ γὰρ νῦν αὐτῆς λείψανον ἐνάμιλλόν ἐστι πρὸς ἡντινοῦν τῷ πάμφορον εὔκαρπόν
111a1 τε εἶναι καὶ τοῖς ζῴοις πᾶσιν εὔβοτον. τότε δὲ πρὸς τῷ
κάλλει καὶ παμπλήθη ταῦτα ἔφερεν. πῶς οὖν δὴ τοῦτο
πιστόν, καὶ κατὰ τί λείψανον τῆς τότε γῆς ὀρθῶς ἂν λέγοιτο; πᾶσα ἀπὸ τῆς ἄλλης ἠπείρου μακρὰ προτείνουσα εἰς
5 τὸ πέλαγος οἷον ἄκρα κεῖται· τὸ δὴ τῆς θαλάττης ἀγγεῖον
περὶ αὐτὴν τυγχάνει πᾶν ἀγχιβαθὲς ὄν.

110e3 ἀρετῇ κ.τ.λ., 'every [other] country was inferior to this one in
fertility'.
111a1–c8 This passage provides evidence of an interest in prehistory
in Plato's late works. It also enables Plato to present Critias

as treating the subject of prehistory in a more credible and investigative way than in his earlier summary of the Atlantis story (*Ti.* 22b–23c; see also [18], esp. n. 34, [26], esp. n. 66. The reconstruction of past soil erosion (and of a reduced water supply, 111d, 112d) is consistent with the theory of periodic natural catastrophes (see *Criti.* 109d–110a; *Ti.* 22c–23b; *Laws* 677–678). The concern with providing empirical proof for the inferences drawn (note τεκμήριον, πιστόν, φανερὰ τεκμήρια, σημεῖα in 110e6, 111a3, 111c3–4, 111d7) is another sign of Plato's interest in the techniques of prehistorical enquiry.

πολλῶν οὖν

γεγονότων καὶ μεγάλων κατακλυσμῶν ἐν τοῖς ἐνακισχιλίοις
ἔτεσι – τοσαῦτα γὰρ πρὸς τὸν νῦν ἀπ' ἐκείνου τοῦ χρόνου

111b1   γέγονεν ἔτη – τὸ τῆς γῆς ἐν τούτοις τοῖς χρόνοις καὶ πάθεσιν
ἐκ τῶν ὑψηλῶν ἀπορρέον οὔτε χῶμα, ὡς ἐν ἄλλοις τόποις,
προχοῖ λόγου ἄξιον ἀεί τε κύκλῳ περιρρέον εἰς βάθος
ἀφανίζεται· λέλειπται δή, καθάπερ ἐν ταῖς σμικραῖς νή-

5   σοις, πρὸς τὰ τότε τὰ νῦν οἷον νοσήσαντος σώματος ὀστᾶ,
περιερρυηκυίας τῆς γῆς ὅση πίειρα καὶ μαλακή, τοῦ λεπτοῦ
σώματος τῆς χώρας μόνου λειφθέντος.

111b1–3   τὸ τῆς γῆς … ἀπορρέον (lit. 'the portion of land flowing down'); translate as 'the topsoil washed down'. ἀεί τε κύκλῳ περιρρέον, 'rolling continually over and over' (i.e. rolling continually down the slope into the deep sea).

111b4   καθάπερ κ.τ.λ., like the many rocky small islands (in the Cyclades, for instance) which are virtually denuded of soil and vegetation.

τότε δὲ ἀκέραιος

111c1   οὖσα τά τε ὄρη γηλόφους ὑψηλοὺς εἶχε, καὶ τὰ φελλέως
νῦν ὀνομασθέντα πεδία πλήρη γῆς πιείρας ἐκέκτητο, καὶ
πολλὴν ἐν τοῖς ὄρεσιν ὕλην εἶχεν, ἧς καὶ νῦν ἔτι φανερὰ

τεκμήρια· τῶν γὰρ ὀρῶν ἔστιν ἃ νῦν μὲν ἔχει μελίτταις
5   μόναις τροφήν, χρόνος δ' οὐ πάμπολυς ὅτε δένδρων † αὐτόθεν εἰς οἰκοδομήσεις τὰς μεγίστας ἐρεψίμων τμηθέντων
στεγάσματ' ἐστὶν ἔτι σᾶ.

111b7–c2   Understand γῆ (with ἀκέραιος οὖσα) as subject of the verbs:
'it had as mountains [or, instead of mountains] lofty mounds,
and what is now called the plains of Phelleus [a stony region
of Attica] were full of rich soil'. I read Phelleus with a capital
letter, unlike Burnet 1902: on the term, see Nesselrath 2006,
196–202.

111c4   ἔστιν ἃ = ἔνια: LSJ, εἰμί IV.

111c5   ὅτε is used here where we might expect ἐξ'οὗ ('it is not long
since'). After δένδρων, the correct textual reading is unclear,
and some words may have dropped out. But we can translate,
'trees were cut down from those parts as roof timbers
[ἐρεψίμων] for the biggest buildings, and the roofs still survive'.
On this passage, see also Nesselrath 2006, 202–04.

πολλὰ δ' ἦν ἄλλ' ἥμερα ὑψηλὰ
δένδρα, νομὴν δὲ βοσκήμασιν ἀμήχανον ἔφερεν. καὶ δὴ καὶ
111d1   τὸ κατ' ἐνιαυτὸν ὕδωρ ἐκαρποῦτ' ἐκ Διός, οὐχ ὡς νῦν
ἀπολλῦσα ῥέον ἀπὸ ψιλῆς τῆς γῆς εἰς θάλατταν, ἀλλὰ
πολλὴν ἔχουσα καὶ εἰς αὐτὴν καταδεχομένη, τῇ κεραμίδι
στεγούσῃ γῇ διαταμιευομένη, τὸ καταποθὲν ἐκ τῶν ὑψηλῶν
5   ὕδωρ εἰς τὰ κοῖλα ἀφιεῖσα κατὰ πάντας τοὺς τόπους παρείχετο ἄφθονα κρηνῶν καὶ ποταμῶν νάματα, ὧν καὶ νῦν ἔτι ἐπὶ
ταῖς πηγαῖς πρότερον οὔσαις ἱερὰ λελειμμένα ἐστὶν σημεῖα
ὅτι περὶ αὐτῆς ἀληθῆ λέγεται τὰ νῦν.

111d1   ἐκαρποῦτ', 'the land took the benefit of, it reaped the fruit of':
supply γῆ as subject.

111e1 Τὰ μὲν οὖν τῆς ἄλλης χώρας φύσει τε οὕτως εἶχε,
καὶ διεκεκόσμητο ὡς εἰκὸς ὑπὸ γεωργῶν μὲν ἀληθινῶν καὶ
πραττόντων αὐτὸ τοῦτο, φιλοκάλων δὲ καὶ εὐφυῶν, γῆν δὲ
ἀρίστην καὶ ὕδωρ ἀφθονώτατον ἐχόντων καὶ ὑπὲρ τῆς γῆς
ὥρας μετριώτατα κεκραμένας·

111e3 The farmers are naturally suited to their job (εὐφυῶν, see also
110c) but also motivated by a desire to do a good job, to grow
fine crops (φιλοκάλων). We may have a hint here of Plato's ideal
in the *Republic* of a city united by common aspiration to an
ideal standard of goodness or beauty (e.g. *Republic* 401b–d).

111e4 ἀφθονώτατον, see also ἄφθονα in d6, ἄφθονον in 112d2. A
profusion of water, as well as of crops, is common in idealized
pictures of the past (e.g. Phaeacia in Homer, *Odyssey* 7.114–131);
for ἄφθονον as a key term in such pictures, see Hesiod, *Works
and Days* 117–18.

111e5 ὥρας κ.τ.λ., the idea that Athens in particular, and Greece in
general, had a 'climate that was most moderately blended [or
harmonized]' was commonplace (see Euripides, *Medea* 825–43;
Aristotle, *Politics* 7.7, 1327b29–32); but it adds to the 'ideal' quality
of primaeval Attica (see the note on 111e4 and *Ti.* 24c6–7).

5 τὸ δ' ἄστυ κατῳκισμένον ὧδ'
ἦν ἐν τῷ τότε χρόνῳ. πρῶτον μὲν τὸ τῆς ἀκροπόλεως εἶχε
112a1 τότε οὐχ ὡς τὰ νῦν ἔχει. νῦν μὲν γὰρ μία γενομένη νὺξ
ὑγρὰ διαφερόντως γῆς αὐτὴν ψιλὴν περιτήξασα πεποίηκε,
σεισμῶν ἅμα καὶ πρὸ τῆς ἐπὶ Δευκαλίωνος φθορᾶς τρίτου
πρότερον ὕδατος ἐξαισίου γενομένου· τὸ δὲ πρὶν ἐν ἑτέρῳ
5 χρόνῳ μέγεθος μὲν ἦν πρὸς τὸν Ἠριδανὸν καὶ τὸν Ἰλισὸν
ἀποβεβηκυῖα καὶ περιειληφυῖα ἐντὸς τὴν Πύκνα καὶ τὸν
Λυκαβηττὸν ὅρον ἐκ τοῦ καταντικρὺ τῆς Πυκνὸς ἔχουσα,
γεώδης δ' ἦν πᾶσα καὶ πλὴν ὀλίγου ἐπίπεδος ἄνωθεν.

112a1–4 See *Ti.* 25c6–d3, where this natural disaster is said to have ended
the war between Athens and Atlantis. The flood of Deucalion

147

is presented at *Ti.* 23b5–6 (referring back to 22a7), as being the only one the Greek people are aware of.

112a6–7 'had Mount Lycabettus at its border on the side opposite the Pnyx'. Critias expands the Acropolis of historical times to take up much of the area of the city of Athens, no doubt to provide room to accommodate his 20,000 guardians (112d7–8). πλὴν ὀλίγον, 'almost entirely'.

112b1 ᾠκεῖτο δὲ τὰ μὲν ἔξωθεν, ὑπ' αὐτὰ τὰ πλάγια αὐτῆς, ὑπὸ τῶν δημιουργῶν καὶ τῶν γεωργῶν ὅσοι πλησίον ἐγεώργουν· τὰ δ' ἐπάνω τὸ μάχιμον αὐτὸ καθ' αὑτὸ μόνον γένος περὶ τὸ τῆς Ἀθηνᾶς Ἡφαίστου τε ἱερὸν κατῳκήκειν, οἷον μιᾶς οἰκίας κῆπον ἑνὶ περιβόλῳ προσπεριβεβλημένοι.

112b3–5 'But the military class alone, by itself [αὐτὸ καθ'αὑτὸ], had occupied the upper parts [τὰ δ'ἐπάνω] around the sanctuary of Athena and Hephaestus, which they had also surrounded [προσπεριβεβλημένοι: understand the members of the fighting class as plural subject] as though it were the garden of a single house, with a single enclosing wall'. Critias emphasizes the separateness and unity of the guardian class in every feature of their life.

5   τὰ γὰρ
πρόσβορρα αὐτῆς ᾤκουν οἰκίας κοινὰς καὶ συσσίτια χειμερινὰ κατασκευασάμενοι, καὶ πάντα ὅσα πρέπον τ' ἦν τῇ κοινῇ
112c1 πολιτείᾳ δι' οἰκοδομήσεων ὑπάρχειν αὐτῶν καὶ τῶν ἱερῶν, ἄνευ χρυσοῦ καὶ ἀργύρου – τούτοις γὰρ οὐδὲν οὐδαμόσε προσεχρῶντο, ἀλλὰ τὸ μέσον ὑπερηφανίας καὶ ἀνελευθερίας μεταδιώκοντες κοσμίας ᾠκοδομοῦντο οἰκήσεις, ἐν αἷς αὐτοί τε
5 καὶ ἐκγόνων ἔκγονοι καταγηρῶντες ἄλλοις ὁμοίοις τὰς αὐτὰς ἀεὶ παρεδίδοσαν – τὰ δὲ πρὸς νότου, κήπους καὶ γυμνάσια συσσίτιά τε ἀνέντες οἷα θέρους, κατεχρῶντο ἐπὶ ταῦτα αὐτοῖς.

112b7–c6   καὶ πάντα κ.τ.λ., 'everything which was needed [lit. 'which was appropriate to be available to them', ὑπάρχειν] for their common way of life [πολιτείᾳ] in the form of [lit. 'by means of'] housing for themselves and their priests.' The moderation and stability of the guardians' way of life and the absence of precious metals (see also *Ti.* 18b; *Republic* 416–417b) form a pointed contrast to the lavish lifestyle of the ruling class in Atlantis (115c–117c). As becomes clear, this lavish lifestyle carries with it the threat of internal conflict and political instability (121a–b7); see also [29].

112c6–7   'As for the southern side, when they abandoned their gardens, gymnasia and dining halls, as is natural in summer [οἷα θέρους], they used this area for these purposes [ἐπὶ ταῦτα]'. That is, they spent the summer wholly in the open air, in preparation, presumably, for military campaigns, which were normally undertaken in summer in ancient Greece.

κρήνη δ' ἦν μία κατὰ τὸν τῆς νῦν ἀκροπόλεως τόπον, ἧς
112d1   ἀποσβεσθείσης ὑπὸ τῶν σεισμῶν τὰ νῦν νάματα μικρὰ κύκλῳ
καταλέλειπται, τοῖς δὲ τότε πᾶσιν παρεῖχεν ἄφθονον ῥεῦμα,
εὐκρὰς οὖσα πρὸς χειμῶνά τε καὶ θέρος. τούτῳ δὴ κατῴκουν
τῷ σχήματι, τῶν μὲν αὐτῶν πολιτῶν φύλακες, τῶν δὲ ἄλλων
5   Ἑλλήνων ἡγεμόνες ἑκόντων, πλῆθος δὲ διαφυλάττοντες ὅτι
μάλιστα ταὐτὸν αὑτῶν εἶναι πρὸς τὸν ἀεὶ χρόνον ἀνδρῶν
καὶ γυναικῶν, τὸ δυνατὸν πολεμεῖν ἤδη καὶ τὸ ἔτι, περὶ δύο
112e1   μάλιστα ὄντας μυριάδας.

112d4–5   τῶν δὲ ἄλλων κ.τ.λ., see *Ti.* 25c. Note ἑκόντων; Plato's Athens is not a 'tyrant' city, which dominated its 'allies', as it had become by the mid-fifth century and the time of the Peloponnesian War (e.g. Thucydides 3.37, also 6.76.4, Hermocrates speaking). For Atlantis as a would-be tyrant city, see *Ti.* 25a5–b2, and (implicitly) *Criti.* 121b6–7.

112d7   τὸ δυνατὸν κ.τ.λ., 'who were already or still of military age' (lit. 'capable of fighting'), that is, those neither within the age limits appropriate for active combat.

Οὗτοι μὲν οὖν δὴ τοιοῦτοί τε ὄντες αὐτοὶ καί τινα τοιοῦτον
ἀεὶ τρόπον τήν τε αὐτῶν καὶ τὴν Ἑλλάδα δίκῃ διοικοῦντες,
ἐπὶ πᾶσαν Εὐρώπην καὶ Ἀσίαν κατά τε σωμάτων κάλλη
5   καὶ κατὰ τὴν τῶν ψυχῶν παντοίαν ἀρετὴν ἐλλόγιμοί τε
ἦσαν καὶ ὀνομαστότατοι πάντων τῶν τότε· τὰ δὲ δὴ τῶν
ἀντιπολεμησάντων αὐτοῖς οἷα ἦν ὥς τε ἀπ' ἀρχῆς ἐγένετο,
μνήμης ἂν μὴ στερηθῶμεν ὧν ἔτι παῖδες ὄντες ἠκούσαμεν,
εἰς τὸ μέσον αὐτὰ νῦν ἀποδώσομεν ὑμῖν τοῖς φίλοις εἶναι
10   κοινά.

112e3   δίκῃ διοικοῦντες, see also the way the world was apportioned
between the gods (δίκης κλήροις, 109b5), and contrast the
disruptive imperialism of Atlantis (ὕβρει πορευομένην, *Ti.*
24e2–3).

112e6–10 'As for the condition of their opponents, what sort it was and
how it became so from the beginning [οἷα ἦν ὥς τε κ.τ.λ.],
unless I have lost the memory of what I heard when I was still
a child [ἂν = ἐὰν, distinct fut. condition, AM 180, RG 402], I
shall now publicly [εἰς τὸ μέσον] hand over these things to be
common property with you, my friends'. εἶναι is either infin.
of purpose (G 1532) or governed by ἀποδώσομεν in the sense of
'allow' (LSJ, ἀποδίδωμι 4), e.g. 'I shall allow these things to be
yours'. The phrase κοινὰ τὰ τῶν φίλων ('friends have all things
in common') is proverbial in Greek.

113a1   Τὸ δ' ἔτι βραχὺ πρὸ τοῦ λόγου δεῖ δηλῶσαι, μὴ πολλάκις
ἀκούοντες Ἑλληνικὰ βαρβάρων ἀνδρῶν ὀνόματα θαυμάζητε·
τὸ γὰρ αἴτιον αὐτῶν πεύσεσθε. Σόλων, ἅτ' ἐπινοῶν εἰς τὴν
αὐτοῦ ποίησιν καταχρήσασθαι τῷ λόγῳ, διαπυνθανόμενος τὴν
5   τῶν ὀνομάτων δύναμιν, ηὗρεν τούς τε Αἰγυπτίους τοὺς πρώ-
τους ἐκείνους αὐτὰ γραψαμένους εἰς τὴν αὐτῶν φωνὴν
μετενηνοχότας, αὐτός τε αὖ πάλιν ἑκάστου τὴν διάνοιαν ὀνό-
113b1   ματος ἀναλαμβάνων εἰς τὴν ἡμετέραν ἄγων φωνὴν ἀπεγρά-
φετο· καὶ ταῦτά γε δὴ τὰ γράμματα παρὰ τῷ πάππῳ τ' ἦν
καὶ ἔτ' ἐστὶν παρ' ἐμοὶ νῦν, διαμεμελέτηταί τε ὑπ' ἐμοῦ παιδὸς

5
ὄντος. ἂν οὖν ἀκούητε τοιαῦτα οἷα καὶ τῇδε ὀνόματα, μηδὲν
ὑμῖν ἔστω θαῦμα· τὸ γὰρ αἴτιον αὐτῶν ἔχετε. μακροῦ δὲ δὴ
λόγου τοιάδε τις ἦν ἀρχὴ τότε.

113b2
The sudden appearance of a manuscript here is not entirely
consistent with the earlier stress on the oral memorization of the
story (*Ti.* 26b–c). Admittedly, the manuscript may be introduced
simply to explain how Critias can present, accurately and in Greek
form, so many names from non-Greek prehistory. However, the
minor inconsistency may indicate that Critias's earlier claim to
present a historically accurate account is not one we are meant to
take very seriously (see also the note on 108e2).

Critias 113b–119b:
Critias's description of the physical features of Atlantis

After the opening section on the divine origin of the ruling family of Atlantis
(113c–114c), there is an extended and graphic description of the physical
features of Atlantis, both natural and constructed. As in primaeval Athens,
and even more so, there is stress on the profusion of natural resources, both
vegetable and mineral (114e–115c, 117a–b, 118b, e). However, there is yet more
emphasis on the remarkable physical layout created by Poseidon and its
transformation by the Atlantean kings, and on the scale, elaborateness and
splendour of their engineering and architecture (115c–117a, 117c–e, 118c–e). By
contrast with primaeval Athens, characterized by unity, stability and relative
simplicity, Atlantis's physical form is marked by organized complexity,
transformation over time, and great lavishness ([29]).

Καθάπερ ἐν τοῖς πρόσθεν ἐλέχθη περὶ τῆς τῶν θεῶν
λήξεως, ὅτι κατενείμαντο γῆν πᾶσαν ἔνθα μὲν μείζους
113c1
λήξεις, ἔνθα δὲ καὶ ἐλάττους, ἱερὰ θυσίας τε αὐτοῖς κατα-
σκευάζοντες, οὕτω δὴ καὶ τὴν νῆσον Ποσειδῶν τὴν Ἀτλαντίδα
λαχὼν ἐκγόνους αὐτοῦ κατῴκισεν ἐκ θνητῆς γυναικὸς γεν-
νήσας ἔν τινι τόπῳ τοιῷδε τῆς νήσου. πρὸς θαλάττης μέν,

5 κατὰ δὲ μέσον πάσης πεδίον ἦν, ὃ δὴ πάντων πεδίων
κάλλιστον ἀρετῇ τε ἱκανὸν γενέσθαι λέγεται, πρὸς τῷ πεδίῳ
δὲ αὖ κατὰ μέσον σταδίους ὡς πεντήκοντα ἀφεστὸς ἦν ὄρος
βραχὺ πάντῃ.

113b5-6   As in the case of Athens (109c), Critias begins with the divine
foundation of Atlantis.

113c   The kings of Atlantis are actually descended from a god,
Poseidon, and are not just the recipients of a divinely guided
character and social framework as the founders of Athens are
(109c, 110b5-c2). However, like the original Athenians (see the
note on 110a7-b5, second paragraph), they are autochthonous
(born from the land), in that Poseidon's human sexual partner
had an earth-born father (113c8-d2; note also the name of her
son, Autochthon, 114c1). This divine ancestry helps to account
for their fabulous luxury and technological power (on the latter,
see 118c and compare 113d5-e1); but when the divine element in
their make-up is weakened through successive generations, this
god-like wealth leads to (human) moral problems (121a-b).

113c4-8   'On the coast [lit. 'towards the sea'], in the middle of the whole
island [understand νήσου]', that is, at the mid-point of the
whole coast, not the exact centre of this huge island (see Fig. 4),
'was a plain, which is said to have been the most beautiful of all
plains and adequate too in its fertility. And, in turn, near the
plain and in the middle of it [i.e. at the mid-point of the coastal
strip on the east–west axis], about [LSJ, ὡς, E] fifty stades
[inland] was a mountain, not very high at any point'.

οὕτω δ' ἦν ἔνοικος τῶν ἐκεῖ κατὰ ἀρχὰς ἐκ
113d1   γῆς ἀνδρῶν γεγονότων Εὐήνωρ μὲν ὄνομα, γυναικὶ δὲ συνοικῶν
Λευκίππῃ· Κλειτὼ δὲ μονογενῆ θυγατέρα ἐγεννησάσθην.
ἤδη δ' εἰς ἀνδρὸς ὥραν ἡκούσης τῆς κόρης ἥ τε μήτηρ
τελευτᾷ καὶ ὁ πατήρ, αὐτῆς δὲ εἰς ἐπιθυμίαν Ποσειδῶν
5   ἐλθὼν συμμείγνυται, καὶ τὸν γήλοφον, ἐν ᾧ κατῴκιστο,
ποιῶν εὐερκῆ περιρρήγνυσιν κύκλῳ, θαλάττης γῆς τε ἐναλλὰξ

ἐλάττους μείζους τε περὶ ἀλλήλους ποιῶν τροχούς, δύο μὲν
γῆς, θαλάττης δὲ τρεῖς οἷον τορνεύων ἐκ μέσης τῆς νήσου,
113e1   πάντῃ ἴσον ἀφεστῶτας, ὥστε ἄβατον ἀνθρώποις εἶναι· πλοῖα
γὰρ καὶ τὸ πλεῖν οὔπω τότε ἦν.

113d1–2   Many of the names of the Atlantean royal family imply
magnificence or strength, such as Evenor ('good' or 'brave
man') and Cleito (compare κλειτός, 'famous' or 'splendid').
Leucippe evokes the Atlantean horses, and horses were
especially associated with Poseidon (see 116e1, 117c3–6).

113d6–8   'he fortified the mound, where she had been settled, by
enclosing it [lit. 'by breaking it off all round, from the
neighbouring area'] all around [lit. 'in a circle'], making rings
of sea and land alternately, of increasing size, one around the
other, two of land and three of sea, at all points equidistant
from each other, like a man using a turning lathe from the
centre of the island'. See Fig. 3. The phrase ἐκ μέσης νήσου is
ambiguous, suggesting either the mid-point of the coastal area
of the great plain (see c4–8), or the middle of the 'island' he
has created around the hill (see τήν τε ἐν μέσῳ νῆσον, e2–3).
However, on either view, the phrase may echo the description
of the work of the craftsman-god in Timaeus's creation
account, who made the world σφαιροειδές, ἐκ μέσου πάντῃ
πρὸς τελευτὰς ἴσον ἀπέχον, κυκλοτερὲς αὐτὸ ἐτορνεύσατο
(*Ti.* 33b4–5). For the suggestion that Critias's full version is in
various ways influenced by Timaeus's cosmological account,
see [25].

Despite this echo, it is not clear that Plato intends us to take
a favourable view of Poseidon's elaborate engineering (which his
descendants continue, 115c–116a, 118c–e). In primaeval Athens,
which is characterized by unity and stability, the agriculture
and city plan is adapted to the natural resources available
(111e–112d). By contrast, Poseidon and the Atlantean kings
superimpose on the natural landscape an architectural (and
political) superstructure of lavish variety and mathematical
complexity (see the notes on 118c2–3, 119a8–b6). This

construction eventually collapses (in the sense that its moral and political cohesion falls apart), unable to bear the 'weight' of the massive wealth and power they have acquired (121a1–b7).

αὐτὸς δὲ τήν τε ἐν μέσῳ
νῆσον οἷα δὴ θεὸς εὐμαρῶς διεκόσμησεν, ὕδατα μὲν διττὰ
ὑπὸ γῆς ἄνω πηγαῖα κομίσας, τὸ μὲν θερμόν, ψυχρὸν δὲ ἐκ
5   κρήνης ἀπορρέον ἕτερον, τροφὴν δὲ παντοίαν καὶ ἱκανὴν ἐκ
τῆς γῆς ἀναδιδούς.

113e2–6   There is some suggestion in this passage that Poseidon created an isolated and self-sufficient paradise (insulated from the sea, which is presented in Plato's *Laws* 705a–b as a source of corrupting influences), and that the Atlanteans were thus betraying Poseidon's intentions in connecting their 'ancient mother city' to the sea and trade routes (115c–e; see also [30] on the land-sea contrast in the story). In the same way, Poseidon places his son the Cyclops on an island that yields food and drink without need for cultivation, and without the use of ships that could enable him to take over a neighbouring island that is suitable for agricultural development (Homer, *Odyssey* 9.105–39). However, in general, the Atlantean kings' engineering works are presented as a continuation of those of their ancestor-god (see the note on 113d6–8). Also, despite *Odyssey* 9.125–29, the sea-god Poseidon is not naturally imagined as antagonistic to contact with the sea.

παίδων δὲ ἀρρένων πέντε γενέσεις διδύ-
μους γεννησάμενος ἐθρέψατο, καὶ τὴν νῆσον τὴν Ἀτλαντίδα
πᾶσαν δέκα μέρη κατανείμας τῶν μὲν πρεσβυτάτων τῷ προ-
114a1   τέρῳ γενομένῳ τήν τε μητρῴαν οἴκησιν καὶ τὴν κύκλῳ λῆξιν,
πλείστην καὶ ἀρίστην οὖσαν, ἀπένειμε, βασιλέα τε τῶν ἄλλων
κατέστησε, τοὺς δὲ ἄλλους ἄρχοντας, ἑκάστῳ δὲ ἀρχὴν πολλῶν ἀνθρώπων καὶ τόπον πολλῆς χώρας ἔδωκεν.

113e6–114a4 If Plato has any historical model for this tenfold division, it is
perhaps the Cleisthenic division of the Athenian population
into ten tribes in 508 (Herodotus 5.69); but the political
structure resembles, rather, the Persian empire, with a number
of separate rulers ('satraps'), each governing his own territory,
but under the supreme command of one man (on the allusions
to the Persian empire, see also the notes on 115c4–116c2,
116c9–117a3).

ὀνόματα
5   δὲ πᾶσιν ἔθετο, τῷ μὲν πρεσβυτάτῳ καὶ βασιλεῖ τοῦτο οὗ
δὴ καὶ πᾶσα ἡ νῆσος τό τε πέλαγος ἔσχεν ἐπωνυμίαν,
Ἀτλαντικὸν λεχθέν, ὅτι τοὔνομ᾽ ἦν τῷ πρώτῳ βασιλεύσαντι
114b1 τότε Ἄτλας· τῷ δὲ διδύμῳ μετ᾽ ἐκεῖνόν τε γενομένῳ, λῆξιν
δὲ ἄκρας τῆς νήσου πρὸς Ἡρακλείων στηλῶν εἰληχότι ἐπὶ
τὸ τῆς Γαδειρικῆς νῦν χώρας κατ᾽ ἐκεῖνον τὸν τόπον ὀνομαζο-
μένης, Ἑλληνιστὶ μὲν Εὔμηλον, τὸ δ᾽ ἐπιχώριον Γάδειρον,
ὅπερ τ᾽ ἦν ἐπίκλην ταύτῃ ὄνομ᾽ ἂ⟨ν⟩ παράσχοι.

114a4–b5   'He gave names to all of them, to the oldest, their king, that
from which the whole island and sea acquired its designation;
it was called Atlantic [Ἀτλαντικὸν agreeing with τό πέλαγος],
because the name of the first king at that time was Atlas; and
to his twin brother, born after him, who took as his share the
edge of the island on the side of the Pillars of Heracles, facing
the region now called Gadiran [i.e. of Gadira = Cádiz, in Spain]
[which is named] after that place [i.e. that part of Atlantis], he
gave the name [supply ὀνόματα … ἔθετο from a4–5] Eumelus
in Greek but Gadirus in the language of that country, the very
name which must have provided this designation [Gadira] also'.
ἐπὶ τὸ τῆς κ.τ.λ. (b2–3) is odd: it looks as though Plato intended
to say 'facing that part of the land [i.e. Europe] which is now
called Gadiran [Γαδειρικόν]' but allowed the adjective to be
attracted to the case of the noun χώρας instead of τὸ; I have
translated as if Plato had written ἐπὶ την … In the last clause,

I prefer the reading of ms. F (ὅπερ τ᾿ἄν ἐπίκλησιν ταύτην ὄνομα παράσχοι) as being more natural than that adopted in Burnet 1902. For a full discussion of the passage and possible readings, see Nesselrath 2006, 267–74. ἄν ... παράσχοι seems to be a potential aor. opt., referring (unusually) to past time; see Goodwin *SMT*, sections 442–43.

5   τοῖν δὲ
δευτέροιν γενομένοιν τὸν μὲν Ἀμφήρη, τὸν δὲ Εὐαίμονα
ἐκάλεσεν· τρίτοις δέ, Μνησέα μὲν τῷ προτέρῳ γενομένῳ,
114c1 τῷ δὲ μετὰ τοῦτον Αὐτόχθονα· τῶν δὲ τετάρτων Ἐλάσιππον
μὲν τὸν πρότερον, Μήστορα δὲ τὸν ὕστερον· ἐπὶ δὲ τοῖς
πέμπτοις τῷ μὲν ἔμπροσθεν Ἀζάης ὄνομα ἐτέθη, τῷ δ᾿ ὑστέρῳ
Διαπρέπης. οὗτοι δὴ πάντες αὐτοί τε καὶ ἔκγονοι τούτων
5 ἐπὶ γενεὰς πολλὰς ᾤκουν ἄρχοντες μὲν πολλῶν ἄλλων κατὰ
τὸ πέλαγος νήσων, ἔτι δέ, ὥσπερ καὶ πρότερον ἐρρήθη, μέχρι
τε Αἰγύπτου καὶ Τυρρηνίας τῶν ἐντὸς δεῦρο ἐπάρχοντες.

114b5–c4 Of these names, Ampheres (well-fitted on both sides, well-built) and Evaemon (of good blood) suggest inherited physical qualities (see also Autochthon, c1). Mneseus (the one who remembers) and Mestor (adviser) suggest mental qualities. Azäes (parched, dark-skinned?) and Diaprepes (magnificent) suggest qualities of appearance. Elasippus (driver of horses), like Eumelus (rich in sheep), suggests Atlantis's animal wealth (see also Brisson 1970, 422–24).

114c6–7 See *Ti.* 25a7–b2.

114d1 Ἄτλαντος δὴ πολὺ μὲν ἄλλο καὶ τίμιον γίγνεται γένος,
βασιλεὺς δὲ ὁ πρεσβύτατος ἀεὶ τῷ πρεσβυτάτῳ τῶν ἐκγόνων
παραδιδοὺς ἐπὶ γενεὰς πολλὰς τὴν βασιλείαν διέσῳζον,
πλοῦτον μὲν κεκτημένοι πλήθει τοσοῦτον, ὅσος οὔτε πω
5 πρόσθεν ἐν δυναστείαις τισὶν βασιλέων γέγονεν οὔτε ποτὲ
ὕστερον γενέσθαι ῥάδιος, κατεσκευασμένα δὲ πάντ᾿ ἦν αὐτοῖς

ὅσα ἐν πόλει καὶ ὅσα κατὰ τὴν ἄλλην χώραν ἦν ἔργον κατασκευάσασθαι.

114d1 μὲν ἄλλο, 'in general' (lit. 'in another respect' but suggesting 'in
other respects'), matching the δὲ clause in d2–3.

114d7–8 ἦν ἔργον κατασκευάσασθαι, 'they needed' (lit. 'there was a need
for them to provide for themselves').

    πολλὰ μὲν γὰρ διὰ τὴν ἀρχὴν αὐτοῖς προσῄειν
114e1 ἔξωθεν, πλεῖστα δὲ ἡ νῆσος αὐτὴ παρείχετο εἰς τὰς τοῦ βίου
κατασκευάς, πρῶτον μὲν ὅσα ὑπὸ μεταλλείας ὀρυττόμενα
στερεὰ καὶ ὅσα τηκτὰ γέγονε, καὶ τὸ νῦν ὀνομαζόμενον
μόνον – τότε δὲ πλέον ὀνόματος ἦν τὸ γένος ἐκ γῆς ὀρυττό-
5 μενον ὀρειχάλκου κατὰ τόπους πολλοὺς τῆς νήσου, πλὴν
χρυσοῦ τιμιώτατον ἐν τοῖς τότε ὄν – καὶ ὅσα ὕλη πρὸς τὰ
τεκτόνων διαπονήματα παρέχεται, πάντα φέρουσα ἄφθονα,
τά τε αὖ περὶ τὰ ζῷα ἱκανῶς ἥμερα καὶ ἄγρια τρέφουσα. καὶ
δὴ καὶ ἐλεφάντων ἦν ἐν αὐτῇ γένος πλεῖστον· νομὴ γὰρ τοῖς
10 τε ἄλλοις ζῴοις, ὅσα καθ' ἕλη καὶ λίμνας καὶ ποταμούς, ὅσα
115a1 τ' αὖ κατ' ὄρη καὶ ὅσα ἐν τοῖς πεδίοις νέμεται, σύμπασιν
παρῆν ἄδην, καὶ τούτῳ κατὰ ταὐτὰ τῷ ζῴῳ, μεγίστῳ πεφυκότι
καὶ πολυβορωτάτῳ.

114e3 στερεὰ, 'solid', probably stone or marble (see 116a6–b2);
τηκτὰ, 'fusible', e.g. bronze or tin (see 116b5–c2); 'orichalch'
('mountain-bronze') normally means brass or copper in Greek
but Plato hints at the existence of some more precious (and
more fabulous) metal than that. Contrast this wealth of mined
metals with the fact that the ruling group (the guardian class)
in primaeval Athens makes no use of gold and silver (112c2–3).

114e6–8 Plato's picture of Atlantis's natural fertility is idyllic, recalling
the garden of Phaeacia in Homer (*Odyssey* 7.113–32); compare
also Hesiod, *Works and Days* 117–18 with 114e8, πάντα φέρουσα
ἄφθονα. See also the note on 111e4, and 117a, 118b. But it may
be implied that the fertility is really *too* lavish: it is capable of

feeding many elephants, 'the most voracious' of beasts (115a3), and encourages eating for its own sake, for amusement or pleasure (115b2–4) instead of need. Compare the search for amusement through variety in the use of stones in buildings (116b), and contrast the simple moderation of daily life in Athens (112c). For the effect of natural environment on moral character, see 109c8–d1, also *Laws* 704b–705b.

114e9   γένος πλεῖστον, 'the species of elephants was numerous there'.

                     πρὸς δὲ τούτοις, ὅσα εὐώδη τρέφει που
γῆ τὰ νῦν, ῥιζῶν ἢ χλόης ἢ ξύλων ἢ χυλῶν στακτῶν εἴτε
5   ἀνθῶν ἢ καρπῶν, ἔφερέν τε ταῦτα καὶ ἔτρεφεν εὖ· ἔτι δὲ τὸν
ἥμερον καρπόν, τόν τε ξηρόν, ὃς ἡμῖν τῆς τροφῆς ἕνεκά ἐστιν,
καὶ ὅσοις χάριν τοῦ σίτου προσχρώμεθα – καλοῦμεν δὲ αὐτοῦ
115b1   τὰ μέρη σύμπαντα ὄσπρια – καὶ τὸν ὅσος ξύλινος, πώματα
καὶ βρώματα καὶ ἀλείμματα φέρων, παιδιᾶς τε ὃς ἕνεκα
ἡδονῆς τε γέγονε δυσθησαύριστος ἀκροδρύων καρπός, ὅσα τε
παραμύθια πλησμονῆς μεταδόρπια ἀγαπητὰ κάμνοντι τίθεμεν,
5   ἅπαντα ταῦτα ἡ τότε [ποτὲ] οὖσα ὑφ' ἡλίῳ νῆσος ἱερὰ καλά
τε καὶ θαυμαστὰ καὶ πλήθεσιν ἄπειρ' ἔφερεν.

115a4   χυλῶν στακτῶν, 'gums exuded by'.

115a6–7   τόν τε ξηρόν, 'both the dry type which we use as our basic source of nutrition [i.e. grain], and the things we use in addition [προσχρώμεθα] as foodstuff – we call them as a whole pulses'.

115b1–4   1) 'the fruit of trees [τὸν ὅσος ξύλινος κ.τ.λ.] which provides drinks, foods and oils, and 2) the fruit from treetops, which is hard to store and which is used for amusement and pleasure [παιδιᾶς τε ὃς κ.τ.λ.], and 3) what we offer as welcome dessert to someone who is suffering to soothe his fullness [ὅσα τε παραμύθια κ.τ.λ.]'. It is not clear if the person is suffering [κάμνοντι] from fatigue or from having eaten too much. The items that seem intended are, perhaps: 1) the olive, 2) the pomegranate and 3) the lemon. For the implied puritanism in this description, see the note on 114e6–8.

115b5   The ms. contains ποτὲ, but this seems to be a scribe's addition, suggested by τότε, and is usually excluded by editors, as it is here. However, it is retained by Nesselrath 2006, 306.

ταῦτα οὖν

λαμβάνοντες πάντα παρὰ τῆς γῆς κατεσκευάζοντο τά τε

115c1   ἱερὰ καὶ τὰς βασιλικὰς οἰκήσεις καὶ τοὺς λιμένας καὶ τὰ
νεώρια καὶ σύμπασαν τὴν ἄλλην χώραν, τοιᾷδ' ἐν τάξει
διακοσμοῦντες.
Τοὺς τῆς θαλάττης τροχούς, οἳ περὶ τὴν ἀρχαίαν ἦσαν

5   μητρόπολιν, πρῶτον μὲν ἐγεφύρωσαν, ὁδὸν ἔξω καὶ ἐπὶ τὰ
βασίλεια ποιούμενοι. τὰ δὲ βασίλεια ἐν ταύτῃ τῇ τοῦ θεοῦ
καὶ τῶν προγόνων κατοικήσει κατ' ἀρχὰς ἐποιήσαντο εὐθύς,
ἕτερος δὲ παρ' ἑτέρου δεχόμενος, κεκοσμημένα κοσμῶν,

115d1   ὑπερεβάλλετο εἰς δύναμιν ἀεὶ τὸν ἔμπροσθεν, ἕως εἰς ἔκπληξιν μεγέθεσιν κάλλεσίν τε ἔργων ἰδεῖν τὴν οἴκησιν
ἀπηργάσαντο.

115c4–116a1   See Fig. 3. This description is reminiscent of Herodotus's accounts of Ecbatana and Babylon (1.98, 1.179–81), as well as Xerxes's engineering feats (Herodotus 7.23–25., 7.33–37, see also 118c). Note also the εἶδος … βαρβαρικὸν of the temple of Poseidon (116d2). See also Friedländer 1956, 319–20; Pradeau 1997, 172–73. However, the description is also reminiscent of the fifth-century construction of walls and ports at Athens, and particularly of Hippodamus's new town plan and harbour complex at the Peiraeus (see also 117d5–e8 and Pradeau 1997, 272–76). The combination of the two allusions may be significant in its own right, since fifth-century Athens, once it had defeated Persia, was accused of becoming the new Persia, in imposing its hegemony on other Greek states (for this accusation, see Thucydides 6.76.4, Hermocrates speaking). See also [30].

115c8   κεκοσμημένα κ.τ.λ., 'improving what was already improved' (or 'decorating what was already decorated'), 'each produced

something superior to his predecessor, as far as he could'.
Again, contrast this competition in ostentation with the
stability and simplicity of primaeval Athens.

115d1-2   εἰς ἔκπληξιν … ἰδεῖν. This phrase seems modelled on the
common θαῦμα ἰδεῖν, 'a wonder to behold' (RG 394 (iii), AM
89); the εἰς denotes purpose (LSJ, εἰς, V 2): 'they made their
residence an object of [lit. 'something that aimed to produce']
astonishment to look at'.

          διώρυχα μὲν γὰρ ἐκ τῆς θαλάττης ἀρχό-
μενοι τρίπλεθρον τὸ πλάτος, ἑκατὸν δὲ ποδῶν βάθος, μῆκος
5   δὲ πεντήκοντα σταδίων, ἐπὶ τὸν ἐξωτάτω τροχὸν συνέτρησαν,
καὶ τὸν ἀνάπλουν ἐκ τῆς θαλάττης ταύτῃ πρὸς ἐκεῖνον ὡς εἰς
λιμένα ἐποιήσαντο, διελόντες στόμα ναυσὶν ταῖς μεγίσταις
ἱκανὸν εἰσπλεῖν.

115d6-7   'and in this way [ταύτῃ] they created access [ἀνάπλουν] to it
[the outermost ring] from the sea, as though to a harbour'.
In the translation, the πλέθρον has been converted to its
equivalent in feet (100), though the more commonly used stade
(στάδιον) (about 200 yards) has not been converted.

          καὶ δὴ καὶ τοὺς τῆς γῆς τροχούς, οἳ τοὺς
115e1   τῆς θαλάττης διεῖργον, κατὰ τὰς γεφύρας διεῖλον ὅσον μιᾷ
τριήρει διέκπλουν εἰς ἀλλήλους, καὶ κατεστέγασαν ἄνωθεν
ὥστε τὸν ὑπόπλουν κάτωθεν εἶναι· τὰ γὰρ τῶν τῆς γῆς
τροχῶν χείλη βάθος εἶχεν ἱκανὸν ὑπερέχον τῆς θαλάττης.
5   ἦν δὲ ὁ μὲν μέγιστος τῶν τροχῶν, εἰς ὃν ἡ θάλαττα
συνετέτρητο, τριστάδιος τὸ πλάτος, ὁ δ᾽ ἑξῆς τῆς γῆς ἴσος
ἐκείνῳ· τοῖν δὲ δευτέροιν ὁ μὲν ὑγρὸς δυοῖν σταδίοιν πλάτος,
ὁ δὲ ξηρὸς ἴσος αὖ πάλιν τῷ πρόσθεν ὑγρῷ· σταδίου δὲ ὁ
161a1   περὶ αὐτὴν τὴν ἐν μέσῳ νῆσον περιθέων. ἡ δὲ νῆσος, ἐν
ᾗ τὰ βασίλεια ἦν, πέντε σταδίων τὴν διάμετρον εἶχεν.

115d8–e3   'In addition, in the rings of land that separated the rings of
           water, at the bridges, they made gaps [διεῖλον] big enough to
           allow one trireme at a time to sail through from one ring of
           water to the next [εἰς ἀλλήλους], and roofed the gaps over above
           to make an underground naval passage [ὑπόπλουν].' Critias
           imagines the series of bridges and underpasses forming a main
           road from the canal (from the sea) to the central island (see
           also c4–6). As Fig. 3 shows, he has overlooked the fact that the
           bridge over the outer ring of water passes directly on to the
           canal and has no obvious means of support on the outer side.
           The bridge is only one hundred feet (one πλέθρον) (116a3–4); the
           canal from the sea is three hundred feet (three πλέθρα) (115d4).

           ταύτην δὴ κύκλῳ καὶ τοὺς τροχοὺς καὶ τὴν γέφυραν πλε-
           θριαίαν τὸ πλάτος οὖσαν ἔνθεν καὶ ἔνθεν λιθίνῳ περιε-
     5   βάλλοντο τείχει, πύργους καὶ πύλας ἐπὶ τῶν γεφυρῶν κατὰ
           τὰς τῆς θαλάττης διαβάσεις ἑκασταχόσε ἐπιστήσαντες· τὸν
           δὲ λίθον ἔτεμνον ὑπὸ τῆς νήσου κύκλῳ τῆς ἐν μέσῳ καὶ ὑπὸ
           τῶν τροχῶν ἔξωθεν καὶ ἐντός, τὸν μὲν λευκόν, τὸν δὲ μέλανα,
  116b1   τὸν δὲ ἐρυθρὸν ὄντα, τέμνοντες δὲ ἅμ᾽ ἠργάζοντο νεωσοίκους
           κοίλους διπλοῦς ἐντός, κατηρεφεῖς αὐτῇ τῇ πέτρᾳ.

116a3–6   Plato seems to imagine a defensive system on each island, facing
           outwards to repel external attack. The inner island (ταύτην) and
           the two rings of land are each surrounded (κύκλῳ) by a wall
           of stone; and the three walls are each decorated with different
           types of precious metal (b5–c2). In each island, the wall stops at
           either side of the bridges (ἔνθεν καὶ ἔνθεν); while on (or at) the
           bridges themselves (ἐπὶ τῶν γεφυρῶν), there are guardhouses
           and gates at each of the underpasses for the canal from the sea
           (κατὰ τὰς τῆς θαλάττης διαβάσεις), at each side (ἑκασταχόσε) of
           the start of the underpasses. The gates must actually be on the
           bridges, the guardhouses at each side (see Fig. 3).
116a6–b2   Stone for the wall, and for buildings, was quarried 'from
           beneath the central island, all around it [κύκλῳ] and from the

two rings of land, both outside and inside each ring ... and, as they quarried, they hollowed out interior [ἐντός] double dockyards, roofed over by the rock itself'. The dockyards may be double (διπλοῦς) 1) because they hold two triremes at one time, 2) because they consist of a dry and wet dock or 3) because they are placed on both sides of the two island rings, formed by the quarried sides of the rings. Their exact locations are not specified.

καὶ τῶν

οἰκοδομημάτων τὰ μὲν ἁπλᾶ, τὰ δὲ μειγνύντες τοὺς λίθους
ποικίλα ὕφαινον παιδιᾶς χάριν, ἡδονὴν αὐτοῖς σύμφυτον
5   ἀπονέμοντες· καὶ τοῦ μὲν περὶ τὸν ἐξωτάτω τροχὸν τείχους
χαλκῷ περιελάμβανον πάντα τὸν περίδρομον, οἷον ἀλοιφῇ
προσχρώμενοι, τοῦ δ' ἐντὸς καττιτέρῳ περιέτηκον, τὸν δὲ
116c1 περὶ αὐτὴν τὴν ἀκρόπολιν ὀρειχάλκῳ μαρμαρυγὰς ἔχοντι
πυρώδεις.

116b3-5   τὰ δὲ κ.τ.λ., 'they made others varied by combining [different types of] stones for the sake of amusement, giving the buildings [αὐτοῖς] an inherent attractiveness'. ἡδονὴν here signifies the quality which produces pleasure rather than the experience of pleasure. The pleasure is 'inherent' (σύμφυτον) because it consists in the attractiveness of the combination of the stones themselves, not in any added ornament (whereas the city walls are decorated with precious metals, b5–c2). For Plato's attitude to this variety and ornamentation, see the note on 114e6–8.

116b6-7   οἷον ἀλοιφῇ προσχρώμενοι, 'as though applying varnish', i.e., they 'smeared' a veneer of bronze over the wall.

Τὰ δὲ δὴ τῆς ἀκροπόλεως ἐντὸς βασίλεια κατεσκευασμένα
ὧδ' ἦν. ἐν μέσῳ μὲν ἱερὸν ἅγιον αὐτόθι τῆς τε Κλειτοῦς
5   καὶ τοῦ Ποσειδῶνος ἄβατον ἀφεῖτο, περιβόλῳ χρυσῷ περι-
βεβλημένον, τοῦτ' ἐν ᾧ κατ' ἀρχὰς ἐφίτυσαν καὶ ἐγέννησαν

τὸ τῶν δέκα βασιλειδῶν γένος· ἔνθα καὶ κατ' ἐνιαυτὸν ἐκ
πασῶν τῶν δέκα λήξεων ὡραῖα αὐτόσε ἀπετέλουν ἱερὰ
ἐκείνων ἑκάστῳ.

116c5   ἀφεῖτο, it had been 'released' from normal use, i.e. dedicated or
consecrated: LSJ, ἀφίημι, II 1e (pass. plpf.).

                   τοῦ δὲ Ποσειδῶνος αὐτοῦ νεὼς ἦν, σταδίου
116d1   μὲν μῆκος, εὖρος δὲ τρίπλεθρος, ὕψος δ' ἐπὶ τούτοις
σύμμετρον ἰδεῖν, εἶδος δέ τι βαρβαρικὸν ἔχοντος. πάντα
δὲ ἔξωθεν περιήλειψαν τὸν νεὼν ἀργύρῳ, πλὴν τῶν ἀκρω-
τηρίων, τὰ δὲ ἀκρωτήρια χρυσῷ· τὰ δ' ἐντός, τὴν μὲν ὀροφὴν
5   ἐλεφαντίνην ἰδεῖν πᾶσαν χρυσῷ καὶ ἀργύρῳ καὶ ὀρειχάλκῳ
πεποικιλμένην, τὰ δὲ ἄλλα πάντα τῶν τοίχων τε καὶ κιόνων
καὶ ἐδάφους ὀρειχάλκῳ περιέλαβον.

116c9-d2   The layout of the temple, with a great cult statue decorated
with precious metals, and with other statues inside and outside,
corresponds to the normal Greek pattern (and might remind
an Athenian reader of the Parthenon, in particular). But the
temple is 'barbaric' in the lavishness of its decoration (compare
the free use of gold in the temple of Babylon, Herodotus 1.183)
and in its scale. It is three times the size of the Parthenon; and,
among Greek temples, only that of Artemis at Ephesus was
as large, and that had been enriched by the contributions of
the fabulously wealthy king Croesus of Lydia (see Rivaud 1925,
248-49; Pradeau 1997, 274-76). For the fusion of Oriental and
Greek themes, see the note on 115c4-116c1.

116d2-7   σύμμετρον ἰδεῖν (like θαῦμα ἰδεῖν, see the note on 115d1-2),
'proportionate [i.e. 'in proportion'] in height to look at'. See also
d5, ἐλεφαντίνην ἰδεῖν; here ἰδεῖν is included because Plato is
describing the visible surface of the ceiling: 'they overlaid the
ceiling [supply περιήλειψαν from d3] [and made it] a complete
surface of ivory [lit. 'wholly ivory to look at'] decorated with
gold, etc.' τὰ δ' ἐντός (d4), acc. of respect, 'as for the interior'.

χρυσᾶ δὲ ἀγάλματα
ἐνέστησαν, τὸν μὲν θεὸν ἐφ᾽ ἅρματος ἑστῶτα ἓξ ὑποπτέρων
116e1 ἵππων ἡνίοχον, αὐτόν τε ὑπὸ μεγέθους τῇ κορυφῇ τῆς ὀροφῆς
ἐφαπτόμενον, Νηρῇδας δὲ ἐπὶ δελφίνων ἑκατὸν κύκλῳ –
τοσαύτας γὰρ ἐνόμιζον αὐτὰς οἱ τότε εἶναι – πολλὰ δ᾽ ἐντὸς
ἄλλα ἀγάλματα ἰδιωτῶν ἀναθήματα ἐνῆν. περὶ δὲ τὸν νεὼν
5 ἔξωθεν εἰκόνες ἁπάντων ἔστασαν ἐκ χρυσοῦ, τῶν γυναικῶν
καὶ αὐτῶν ὅσοι τῶν δέκα ἐγεγόνεσαν βασιλέων, καὶ πολλὰ
ἕτερα ἀναθήματα μεγάλα τῶν τε βασιλέων καὶ ἰδιωτῶν ἐξ
αὐτῆς τε τῆς πόλεως καὶ τῶν ἔξωθεν ὅσων ἐπῆρχον. βωμός
117a1 τε δὴ συνεπόμενος ἦν τὸ μέγεθος καὶ τὸ τῆς ἐργασίας ταύτῃ
τῇ κατασκευῇ, καὶ τὰ βασίλεια κατὰ τὰ αὐτὰ πρέποντα μὲν
τῷ τῆς ἀρχῆς μεγέθει, πρέποντα δὲ τῷ περὶ τὰ ἱερὰ κόσμῳ.

116e1–2 Pheidias's great cult statue of Zeus at Olympia also 'nearly touched the roof with his head' (Strabo 8.353). The sculptor Scopas, a contemporary of Plato, created a group including Poseidon and Nereids on dolphins (Pliny, *Natural History* 36.26). The normal number of Nereids was 50, but everything is bigger in Atlantis (see Rivaud 1925, 248).

ταῖς δὲ δὴ κρήναις, τῇ τοῦ ψυχροῦ καὶ τῇ τοῦ θερμοῦ νάματος,
5 πλῆθος μὲν ἄφθονον ἐχούσαις, ἡδονῇ δὲ καὶ ἀρετῇ τῶν ὑδάτων
πρὸς ἑκατέρου τὴν χρῆσιν θαυμαστοῦ πεφυκότος, ἐχρῶντο
περιστήσαντες οἰκοδομήσεις καὶ δένδρων φυτεύσεις πρε-
117b1 πούσας ὕδασι, δεξαμενάς τε αὖ τὰς μὲν ὑπαιθρίους, τὰς δὲ
χειμερινὰς τοῖς θερμοῖς λουτροῖς ὑποστέγους περιτιθέντες,
χωρὶς μὲν βασιλικάς, χωρὶς δὲ ἰδιωτικάς, ἔτι δὲ γυναιξὶν
ἄλλας καὶ ἑτέρας ἵπποις καὶ τοῖς ἄλλοις ὑποζυγίοις, τὸ
πρόσφορον τῆς κοσμήσεως ἑκάστοις ἀπονέμοντες.

117a–b The plumbing in Atlantis has been seen as reminiscent of Minoan Crete (see [46]); more obvious are the echoes of the royal gardens of Phaeacia (see the note on 114e6–8). Also, the walls and roof of the palace of Phaeacia are decorated with

precious metals (compare Homer, *Odyssey* 7.83–93 and *Criti.*
116b5–c2, c5–d7), and the Phaeacian royal family has Poseidon
as its ancestor (compare *Odyssey* 7.56–63 and *Criti.* 113d–114c).

117a5 ἡδονῇ κ.τ.λ., θαυμαστοῦ πεφυκότος agrees with νάματος;
each of the springs 'was wonderfully suited by nature, in the
flavour [ἡδονῇ] and quality of the waters, for the use to which
it was put [πρὸς ἑκατέρου τὴν χρῆσιν]', that is, principally, cold
drinking water and warm washing water (compare Homer, *Iliad*
22.147–56).

117b1–2 δεξαμενάς τε αὖ κ.τ.λ., 'and they also constructed around them
[the springs] pools, some open to the air [presumably drawing
on the cold spring, for summer use], and others roofed over for
winter use as [lit. 'for'] warm baths'.

117b4–5 τὸ πρόσφορον κ.τ.λ., 'they assigned [in each case] the type of
decoration appropriate to each group'.

5   τὸ δὲ
ἀπορρέον ἦγον ἐπὶ τὸ τοῦ Ποσειδῶνος ἄλσος, δένδρα παντο-
δαπὰ κάλλος ὕψος τε δαιμόνιον ὑπ' ἀρετῆς τῆς γῆς ἔχοντα,
καὶ ἐπὶ τοὺς ἔξω κύκλους δι' ὀχετῶν κατὰ τὰς γεφύρας
117c1 ἐπωχέτευον· οὗ δὴ πολλὰ μὲν ἱερὰ καὶ πολλῶν θεῶν, πολλοὶ
δὲ κῆποι καὶ πολλὰ γυμνάσια ἐκεχειρούργητο, τὰ μὲν ἀνδρῶν,
τὰ δὲ ἵππων χωρὶς ἐν ἑκατέρᾳ τῇ τῶν τροχῶν νήσῳ, τά τε
ἄλλα καὶ κατὰ μέσην τὴν μείζω τῶν νήσων ἐξῃρημένος
5 ἱππόδρομος ἦν αὐτοῖς, σταδίου τὸ πλάτος ἔχων, τὸ δὲ μῆκος
περὶ τὸν κύκλον ὅλον ἀφεῖτο εἰς ἅμιλλαν τοῖς ἵπποις.

117c1–2 Contrast the stress on the *many* temples, gods, gardens, etc.,
with the *one* temple, living quarters and garden of Athens's
ruling (guardian) class (112b) (see also [29]).

117c3–6 τὰ δὲ ἵππων χωρὶς κ.τ.λ., 'and areas for exercise [lit. 'gymnasia']
were built, separately for men and horses on each of the two
islands formed by the rings [see 113d], and in particular [lit. 'as
well as the others'] a racecourse was reserved [ἐξῃρημένος] in
the middle of the largest island. It was a stade in width; as for

its length, a space was left free [ἀφεῖτο, see the note on 116c5] around the whole circuit of the land for horse-racing'. Normally (e.g. at Olympia), a racecourse was a stade [in Latin, a *stadium*] in length; in Atlantis, where everything is bigger, it is a stade in width. See Fig. 3; for Poseidon's association with horses, see Brisson 1970, 420.

117d1

5

δορυφορικαὶ δὲ περὶ αὐτὸν ἔνθεν τε καὶ ἔνθεν οἰκήσεις ἦσαν τῷ πλήθει τῶν δορυφόρων· τοῖς δὲ πιστοτέροις ἐν τῷ μικρο-τέρῳ τροχῷ καὶ πρὸς τῆς ἀκροπόλεως μᾶλλον ὄντι διετέτακτο ἡ φρουρά, τοῖς δὲ πάντων διαφέρουσιν πρὸς πίστιν ἐντὸς τῆς ἀκροπόλεως περὶ τοὺς βασιλέας αὐτοὺς ἦσαν οἰκήσεις δεδομέναι. τὰ δὲ νεώρια τριήρων μεστὰ ἦν καὶ σκευῶν ὅσα τριήρεσιν προσήκει, πάντα δὲ ἐξηρτυμένα ἱκανῶς. καὶ τὰ μὲν δὴ περὶ τὴν τῶν βασιλέων οἴκησιν οὕτω κατεσκεύαστο·

117d2

καὶ πρὸς κ.τ.λ., 'more in the direction of' (LSJ, πρός, gen. 2), that is, 'nearer the citadel', which was on the central island. These arrangements show the character of the regime, a military joint monarchy: δορυφόροι (bodyguards) were particularly associated with kings and tyrants (see Rivaud 1925, 269, n. l).

117e1

5

διαβάντι δὲ τοὺς λιμένας ἔξω τρεῖς ὄντας ἀρξάμενον ἀπὸ τῆς θαλάττης ᾔειν ἐν κύκλῳ τεῖχος, πεντήκοντα σταδίους τοῦ μεγίστου τροχοῦ τε καὶ λιμένος ἀπέχον πανταχῇ, καὶ συνέκλειεν εἰς ταὐτὸν πρὸς τὸ τῆς διώρυχος στόμα τὸ πρὸς θαλάττης. τοῦτο δὴ πᾶν συνῳκεῖτο μὲν ὑπὸ πολλῶν καὶ πυκνῶν οἰκήσεων, ὁ δὲ ἀνάπλους καὶ ὁ μέγιστος λιμὴν ἔγεμεν πλοίων καὶ ἐμπόρων ἀφικνουμένων πάντοθεν, φωνὴν καὶ θόρυβον παντοδαπὸν κτύπον τε μεθ᾽ ἡμέραν καὶ διὰ νυκτὸς ὑπὸ πλήθους παρεχομένων.

117d8–e4

διαβάντι, 'as you went past the outer harbours, which were three in number, [you saw] a wall [which] … went in a circle'.

Plato imagines someone travelling along the 'main road' from the citadel, over the three bridges, and beside the canal to the sea, where the outer city wall began (see Fig. 4). The wall 'completed its circuit' (or its 'enclosure', συνέκλειεν) by returning to itself (or to the same point it started from, εἰς ταὐτὸν, a variant of ταὐτό), 'at the mouth of the canal' (LSJ, πρός, acc. 2) 'by the sea' (LSJ, πρός, gen. 2).

117e4–8   This picture might well remind an Athenian of the busy commercial port, the Peiraeus, and the occupied area inside the Long Walls from Athens to Peiraeus. In Plato's *Gorgias* (518e–519a), Socrates presents the fifth-century construction of Peiraeus and the Long Walls as promoting materialistic greed and thus the moral deterioration of Athens's character. From a conservative Athenian standpoint, this conversion of Atlantis into a mercantile port and maritime power would have been viewed negatively and may be seen in this way by Critias (see [30–31]). However, it is open to question whether Plato himself shared such a conservative standpoint and how central to his concerns in the story these allusions to fifth-century Athens are (see [32–34]).

Τὸ μὲν οὖν ἄστυ καὶ τὸ περὶ τὴν ἀρχαίαν οἴκησιν σχεδὸν
10   ὡς τότ' ἐλέχθη νῦν διεμνημόνευται· τῆς δ' ἄλλης χώρας
118a1   ὡς ἡ φύσις εἶχεν καὶ τὸ τῆς διακοσμήσεως εἶδος, ἀπομνη-
μονεῦσαι πειρατέον. πρῶτον μὲν οὖν ὁ τόπος ἅπας ἐλέγετο
σφόδρα τε ὑψηλὸς καὶ ἀπότομος ἐκ θαλάττης, τὸ δὲ περὶ
τὴν πόλιν πᾶν πεδίον, ἐκείνην μὲν περιέχον, αὐτὸ δὲ κύκλῳ
5   περιεχόμενον ὄρεσιν μέχρι πρὸς τὴν θάλατταν καθειμένοις,
λεῖον καὶ ὁμαλές, πρόμηκες δὲ πᾶν, ἐπὶ μὲν θάτερα τρισχι-
λίων σταδίων, κατὰ δὲ μέσον ἀπὸ θαλάττης ἄνω δισχιλίων.
118b1   ὁ δὲ τόπος οὗτος ὅλης τῆς νήσου πρὸς νότον ἐτέτραπτο,
ἀπὸ τῶν ἄρκτων κατάβορρος.

117e10   ὡς τότ' ἐλέχθη, 'what [lit. 'as'] was reported then' (by the Egyptian priests to Solon, and so, eventually, to Critias).

118a6–7   See Fig. 4.

τὰ δὲ περὶ αὐτὸν ὄρη τότε
ὑμνεῖτο πλῆθος καὶ μέγεθος καὶ κάλλος παρὰ πάντα τὰ νῦν
ὄντα γεγονέναι, πολλὰς μὲν κώμας καὶ πλουσίας περιοίκων
5 ἐν ἑαυτοῖς ἔχοντα, ποταμοὺς δὲ καὶ λίμνας καὶ λειμῶνας
τροφὴν τοῖς πᾶσιν ἡμέροις καὶ ἀγρίοις ἱκανὴν θρέμμασιν,
ὕλην δὲ καὶ πλήθει καὶ γένεσι ποικίλην σύμπασίν τε τοῖς
ἔργοις καὶ πρὸς ἕκαστα ἄφθονον.

118b2   τὰ δὲ κ.τ.λ., 'the surrounding mountains of that time were
praised for their number, size and beauty [acc. of respect, RG
335, AM 12], and said to go beyond [παρὰ] all those which exist
today'. This 'praise' presumably came from the Egyptian priests
(see also the note on 117e10)
118b7–8   'wood which was, in its quantity [πλήθει] and the variety of its
types, abundant [ἄφθονον] both for all kinds of work and for
each individual requirement [πρὸς ἕκαστα]'. For 'abundant' (or
'profuse', ἄφθονον) as a typically idyllic adj., see 117a5 and notes
on 111e4, 114e6–8.

ὧδε οὖν τὸ πεδίον φύσει
118c1   καὶ ὑπὸ βασιλέων πολλῶν ἐν πολλῷ χρόνῳ διεπεπόνητο.
τετράγωνον μὲν αὖθ' ὑπῆρχεν τὰ πλεῖστ' ὀρθὸν καὶ πρόμηκες,
ὅτι δὲ ἐνέλειπε, κατηύθυντο τάφρου κύκλῳ περιορυχθείσης·
τὸ δὲ βάθος καὶ πλάτος τό τε μῆκος αὐτῆς ἄπιστον μὲν
5 λεχθέν, ὡς χειροποίητον ἔργον, πρὸς τοῖς ἄλλοις διαπονή-
μασι τοσοῦτον εἶναι, ῥητέον δὲ ὅ γε ἠκούσαμεν·

118c2–3   'It was originally, as I said [lit. 'again': αὖθ = αὖτε before
aspiration, as in ms. a, though not in Burnet 1902], mostly
quadrilateral, with straight sides, and oblong in shape. Where
[lit. 'in that, in so far as, because'] it fell short of this [i.e.
geometric regularity], they made it straight by digging a canal
[gen. abs.] around [κύκλῳ]'. In their ambitious engineering
projects, the Atlanteans continue the original foundation of
Poseidon (see διακοσμήσεως at 118a1 and 113e3, and the note

on 113d6-8, e2-6). These grandiose projects are reminiscent of the Persian king Xerxes's preparations for war (Herodotus 7.23–25, 33–37), and also of Egypt's elaborate irrigation system (Herodotus 2.99, 108, 158; see also Pradeau 1997, 174–75).

118c4-6 'As for its depth, width and length, what was claimed is incredible – for [lit. 'as', ὡς] a work of human hands – that it should be so great in addition to the other labours' (i.e. those described in 115c–117b: τοσοῦτον εἶναι, ind. statement after λεχθέν). 'But we must in any case [γε] report [ῥητέον δὲ] what we have been told [incredible though it may seem]'.

πλέθρου
μὲν γὰρ βάθος ὀρώρυκτο, τὸ δὲ πλάτος ἁπάντη σταδίου,
118d1 περὶ δὲ πᾶν τὸ πεδίον ὀρυχθεῖσα συνέβαινεν εἶναι τὸ μῆκος
σταδίων μυρίων. τὰ δ' ἐκ τῶν ὀρῶν καταβαίνοντα ὑπο-
δεχομένη ῥεύματα καὶ περὶ τὸ πεδίον κυκλωθεῖσα, πρὸς τὴν
πόλιν ἔνθεν τε καὶ ἔνθεν ἀφικομένη, ταύτῃ πρὸς θάλατταν
μεθεῖτο ἐκρεῖν.

118d1 The outer canal is 10,000 stades long and oblong, hence probably 3,000 by 2,000 stades; total area enclosed = 6 million sq. stades.

118d4 ἔνθεν καὶ ἔνθεν, 'reached the city on both sides' (see Fig. 4).

5 ἄνωθεν δὲ ἀπ' αὐτῆς τὸ πλάτος μάλιστα
ἑκατὸν ποδῶν διώρυχες εὐθεῖαι τετμημέναι κατὰ τὸ πεδίον
πάλιν εἰς τὴν τάφρον τὴν πρὸς θαλάττης ἀφεῖντο, ἑτέρα
δὲ ἀφ' ἑτέρας αὐτῶν σταδίους ἑκατὸν ἀπεῖχεν· ᾗ δὴ τήν
118e1 τε ἐκ τῶν ὀρῶν ὕλην κατῆγον εἰς τὸ ἄστυ καὶ τἆλλα δὲ
ὡραῖα πλοίοις κατεκομίζοντο, διάπλους ἐκ τῶν διωρύχων
εἰς ἀλλήλας τε πλαγίας καὶ πρὸς τὴν πόλιν τεμόντες. καὶ
δὶς δὴ τοῦ ἐνιαυτοῦ τὴν γῆν ἐκαρποῦντο, χειμῶνος μὲν τοῖς
5 ἐκ Διὸς ὕδασι χρώμενοι, θέρους δὲ ὅσα γῆ φέρει τὰ ἐκ
τῶν διωρύχων ἐπάγοντες νάματα.

118d5–e3 ἄνωθεν, 'further inland'. Plato's system of channels consists of two series; the first runs north to south, and they 'discharged their waters back into the [main] canal on the seaward side' (d5–8). There is also a second series of cross-channels (διάπλους) connecting the first series (ἐκ τῶν διωρύχων εἰς ἀλλήλας) and at right angles to them (πλαγίους), thus enabling the movement of goods to the city (πρὸς τὴν πόλιν) (d8–e3). (I have adopted πλαγίους, rather than the πλαγίας of Burnet 1902, following Nesselrath 2006, 379–80.) The cross-channels run west to east; Plato does not say how far apart they are, but presumably they are 100 stades apart, like the first series. For the whole system, see Fig. 4 (based on Friedlander 1958, 314–6, Fig. 10). It creates a complex of land units, total 600, each one 10,000 sq. stades in area.

πλῆθος δέ, τῶν μὲν
ἐν τῷ πεδίῳ χρησίμων πρὸς πόλεμον ἀνδρῶν ἐτέτακτο τὸν
119a1 κλῆρον ἕκαστον παρέχειν ἄνδρα ἡγεμόνα, τὸ δὲ τοῦ κλήρου
μέγεθος εἰς δέκα δεκάκις ἦν στάδια, μυριάδες δὲ συμπάντων
τῶν κλήρων ἦσαν ἕξ· τῶν δ' ἐκ τῶν ὀρῶν καὶ τῆς ἄλλης
χώρας ἀπέραντος μὲν ἀριθμὸς ἀνθρώπων ἐλέγετο, κατὰ
5 δὲ τόπους καὶ κώμας εἰς τούτους τοὺς κλήρους πρὸς τοὺς
ἡγεμόνας ἅπαντες διενενέμηντο.

118e6–119a5 πλῆθος δέ κ.τ.λ., 'As for the number of men on the plain fit to serve in war, it had been laid down [ἐτέτακτο, impersonal] that each district should provide one leader; the size of the district was ten square stades [lit. 'ten by ten stades', δέκα δεκάκις; for εἰς with numerals as distributive = 'in each case', see LSJ, εἰς, III 2], and the total number of districts was sixty thousand'. Plato seems to imagine each of the 600 land units created by the channel system being subdivided into 100 districts. These 60,000 districts are then used as the basis of military organization (τούτους τοὺς κλήρους, 119a5).

τὸν οὖν ἡγεμόνα ἦν τε-
ταγμένον εἰς τὸν πόλεμον παρέχειν ἕκτον μὲν ἅρματος
πολεμιστηρίου μόριον εἰς μύρια ἅρματα, ἵππους δὲ δύο καὶ
119b1   ἀναβάτας, ἔτι δὲ συνωρίδα χωρὶς δίφρου καταβάτην τε
μικράσπιδα καὶ τὸν ἀμφοῖν μετ' ἐπιβάτην τοῖν ἵπποιν
ἡνίοχον ἔχουσαν, ὁπλίτας δὲ δύο καὶ τοξότας σφενδονήτας
τε ἑκατέρους δύο, γυμνῆτας δὲ λιθοβόλους καὶ ἀκοντιστὰς
5   τρεῖς ἑκατέρους, ναύτας δὲ τέτταρας εἰς πλήρωμα διακοσίων
καὶ χιλίων νεῶν. τὰ μὲν οὖν πολεμιστήρια οὕτω διετέτακτο
τῆς βασιλικῆς πόλεως, τῶν δὲ ἐννέα ἄλλα ἄλλως, ἃ μακρὸς
ἂν χρόνος εἴη λέγειν.

119a8–b6   ἵππους κ.τ.λ., 'two horses and riders' [i.e. cavalrymen] and,
besides, a pair of horses without a chariot but equipped with
[ἔχουσαν] a foot soldier [one who dismounts, καταβάτης] with
a small shield, and a charioteer for both horses [who stands]
behind [μετ'] the chariot fighter [one who goes mounted,
ἐπιβάτης]; two hoplites; archers and slingers, two of each [of the
two types of fighter, ἑκατέρους]; lightly armed stone-throwers
and javelin-throwers, three of each [of the two types of fighter,
ἑκατέρους]'. The presentation of the charioteer as standing
behind the chariot fighter instead of in front of him (to manage
the horses) is rather puzzling; some editors omit the words
μετ' ἐπιβάτην, leaving only the charioteer (see Nesselrath 2006,
388–90). In general, the military arrangements are barbaric
rather than Greek (with slingers and stone-throwers), though
chariots are found in Homer. The massive scale of the forces
involved evokes the vast forces assembled by Xerxes for his
invasion of Greece (Herodotus 7.60, 87, 89, 184–85, 187; see also
Pradeau 1997, 175–76).

    Scholars have speculated about the possible significance
of these (and other) numbers in Plato's account of Atlantis.
Some see a systematic alternation of even and odd, as here,
emphasized by the wording, ἑκατέρους δύο … τρεῖς ἑκατέρους;
or the pair of horses (συνωρίδα, also ἀμφοῖν) equipped,
unusually, with three soldiers. See also the plain of Atlantis,

2,000 by 3,000 stades in area (118a6–7); and, especially, the
meetings of the Atlantean kings, held 'in the fifth and then the
sixth year, alternately, giving an equal share to the even and
the odd' (119d3–4). This systematic alternation may be seen
as typical of Atlantis's (over-)complicated structure; see the
note on 113d6–8; [29], esp. n. 72; Brisson 1970, 429–30; Pradeau
1997, 93–95.

Critias 119c–121c:
the political structure of Atlantis and its moral decline

Critias describes the procedures by which Atlantean kings regulated their
mutual relations by reference to laws laid down by Poseidon. For some time,
the system worked well; but when the divine element in the kings' nature
became diluted, they gave themselves up to unjust greed and love of power,
and this poisoned their relations with each other (121a). Zeus intervenes to
punish and, although the text breaks off at this point, we can tell that the
punishment took the form of war with Athens (120d6–8.). In this war, the
Atlanteans were given a chance to express their greed and love of power in
an imperialist attack on Greece, and were punished for this attack, first by
defeat at Athens's hands and then by having their island sunk beneath the
waves (*Timaeus* 24d–25d). Until this point, Critias's description of the two
states has been largely even-handed, with only occasional touches of implied
criticism of Atlantis. However, the sudden moral decline in Atlantis makes
explicit the potential for instability and internal and external conflict latent
in its social structure, which is also implied by the contrast with primaeval
Athens (see [29]). In this way, Critias shows that he has now met Socrates's
original request for a story illustrating the contrast between the ideal of the
Republic and a suitable opponent (*Timaeus* 19b–20c). This may partly explain
why Plato abandons his story in mid-sentence (see final note and [35]).

119c1 Τὰ δὲ τῶν ἀρχῶν καὶ τιμῶν ὧδ᾽ εἶχεν ἐξ ἀρχῆς διακο-
σμηθέντα. τῶν δέκα βασιλέων εἰς ἕκαστος ἐν μὲν τῷ καθ᾽
αὐτὸν μέρει κατὰ τὴν αὐτοῦ πόλιν τῶν ἀνδρῶν καὶ τῶν

πλείστων νόμων ἦρχεν, κολάζων καὶ ἀποκτεινὺς ὅντιν'

5   ἐθελήσειεν· ἡ δὲ ἐν ἀλλήλοις ἀρχὴ καὶ κοινωνία κατὰ ἐπι-
στολὰς ἦν τὰς τοῦ Ποσειδῶνος, ὡς ὁ νόμος αὐτοῖς παρέ-
δωκεν καὶ γράμματα ὑπὸ τῶν πρώτων ἐν στήλῃ γεγραμμένα

119d1 ὀρειχαλκίνῃ, ἣ κατὰ μέσην τὴν νῆσον ἔκειτ' ἐν ἱερῷ Ποσειδῶνος, οἳ δὴ δι' ἐνιαυτοῦ πέμπτου, τοτὲ δὲ ἐναλλὰξ ἕκτου,
συνελέγοντο, τῷ τε ἀρτίῳ καὶ τῷ περιττῷ μέρος ἴσον ἀπονέμοντες, συλλεγόμενοι δὲ περί τε τῶν κοινῶν ἐβουλεύοντο
καὶ ἐξήταζον εἴ τίς τι παραβαίνοι, καὶ ἐδίκαζον.

119c1   ὧδ' εἶχεν κ.τ.λ., 'were organized in this way, from the
beginning', i.e. by Poseidon; for this intransitive use of ἔχω, see
the note on 107b2.

119c2-3 ἐν μὲν κ.τ.λ., 'in his own individual [καθ' αὑτὸν] region and
as regards [κατὰ] his own city'. μέρος denotes the geographical
region, πόλις the political unit (as well as the urban settlement)
allocated to each king.

119c4-5 ὅντιν' ἐθελήσειεν, 'whomever he wanted', aor. opt., indef. rel.,
RG 406 (iii), AM 166. See also d5-6, ὅτε ... μέλλοιεν; e2, ὃν
... ἕλοιεν; 119e5-120a1, ὅτε ... καθαγίζοιεν; 120b4-5, ἐπειδὴ
γίγνοιτο.

119c7   τῶν πρώτων, the immediate descendants of Poseidon
(113e-114c). Compare the role in the foundation of their state
played by the original ἀγαθοί (or θεῖοι) ἄνδες whom the gods
settled in Athens (109d1-2, 110c5-6).

119d3-4 For this systematic alternation of odd and even in Atlantis, see
the note on 119a8-b6, second paragraph.

119d5   εἴ τις τι παραβαίνοι, opt., ind. question in secondary sequence
(RG 167, AM 162), 'if any of them was doing something wrong'
(i.e. acting against the laws governing their mutual relations).

                                        ὅτε δὲ

5 δικάζειν μέλλοιεν, πίστεις ἀλλήλοις τοιάσδε ἐδίδοσαν πρότερον. ἀφέτων ὄντων ταύρων ἐν τῷ τοῦ Ποσειδῶνος ἱερῷ,
μόνοι γιγνόμενοι δέκα ὄντες, ἐπευξάμενοι τῷ θεῷ τὸ κεχα-

119e1   ρισμένον αὐτῷ θῦμα ἑλεῖν, ἄνευ σιδήρου ξύλοις καὶ βρόχοις
ἐθήρευον, ὃν δὲ ἕλοιεν τῶν ταύρων, πρὸς τὴν στήλην προσ-
αγαγόντες κατὰ κορυφὴν αὐτῆς ἔσφαττον κατὰ τῶν γραμμάτων. ἐν δὲ τῇ στήλῃ πρὸς τοῖς νόμοις ὅρκος ἦν μεγάλας
ἀρὰς ἐπευχόμενος τοῖς ἀπειθοῦσιν.

119d–120c   The main object of this ritual seems to be for the kings to
reanimate in themselves the spirit of their divine ancestor,
Poseidon, before judging each other by Poseidon's laws. The
spirit of Poseidon is embodied in his special animal, the bull;
and the kings leave it to Poseidon (by refraining from using
metal weapons) to determine which bull he wants them to
catch, as his substitute. The blood of the bull sanctifies the
column containing Poseidon's laws, as well as the kings, who
drink it before passing judgement. Identification with Poseidon
is heightened by dressing in robes whose colour (dark blue,
κυάνεος) resembles the sea, and by sitting over the embers of a
fire mingled with the bull's blood. See Pradeau 1997, 163–65.

Plato's sources for the composition of this ritual are
discussed by Brisson 1970, 432–35. The general situation is
strongly reminiscent of an incident in early Egyptian history
described in Herodotus 2.147 and 151. A group monarchy was
established whose 12 members met to sanctify their compact
(based on strict regulations governing their mutual relations)
by a ritual involving sacrifice, libation and solemn drinking.
This group monarchy also created an astonishing architectural
and engineering complex (2.148–150). The subsequent sequence
of events described by Herodotus, in which this compact was
destroyed (2.152–54), may also indicate the way Plato intended
to continue his unfinished story (see 121a, esp. 4–5 referring to
the importance of φιλία in maintaining shared prosperity).

119e3–4   κατὰ κορυφὴν κ.τ.λ., 'they cut its throat over the top [of the
column] [LSJ, κατά, acc. I 2], [so that the blood ran] down over
the inscription' (of the law code, LSJ, κατά, gen. II 1).

5   ὅτ' οὖν κατὰ τοὺς
120a1 αὐτῶν νόμους θύσαντες καθαγίζοιεν πάντα τοῦ ταύρου τὰ
μέλη, κρατῆρα κεράσαντες ὑπὲρ ἑκάστου θρόμβον ἐνέβαλλον
αἵματος, τὸ δ' ἄλλ' εἰς τὸ πῦρ ἔφερον, περικαθήραντες τὴν
στήλην· μετὰ δὲ τοῦτο χρυσαῖς φιάλαις ἐκ τοῦ κρατῆρος
5 ἀρυτόμενοι, κατὰ τοῦ πυρὸς σπένδοντες ἐπώμνυσαν δικάσειν
τε κατὰ τοὺς ἐν τῇ στήλῃ νόμους καὶ κολάσειν εἴ τίς τι
πρότερον παραβεβηκὼς εἴη, τό τε αὖ μετὰ τοῦτο μηδὲν τῶν
γραμμάτων ἑκόντες παραβήσεσθαι, μηδὲ ἄρξειν μηδὲ ἄρ-
120b1 χοντι πείσεσθαι πλὴν κατὰ τοὺς τοῦ πατρὸς ἐπιτάττοντι
νόμους.

120a3-5   The kings cleanse the column of blood, and throw all the
surplus blood into the fire, ensuring that the bull's divine
power is not dispersed but concentrated into the fire by whose
embers they pass judgement. The φιάλη, a flat bowl or saucer, is
regularly used for pouring libations in religious ceremonies, and
here the libation is made down into the fire (κατὰ τοῦ πυρὸς,
LSJ, κατά, gen. II 2).

120a5-b2   ἐπώμνυσαν δικάσειν ... κολάσειν ... παραβήσεσθαι κ.τ.λ., fut.
infin. in indirect statement (RG 235, AM 157; for fut. infin. with
verbs of swearing, see G 1286). κολάσειν εἴ τίς ... παραβεβηκὼς
εἴη, if anyone proved to have been an offender, pf. part. + εἴη
(pres. opt., εἰμί), remote fut. condition.

     ταῦτα ἐπευξάμενος ἕκαστος αὐτῶν αὑτῷ καὶ τῷ
ἀφ' αὑτοῦ γένει, πιὼν καὶ ἀναθεὶς τὴν φιάλην εἰς τὸ ἱερὸν
τοῦ θεοῦ, περὶ τὸ δεῖπνον καὶ τἀναγκαῖα διατρίψας, ἐπειδὴ
5 γίγνοιτο σκότος καὶ τὸ πῦρ ἐψυγμένον τὸ περὶ τὰ θύματα
εἴη, πάντες οὕτως ἐνδύντες ὅτι καλλίστην κυανῆν στολήν,
ἐπὶ τὰ τῶν ὁρκωμοσίων καύματα χαμαὶ καθίζοντες, νύκτωρ,
120c1 πᾶν τὸ περὶ τὸ ἱερὸν ἀποσβεννύντες πῦρ, ἐδικάζοντό τε
καὶ ἐδίκαζον εἴ τίς τι παραβαίνειν αὐτῶν αἰτιῷτό τινα·
δικάσαντες δέ, τὰ δικασθέντα, ἐπειδὴ φῶς γένοιτο, ἐν χρυσῷ
πίνακι γράψαντες μετὰ τῶν στολῶν μνημεῖα ἀνετίθεσαν.

120b2-3   τῷ ἀφ' αὑτοῦ γένει, 'his descendants', i.e. the family sprung
           from him.
120b7   ὁρκωμοσίων, like ὅρκια, the sacrifice used at the taking of a
           sacred oath. The embers are those of the fire in which the bull's
           blood has been burnt (and perhaps his limbs too, a1-2).
120c2   εἰ τίς ... αἰτιῷτό τινα, pres. opt., general condition in secondary
           sequence (AM 182).
120c4   μνημεῖα, 'as a memorial [offering]'.

5   νόμοι δὲ πολλοὶ μὲν ἄλλοι περὶ τὰ γέρα τῶν βασιλέων
           ἑκάστων ἦσαν ἴδιοι, τὰ δὲ μέγιστα, μήτε ποτὲ ὅπλα ἐπ'
           ἀλλήλους οἴσειν βοηθήσειν τε πάντας, ἄν πού τις αὐτῶν
           ἔν τινι πόλει τὸ βασιλικὸν καταλύειν ἐπιχειρῇ γένος, κοινῇ
120d1   δέ, καθάπερ οἱ πρόσθεν, βουλευόμενοι τὰ δόξαντα περὶ
           πολέμου καὶ τῶν ἄλλων πράξεων, ἡγεμονίαν ἀποδιδόντες
           τῷ Ἀτλαντικῷ γένει. θανάτου δὲ τὸν βασιλέα τῶν συγ-
           γενῶν μηδενὸς εἶναι κύριον, ὃν ἂν μὴ τῶν δέκα τοῖς ὑπὲρ
5   ἥμισυ δοκῇ.

120c5-b2   The structure of this sentence is this: νόμοι δὲ πολλοὶ ...
           ἦσαν ἴδιοι, τὰ δὲ μέγιστα (= 'there were many other [specific]
           laws but the most important points were that' μήτε ... οἴσειν
           βοηθήσειν τε πάντας (ind. command, AM 161, RG 397 (ii)).
           The infinitives are future rather than the normal present,
           perhaps by analogy with δικάσειν κ.τ.λ., a5-b2; also βοηθήσειν
           τε πάντας stands, in indirect speech, for the main clause of
           a future condition, cf. κολάσειν εἰ τίς κ.τ.λ., a6-7). ἄν [= ἐὰν]
           ἐπιχειρῇ, distinct future condition (RG, 402 (iii), AM 180),
           tense unaltered in secondary sequence (AM 197). κοινῇ δέ ...
           βουλευόμενοι ... ἀποδιδόντες: these participles are loosely
           attached, grammatically, to βοηθήσειν, but seem to introduce
           separate regulations; the change from acc. (πάντας) to nom.
           may be by analogy with the 'swearing' construction in a5-b1,
           as if Plato had written, 'they swore that they would help,
           reaching their decisions in common, etc.'

120d3–5 θανάτου ... εἶναι κύριον, continuation of ind. speech: 'that
the king [τὸν βασιλέα, i.e. the king descended from Atlas and
holding the highest authority, as just mentioned in d2–3] [of
this house] should not have the right to kill any of his relatives'.
ὃν ἂν μὴ ... δοκῇ, indef. rel. clause, 'someone [whose killing]
was not approved', that is, unless the king's right to kill the
relevant person was approved. For this interpretation of the
sentence, see Nesselrath 2006, 427–28 (though he also argues for
an emendation which I do not consider necessary).

Ταύτην δὴ τοσαύτην καὶ τοιαύτην δύναμιν ἐν ἐκείνοις
τότε οὖσαν τοῖς τόποις ὁ θεὸς ἐπὶ τούσδε αὖ τοὺς τόπους
συντάξας ἐκόμισεν ἔκ τινος τοιᾶσδε, ὡς λόγος, προφάσεως.
120e1   ἐπὶ πολλὰς μὲν γενεάς, μέχριπερ ἡ τοῦ θεοῦ φύσις αὐτοῖς
ἐξήρκει, κατήκοοί τε ἦσαν τῶν νόμων καὶ πρὸς τὸ συγγενὲς
θεῖον φιλοφρόνως εἶχον·

120d6–8 'The god' (ὁ θεὸς) is not specified; but in 121b7–c5 the god
who is about to initiate the war seems to be Zeus. It is rather
awkward that in e1 'the god' is certainly Poseidon, but it seems
less likely that he would initiate a war that was so disastrous
for his favoured city. πρόφασις, as in Thucydides 1.23.6, seems
to mean the true reason for the war, rather than a 'pretext' or
'excuse', which πρόφασις can also mean.

120e1–3 αὐτοῖς ἐξήρκει, 'was sufficiently strong in them' to preserve
their original character. καὶ πρὸς κ.τ.λ., 'and were well-disposed
towards the divine [i.e. the divine basis of their constitution] to
which they were related', or 'towards their innate divinity'. The
idea that obedience to the law is like submission to 'divine' rule
is elaborated in *Laws* 713c–714a and 644d–645b; see also Gill
1979a, 158–59.

τὰ γὰρ φρονήματα ἀληθινὰ καὶ
πάντῃ μεγάλα ἐκέκτηντο, πρᾳότητι μετὰ φρονήσεως πρὸς

5   τε τὰς ἀεὶ συμβαινούσας τύχας καὶ πρὸς ἀλλήλους χρώ-
       μενοι, διὸ πλὴν ἀρετῆς πάντα ὑπερορῶντες μικρὰ ἡγοῦντο
121a1 τὰ παρόντα καὶ ῥᾳδίως ἔφερον οἷον ἄχθος τὸν τοῦ χρυσοῦ
       τε καὶ τῶν ἄλλων κτημάτων ὄγκον, ἀλλ' οὐ μεθύοντες ὑπὸ
       τρυφῆς διὰ πλοῦτον ἀκράτορες αὑτῶν ὄντες ἐσφάλλοντο,
       νήφοντες δὲ ὀξὺ καθεώρων ὅτι καὶ ταῦτα πάντα ἐκ φιλίας
5   τῆς κοινῆς μετ' ἀρετῆς αὐξάνεται, τῇ δὲ τούτων σπουδῇ καὶ
       τιμῇ φθίνει ταῦτά τε αὐτὰ κἀκείνη συναπόλλυται τούτοις.
       ἐκ δὴ λογισμοῦ τε τοιούτου καὶ φύσεως θείας παραμενούσης
       πάντ' αὐτοῖς ηὐξήθη ἃ πρὶν διήλθομεν.

120e4–5 πρᾳότητι, 'they reacted with a combination of mildness and
         good sense towards their fortunes as they fell out at any one
         time'.

121a1   τὰ παρόντα, 'their current prosperity'; ἔφερον κ.τ.λ., 'they bore
         without difficulty the bulk of their gold and other possessions,
         as though they were a burden [οἷον ἄχθος]'.

121a2–3 'and they were not intoxicated by luxury, because of their
         wealth. Nor did they lose control of themselves and trip up' (as
         drunks do, LSJ, σφάλλω 1, pass.).

121a4   ταῦτα πάντα, that is, their wealth, likewise τούτων (a5), ταῦτά
         τε αὐτὰ and τούτοις (a6), πάντα (a8). κἀκείνη (a6) is probably
         ἀρετή (or possibly φιλία, or the combination of the two).
         The reference to φιλία suggests that the elaborate methods
         for preserving the mutual relationships between the kings
         (described in 119c–120d) had failed to work. Competition or
         conflict between the kings then led to external aggression,
         presumably animated by the desire of each of the kings to have
         yet more wealth and power. See also the Herodotean parallel for
         this sequence of events in note on 119d–120c, second paragraph.

121a7   λογισμοῦ … φύσεως θείας. By associating these elements, Plato
         implies that reason is the divine element in human nature (and
         hence also the element that is obedient to good legal principles,
         see 120e1–3 and note).

ἐπεὶ δ' ἡ τοῦ θεοῦ
μὲν μοῖρα ἐξίτηλος ἐγίγνετο ἐν αὐτοῖς πολλῷ τῷ θνητῷ καὶ
121b1   πολλάκις ἀνακεραννυμένη, τὸ δὲ ἀνθρώπινον ἦθος ἐπεκράτει,
τότε ἤδη τὰ παρόντα φέρειν ἀδυνατοῦντες ἠσχημόνουν, καὶ
τῷ δυναμένῳ μὲν ὁρᾶν αἰσχροὶ κατεφαίνοντο, τὰ κάλλιστα
ἀπὸ τῶν τιμιωτάτων ἀπολλύντες, τοῖς δὲ ἀδυνατοῦσιν
5   ἀληθινὸν πρὸς εὐδαιμονίαν βίον ὁρᾶν τότε δὴ μάλιστα
πάγκαλοι μακάριοί τε ἐδοξάζοντο εἶναι, πλεονεξίας ἀδίκου
καὶ δυνάμεως ἐμπιμπλάμενοι.

121a9   μοῖρα, 'portion' in their genetic constitution; ἐξίτηλος, 'extinct,
        weakened'.

121b3   ὁρᾶν, the 'sight' is moral insight, see also b5, and a4, ὀξὺ
        καθεώρων. At b4, τῶν τιμιωτάτων also refers to moral insight.

121b4   τοῖς δὲ κ.τ.λ., 'but to those unable to see the life that truly leads
        to happiness' (lit. 'the true life [that leads] to happiness'). This
        stress on the moral insight that looks behind the surface may be
        a comment on how we, as readers, are encouraged to evaluate
        the material splendour of Atlantis.

121b7   δυνάμεως, literally simply 'power' but the term is coupled
        with 'unjust greed for possessions', suggesting that they are
        activated by greed for (yet more) power. Critias's account of the
        moral and political decline of Atlantis is close to the picture
        given in the *Laws* of the decline in Persia that followed the
        reigns of Cyrus and Darius (694a–b, 695b, 697c–698a; see also
        Friedländer 1958, 203–04). The decline that followed Darius's
        reign led directly to the war against Greece (*Laws* 698b–e), and
        this seems to be one of the historical models used by Plato in
        constructing his story (see [30]).

θεὸς δὲ ὁ θεῶν Ζεὺς ἐν
νόμοις βασιλεύων, ἅτε δυνάμενος καθορᾶν τὰ τοιαῦτα,
ἐννοήσας γένος ἐπιεικὲς ἀθλίως διατιθέμενον, δίκην αὐτοῖς
121c1   ἐπιθεῖναι βουληθείς, ἵνα γένοιντο ἐμμελέστεροι σωφρονι-
σθέντες, συνήγειρεν θεοὺς πάντας εἰς τὴν τιμιωτάτην αὐτῶν

οἴκησιν, ἣ δὴ κατὰ μέσον παντὸς τοῦ κόσμου βεβηκυῖα
καθορᾷ πάντα ὅσα γενέσεως μετείληφεν, καὶ συναγείρας
5   εἶπεν—

*   *   *   *   *

121b7	θεὸς κ.τ.λ., for Plato's picture of Zeus as a 'constitutional' monarch (ἐν νόμοις βασιλεύων), see the note on 109b1–5.
121c1	ἵνα γένοιντο, 'to render them self-controlled and more harmonious'; for the idea of punishment as morally corrective, see the note on 106b2–3.
121c4	γενέσεως μετείληφεν, perf. in pres. sense. The phrase refers to Timaeus's theory that the physical world participates in change or 'becoming' (γένεσις), although it is also an image of timeless 'being' (*Ti.* 27d–29d). This indicates the linkage between the Atlantis story and Timaeus's cosmology that has been an implicit feature of Critias's full version of the story (see [25]).

There is no evidence that Plato wrote any more of the *Critias*, or even completed this last sentence. He may have felt that Critias's full version of the story, as far as it went, had met the key aims of Socrates's original request for a story illustrating the contrast between an embodiment of the ideal state of the *Republic* and a suitable opponent. Also, he may have decided that he wanted to pursue the themes that would have been central for the representation of diplomacy and war in the form of a more discursive and investigative philosophical discussion, of the kind he produces in the *Laws*. See [35] and Nesselrath 2006, 34–41.

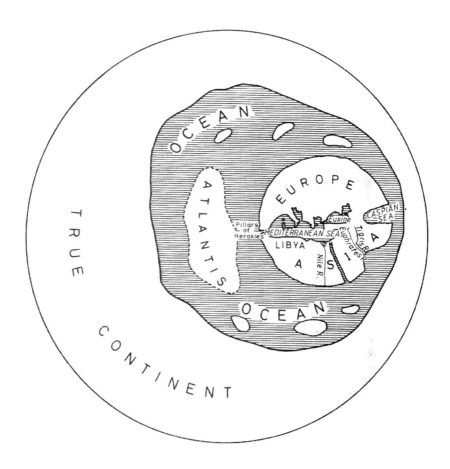

Figure 1: Plato's world view.

Figure 2: The traditional Greek world view
(based on a reconstruction of Hecateus' World Map, *c.* 500 BC).

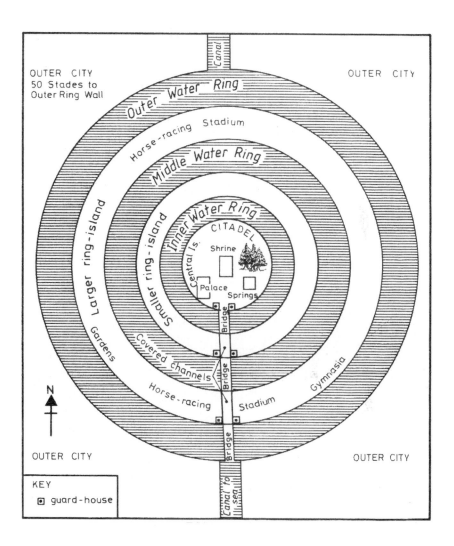

Figure 3: The capital city of Atlantis.

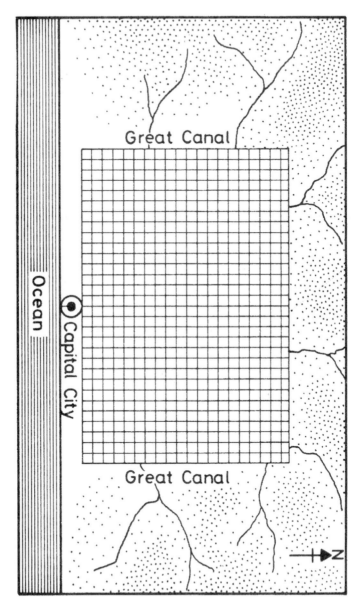

Figure 4: The coastal plain of Atlantis.

Vocabulary

Note on verb forms: In this vocabulary, verb forms other than the basic λύω (i.e. 1ˢᵗ person singular, present indicative active) are related to basic forms (e.g. ἀκούσαιμι: ἀκούω, aor. opt.). Unless otherwise stated, verb forms should be assumed to be 1ˢᵗ person singular (rather than any other person), present (rather than any other tense), indicative (rather than any other mood) and active (rather than any other voice). Other persons, tenses, moods and voices are specified. The basic verb forms are given in uncontracted form (e.g. ἀφικνέομαι not ἀφικνοῦμαι), and so are nouns (e.g. νόος, ὁ not νοῦς, ὁ) and adjectives (ἁπλόος -ῆ -ον, not ἁπλοῦς -ῆ -οῦν).

A

ἄβατος -ον, *inaccessible*
ἀγαθός -ή -όν, *good*
ἄγαλμα, τό, *image, statue honouring a god*
ἀγαπάω, *be satisfied with, tolerate*
ἀγαπητός -ή -όν, *pleasant*
ἀγαπητῶς, *gladly, with relief*
ἀγγεῖον, τό, *basin*
ἅγιος -α -ον, *holy, sacred*
ἀγνοέω, *be ignorant of*
ἄγνοια, ἡ, *ignorance*
ἀγγράμματος -ον, *illiterate*
ἄγριος -α -ον, *wild, savage*
ἄγροικος -ον, *boorish, rude, uncivil*
ἀγχιβαθής -ές, *deep (close to the shore)*
ἄγω, *lead, drive; keep, maintain*
ἀγωνία, ἡ, *contest*

ἀγωνίζομαι (mid.), *compete, contend in*
ἀδελφή, ἡ, *sister*
ἀδελφός, ὁ, *brother*
ἀδελφός -ή -όν, *brotherly, sisterly; akin, cognate*
ἄδην (adv.), *in abundance, to give them their fill*
ἀδιερεύνητος -ον, *impenetrable*
ἄδικος -ον, *unjust*
ἀδυνατέω (+ infin.), *be unable to*
ἀεί, *always, continually, at any time*
ἀείδω, *sing*
ἀήθεια, ἡ, *unusual character*
ἀθλέω, *compete in*
ἄθλιος -α -ον, *wretched, miserable*
ἄθλον, τό, *prize for contest*
ἄθλος, ὁ, *contest, competition*
ἀθρόος -α -ον, *altogether, in a body*

ἀθυμέω, *be feeble, uninspired*
Αἰγυπτιστί, *in the Egyptian language*
Αἴγυπτος, ὁ, *Egypt*
αἷμα, τό, *blood*
αἱρέω, *take*
αἰσθάνομαι (mid.), *perceive, notice*
αἰσχρός -ά -όν, *ugly, immoral*
αἰτέομαι (mid.), *ask for one's own use, claim*
αἰτέω, *ask*
αἰτία, ἡ, *cause, reason*
αἰτιάομαι (mid.), *accuse*
αἴτιον, τό, *cause*
αἰτιῷτο: αἰτιάομαι, 3 s. opt.
ἀκέραιος -ον, *untouched, unharmed*
ἀκήκοα: ἀκούω, pf.
ἀκοή, ἡ, *hearing, report, tradition*
ἀκοντιστής, ὁ, *javelin-thrower*
ἀκούοιτε: ἀκούω, 2 pl. opt.
ἀκούσαιμι: ἀκούω, aor. opt.
ἀκούω *(usually with acc. of thing, gen. of person), hear, listen to*
ἄκρα, ἡ, *headland, cape; edge*
ἀκράτωρ (= ἀκρατής -ές, + gen.), *lacking control over*
ἀκρίβεια, ἡ, *accuracy, precision* (δι᾿ ἀκριβείας, *with accuracy*).
ἀκριβές, τό, *the details*
ἀκριβής -ές, *accurate*
ἀκρόδρυα, τά, *trees growing fruit on their upper branches (e.g. pomegranates)*
ἄκρον, τό, *summit, top; pl. heights*
ἀκρόπολις, ἡ, *citadel; the Acropolis in Athens*
ἄκρος -α -ον, *furthest, the edge of*
ἀκρωτήρια, τά, *pediment sculptures*
ἄκων -ουσα -ον, *unwilling*

ἄλειμμα, τό, *oil*
ἀληθινός -ή -όν, *true, real*
ἀληθής -ές, *true, real*
ἀλλά, *but*
ἀλλὰ γάρ, *but really, but certainly*
ἀλλήλους -ας -α (*and other cases*), *each other*
ἄλλος -η -ο, *other, another, the rest of*
ἀλοιφή, ἡ, *varnish*
ἄλσος, τό, *grove*
ἅμα, *at the same time*
ἀμελέω (+ gen.), *neglect, fail to think about*
ἀμήχανος -ον, *extraordinary, enormous*
ἄμιλλα, ἡ, *competition, race*
ἀμούσικος -ον, *uncultured, uneducated*
ἀμφότερος -α -ον, *either (of two), both*
ἄμφω (dual), *both*
ἄν (particle), *usually with subj. or opt.*
ἀναβάτης, ὁ, *rider, cavalryman*
ἀναγκάζω, *compel, force*
ἀναγκαῖα, τά, *the necessities of life, necessary business*
ἀναγκασθῇ: ἀναγκάζω, 3 s. aor. subj. pass.
ἀνάγκη, ἡ, *necessity* (ἐξ᾿ ἀνάγκης, *of necessity, forcibly*)
ἀνάγω, *conduct, transfer*
ἀναδιδούς -οῦσα -όν: ἀναδίδωμι, part.
ἀναδίδωμι, *produce, yield*
ἀναζήτησις, ἡ (+ gen.), *enquiry into*
ἀναθείς -εῖσα -έν: ἀνατίθημι, aor. part.

ἀνάθημα, τό, *statue set up in honour of a god, dedicatory offering*
ἀνακεράννυμι, *mix up again*
ἀναλαβών -οῦσα -όν: ἀναλαμβάνω, aor. part.
ἀναλαμβάνω, *find out, restore, translate back*
ἀναλαμβάνω πρὸς ἐμαυτὸν, *I run over in my mind, refresh my memory*
ἀναλίσκω, *spend (e.g. money)*
ἀναμιμνῄσκομαι, *see* μιμνῄσκομαι
ἀνάξιος -α -ον (+ gen.), *unworthy of, not deserving*
ἀναπαύομαι (+ gen.), *take rest from*
ἀναπληρόω, *fill, supply*
ἀνάπλοος, ὁ, *canal, access by ship*
ἀνατίθημι, *dedicate, set up as a dedicatory offering*
ἀναφαίνω, *reveal, bring to light*
ἀναφέρω, *report, refer*
ἀνδρείως, *bravely*
ἀνειλλόμενος -η -ον: ἀνειλέω, part. pass.; *as it unrolls, unfolds*
ἀνείς -εῖσα -έν: ἀνίημι, aor. part.
ἀνέκπλυτος -ον, *indelible*
ἀνελευθερία, ἡ, *meanness, servility*
ἀνερωτάω (+ acc. of person, acc. of thing), *question someone about something*
ἄνευ (prep. + gen.), *without*
ἀνευρεῖν: ἀνευρίσκω, aor. infin.
ἀνευρίσκω, *find out, discover*
ἀνήρ, ὁ, *man*
ἄνθος, τό, *flower*
ἀνθρώπινος -η -ον, *human*
ἄνθρωπος, ὁ, *human being*
ἀνίημι, *abandon, leave*
ἀντακούω, *listen in return*

ἀνταποδίδωμι, *give back in return*: ἀνταποδώσειν, fut. infin.
ἀνταπολαμβάνω, *take in return*: ἀνταπολήψεσθαι, fut. infin
ἀνταφεστάω, *feast in return*
ἀντεπέταξα: ἀντεπιτάσσω, aor.
ἀντεπιτάσσω (acc. of thing, dat. of person), *order in return, impose a duty in return*
ἀντί (prep. + gen.), *instead of, in return for*
ἀντιπολεμέω (+ dat.), *fight against, oppose*
ἄνω (prep. + gen.), *above (place), earlier than (time)*
ἄνω (adv.), *inland, further up, above (place), formerly, earlier (time)*
ἄνωθεν (adv.), *further back, further inland, above, down from above (place), earlier (time)*
ἄξιος -α -ον (+ gen.), *worthy of, deserving*
ἄξιος λόγου, *worth speaking about, worth noticing*
ἀξιόω, *think something is right, approve;* (+ infin.), *think oneself worthy of, think one has a claim to*
ἀπαγγέλλω, *report, relate*
ἀπᾴδω, *sing out of tune, strike a false note*
ἀπαλλάσσω, *set free, release;* mid. pass., *finish, leave off*
ἅπας = πᾶς
ἀπατηλός -ή -όν, *deceptive, illusory*
ἀπειθέω (+ dat.), *disobey*
ἀπεικάζω, *make a likeness, reproduce*
ἀπεικασία, ἡ, *production of likeness, representation*

ἄπειμι, *be absent*
ἀπείργω, *prevent*
ἀπειρία, ἡ, *inexperience*
ἄπειρος -ον, *boundless, infinite*
ἀπέραντος -ον, *numberless, infinite*
ἀπεργάζομαι (mid.), *finish, complete*
ἀπευθύνω, *steer, direct*
ἀπήλλαγμαι: ἀπαλλάσσω, perf. pass.
ἄπιστος -ον, *incredible*
ἁπλόος -η -ον, *simple, plain*
ἀπό (prep. + gen.), *from, because of*
ἀποβαίνω, *reach, extend* (in space):
ἀποβεβηκώς -υῖα -ός, pf. part
ἀπογράφομαι, *commit to writing*
ἀποδίδωμι, *give back, provide in return*:
ἀποδοῖεν, 3 pl. aor. opt.
ἀποδοῦναι, aor. infin.
ἀποκτείνυμι (= ἀποκτείνω), *kill*
ἀπολείπομαι (mid. + gen.), *be missing from*
ἀπόλλυμι, *lose*
ἀπομιμέομαι, *represent, copy*
ἀπομνημονεύω, *recall, record, relate from memory*
ἀπονέμω, *allocate, allot*
ἀπορέω (+ gen.), *be in need of*
ἀπορία, ἡ, *lack, difficulty, desperate situation, disaster*
ἄπορος -ον, *difficult, impenetrable*
ἀπορρέον, τό, ἀπορρέω, neut. part., *the outflow*
ἀπορρέω, *flow out, run off*
ἀποσβέννυμι, *extinguish*; pass., *vanish, die*:
ἀποσβεσθείς -εῖσα -έν, aor. part. pass.
ἀποστάς -ᾶσα -άν: ἀφίστημι, 2 aor. (intrans.) part.

ἀποτελέω, *complete, perform one's duty*
ἀπότομος -ον, *sheer, precipitous*
ἀποχρώντως, *enough, adequately*
ἄρα, ἆρα (particle emphasizing question or conclusion), *then, surely*
ἀρά, ἡ, *curse*
ἀργός -ή -ον (+ gen.), *free from (some kind of work)*
ἄργυρος, ὁ, *silver*
ἀρετή, ἡ, *excellence, virtue; (of land) fertility*
ἀριθμέω, *number, count*
ἄριστα (neut. pl. adj. as adv.), *best, in the best way*
ἀριστερά, ἡ, *left hand*
ἄριστος -η -ον, *best*
ἄρκτος, ἡ / ἄρκτοι, αἱ, *the north*
ἅρμα, τό, *chariot, chariot team (of horses)*
ἁρμόζω, *fit*
ἆρ᾽ οὐ (introduces question inviting affirmative answer), *isn't it, didn't we?*
ἆρ᾽ οὖν (emphasizes question or conclusion), *then, surely*
ἄρουρα, ἡ, *land; pl. fields*
ἄρρην -εν, *male*
ἄρτι, *just, recently*
ἄρτιος -α -ον, *even*
ἀρύτομαι (mid.), *draw off (liquid) for oneself*
ἀρχαῖος -α -ον, *ancient*
ἀρχή, ἡ, *beginning; rule, office of government*
ἀρχηγός, ὁ, *founder*
ἄρχομαι (mid.), *begin*
ἄρχω (+ gen.), *begin, lead, rule*

Vocabulary

ἄρχων -ουσα -ον: ἄρχω, part.; as
noun, *male or female ruler*
ἀσαφής -ές, *indistinct, imprecise*
ἀσθένεια, ἡ, *weakeness, illness*
ἄσμενος -η -ον, *glad*
ἀσπίς, ἡ, *shield*
ἄστοχος -ον (+ gen.), *aiming badly
at, missing the target*
ἀστρονομικός -ή -όν, *skilled in
astronomy*
ἄστυ, τό, *city, town*
ἀσχημονέω, *disgrace oneself*
Ἀσωπός, ὁ, *river Asopus*
ἄτε, *seeing that, because*
ἀτιμάζω, *dishonour, despise*
ἄτοπος -ον, *strange, extraordinary*
αὖ, αὖτε, αὖτις, αὖθις, *again, at
another time; on the other hand*
αὐξάνω, *increase, strengthen*
αὐτόθεν, *from there*
αὐτόθι, *there, on the spot*
αὐτόθι ἐν μέσῳ, *in the very middle*
αὐτόν -ήν -ό (= ἑαυτόν -ήν -ό) and
other cases, *himself, herself, itself*
αὐτός -ή -ό (as adj., in all cases;
following def. article), *same,*
e.g. ὁ αὐτὸς ἀνήρ, *the same
man;* (preceding def. article or
following noun, intensive adj.),
e.g. αὐτὸς ὁ ἀνήρ, ὁ ἀνηρ αὐτος,
the man himself; (not in nom.,
reflex. pers pron.), e.g. ὑμᾶς
αὐτούς, *yourselves,* ἡμᾶς αὐτούς,
ourselves; (as pron., not in nom.),
him, her, it, etc.
αὐτόσε, *to that place*
αὐτοῦ (adv.), *here, there*
αὐτόχθων -ον, *born from the earth
itself*

ἀφανής -ές, *unknown, lost in
oblivion*
ἀφανίζομαι (pass.), *vanish,
disappear*
ἀφεῖντο: ἀφίεμαι (mid.), 3 pl. aor.
ἀφεῖτο: ἀφίημι, 3 s. plpf. pass.
ἀφεστώς -υῖα -ός: ἀφίστημι, 2 perf.
(intrans.) part., in pres. sense,
being distant from
ἄφετος -ον, *set free, roaming free
(from work); consecrated*
ἄφθονος -ον, *abundant, plentiful,
profuse*
ἀφθόνως, *generously, profusely*
ἀφιείς -εῖσα -έν: ἀφίημι, part.
ἀφίεμαι (mid.), *discharge, release
from oneself*
ἀφίημι, *release, send forth; release
from normal use, dedicate*
ἀφικνέομαι, *come, arrive at:*
ἀφικόμεθα, 1 pl. aor.
ἀφίκοιτο, 3 s. aor. opt.
ἀφίστημι (intrans. tenses), *be distant
from; stand aside from, desert*
ἀφορίζω, *separate, distinguish*
ἄφωνος -ον, *speechless, without
expressing themselves*
ἀφωρισμένος -η -ον: ἀφορίζω, pf.
part. pass.
ἄχθος, τό, *burden*

B
βάθος, τό, *depth, height*
βαρβαρικός -ή -όν, *non-Greek,
barbaric, foreign*
βάρβαρος -α -ον, *non-Greek,
barbaric, foreign*
βασίλεια, ἡ, *kingdom*
βασιλείδης, ὁ, *prince*

βασίλειον, τό/βασίλεια, τά, *palace, palace buildings*
βασιλεύς, ὁ, *king*
βασιλεύω, *be a king*
βασιλικός -ή -όν, *kingly, royal, regal*
βεβαιόω, *establish securely, fix firmly:*
βεβαιωθῇ, 3 s. aor. subj. pass.
βεβηκώς -υῖα -ός: βαίνω, pf. part., *standing, having taken a stand*
βιάζομαι (mid.), *use force on, master by force*
βίος, ὁ, *life*
βόσκημα, τό, *animal, esp. cow*
βουλεύομαι, *deliberate about, plan*
βουληθείς -εῖσα -εν, βούλομαι, aor. part.
βούλομαι, *want, wish*
βούλημα, *purpose, intention*
βραχύς -εῖα -ύ, *short, small; pl. few:* διὰ βραχέων, *in a few words, briefly*
βρόχος, ὁ, *noose, net*
βρῶμα, τό, *food*
βωμός, ὁ, *altar*

Γ
Γαδειρικός -ή -όν, *of Gadira (modern Cádiz)*
γάμος, ὁ, *wedding*
γάρ, *for*
γὰρ οὖν, *for indeed*
γε, *at least*
(γε μήν, *nevertheless*)
γεγενημένος -η -ον: γίγνομαι, pf. part. (pass. form)
γεγένησθε: γίγνομαι, 2 pl. pf. (pass. form)

γέγονα, γεγονέναι, γεγονώς -υῖα -ός: γίγνομαι, pf., pf. infin., pf. part. (act. form)
γεγραμμένος -η -ον: γράφω, pf. part. pass.
γέγραπται : γράφω, 3 s. pf. pass.
γέμω (+ gen.), *be full of*
γενεά, ἡ, *race, generation*
γενεαλογέω, *trace the lineage (or genealogy)*
γενεαλογηθείς -εῖσα -έν, aor. part. pass.
γενέσθαι: γίγνομαι, aor. infin. (mid. form)
γένεσις, ἡ, *origin, growth, generation, becoming*
γεννάομαι, *produce (as either parent)*
γεννάω, *produce (usually as male parent)*
γέννημα, τό, *child*
γένος, τό, *race, tribe, class, group, species*
γέρας, τό, *privilege*
γέρων, ὁ, *old man*
γέφυρα, ἡ, *bridge*
γεφυρόω, *put a bridge over*
γεώδης -ες, *with deep soil*
γεωργός ὁ, *farmer*
γῆ, ἡ, *earth*
γήλοφος, ὁ, *mound*
γίγνομαι (verb system includes active, middle and passive forms), *be born, come into being, become; take place, occur; be*
γιγνώσκω, *recognize, perceive; (past tenses) know*
γνώσοιτο, 3 s. fut. opt.: γιγνώσκω
γονεύς, ὁ, *father*

Vocabulary

γοῦν (= γε οὖν), *at least, at all events*

γράμματα, τά, *letters, alphabet; piece of writing*

γραφεύς, ὁ, *painter, visual artist*

γραφή, ἡ, *painting, drawing, visual art*

γράφομαι (mid.), *note down, write down for one's future use*

γράφω, *write*

γυμνάσιον, τό, *gymnasium, exercise area*

γυμναστική (adj., τέχνη understood), *athletics*

γυμνής, ὁ, *lightly armed foot soldier*

γυνή, ἡ, *woman*

Δ

δαιμόνιος -α -ον, *miraculous, marvellous*

δαιτυμών, ὁ, *guest*

δέ, *but*

(μέν ... δέ ..., *on the one hand ... on the other*)

δεδεγμένος -η -ον: δέχομαι, pf. part

δεδομένος -η -ον: δίδωμι, pf. part. pass.

δεδόσθω: δίδωμι, 3 s. pf. imp. pass.

δεῖ (impersonal verb), *need to, must*

δεῖπνον, τό, *meal*

δέκα, *ten*

δεκάκις, *ten times*

δεκέτης -ες, *ten years old*

δελφίς, ὁ, *dolphin*

δένδρον, τό, *tree*

δεξαμενή, ἡ, *pool, receptacle for water*

δεξιά, ἡ, *right hand*

δέομαι (mid. + gen. of person and/ or thing), *beg, ask, need*

δέον: δεῖ (part.), *necessary, right*

δεῦρο, *(place) here, to this place; (time) to this point, until now*

δεύτερος -α -ον, *second*

δέχομαι (mid.), *receive, accept*

δή, *indeed, in fact*

δῆλος -η -ον, *clear*

δηλόω, *show, disclose, reveal*

δηλώσω, aor. subj.

δημιουργία, ἡ, *craftsmanship, manufacture*

δημιουργός, ὁ, *craftsman*

διά (prep. + gen.: time, place, manner), *through, by means of (e.g. διά βραχέων, in a few words); at such-and-such intervals of time;* (prep. + acc.), *because of, on account of*

διαβαίνω, *go past, pass over*

διάβασις, ἡ, *passage*

διαγίγνομαι, *survive*

διαδίδωμι, *hand over, allocate:*

διαδοτέον, verbal adj.

διαθεσις, ἡ, *arrangement, order*

διαιρέομαι (mid.), *divide, separate (for oneself)*

διαιρέω, *divide, make a gap*

δίαιτα, ἡ, *way of life, daily life*

διακηκοώς -υῖα -ός: διακούω, pf. part.

διακοσμέω, *organise, order*

διακοσμήσις, ἡ, *ordering, organisation*

διακούω (+ gen.), *hear, learn from someone*

διακωλύω (+ infin.), *prevent (something from happening)*

διαλαγχάνω, *receive as one's lot, divide between them*
διαλαμβάνω, *distribute, divide*
διαμειδάω, *smile*
διαμελέω, *study thouroughly:* διαμεμελέτηται, 3 s. pf. pass.
διάμετρος, ἡ, *diameter*
διαμνημονεύω, *record, recall clearly*
διανέμω, *assign, allocate*
διανοέομαι, *think, suppose*
διάνοια, ἡ, *state of mind, purpose, intention*
διαπεραίνω, *bring to a conclusion*
διάπλοος, ὁ, *cross-channel*
διαπολεμέω (+ dat.), *carry through a war against, continue fighting with*
διαπονέω, *work, make (by working), mould*
διαπόνημα, το, *work, labour*
διαπορεία, ἡ, *journey*
διαπυνθάνομαι (mid.), *find out by questioning, enquire*
διαρκέω, *last, endure*
διασώζω, *preserve, save*
διαταμιεύω, *manage;* (mid.), *store*
διατάσσω, *appoint, assign*
διατίθεμαι (pass. + adverb), *be treated in such-and-such a way, be in such-and-such a state*
διατίθημι, *distribute*
διατρίβω (+ περί), *busy oneself with*
διαφανής -ές, *clear, conspicuous*
διαφερόντως, *exceptionally, distinctively*
διαφέρω (+ gen.), *be different from, be better than*
διαφεύγω, *escape one's notice or memory*

διαφθείρω, *destroy, kill*
διαφορά, ἡ, *distinction, excellence*
διαφυλάττω (+ infin.), *take care that (something should be)*
διδάσκω, *teach*
δίδυμος -η -ον, *twin*
δίδωμι, *give, assign*
διεγένοντο: διαγίγνομαι, 3 pl. aor.
διέθεμεν: διατίθημι, 1 pl. aor.
διειλόμεθα: διαιρέομαι, 1 pl. aor.
δίειμι, *narrate, describe*
διείργω, *separate, divide*
διεκεκόσμητο: διακοσμέω, 3 s. plpf. pass.
διέκπλοος, ὁ, *passage (for navigation)*
διεληλύθαμεν: διέρχομαι, 1 pl. pf.
διελθεῖν: διέρχομαι, aor. infin.
διελών -οῦσα -όν: διαιρέω, aor. part.
διενενέμηντο: διανέμω, 3 pl. plpf. pass.
διέξειμι, *recount, describe*
διέξοδος, ἡ, *course, development*
διεπεπόνητο: διαπονέω 3 s. plpf pass.
διερμήνευσις, ἡ, *negotiation*
διέρχομαι, *describe, recount, tell in detail*
διετέτακτο: διατάσσω, 3 s. plpf. pass.
διεφθάρη: διαφείρω, 3 s. aor. pass.
διηγεῖτο: διηγέομαι, 3 s. impf.
διηγέομαι, *describe, recount*
διήεισθα: δίειμι, 2 s. impf.
δικάζω (+ dat. of person), *pass judgement on*
δίκη, ἡ, *penalty, justice*
διό, *therefore*
διοικέω, *manage, govern, administer*
διόλλυμι, *destroy;* (pass.) *die*

Vocabulary

Διός = Ζεύς (gen.), *of Zeus, of the sky*
διπλόος -η -ον, *double*
δίς, *twice*
δισχιλίοι -αι -α, *two thousand*
διττός -ή -όν, *twin*
δίφρος, ὁ, *chariot*
διῳκηκώς -υῖα -ός: διοικέω, pf. part.
διῶρυξ, ἡ, *canal, ditch*
δοκεῖ (+ dat. of person), *it seems good to someone, someone approves or decides*
δοκέω, *seem*
δόξα, ἡ, *opinion, expectation*
δόξαν λαμβάνω, *form an opinion*
δοξάζομαι (pass. + infin.), *be thought to be*
δόξαντα, τά: δοκεῖ, neut. pl. aor. part; the *things that seemed best, the resolutions, decisions*
δόρυ, τό, *spear*
δορυφορικός, -ή -όν, *of the bodyguards*
δορύφορος, ὁ, *bodyguard*
δοτέον: δίδωμι, verbal adj.
δουλόω, *enslave;* (mid.), *enslave for oneself*
δουλωθῆναι, aor. infin. pass.
δούς, δοῦσα, δόν: δίδωμι, aor. part.
δρατέον: δράω, verbal adj.
δράω, *do*
δύναιντο: δύναμαι, 3 pl. opt.
δύναμαι, *be able*
δύναμις, ἡ, *power*
(κατὰ δύναμιν, *to the limits of one's power, as far as possible*)
δυναστεία, ἡ, *royal line, dynasty*
δυναστής, ὁ, *ruler*
δυνατός -ή -όν, *able*
δύο, *two*

δυσθησαύριστος -ον, *hard to store*
δύω, *sink*
δωρεά, ἡ, *gift, present*

E

ἑαυτόν -ήν -ό (+ other cases), *himself, herself, itself*
ἐγγύς (adv.), *near, nearly*
ἐγεννησάσθην: γεννάομαι, dual aor.
ἐγενόμην: γίγνομαι, aor. (mid. form)
ἔγκαυμα, τό, *mark burnt by 'encaustic' painting*
ἐγκωμιάζω, *praise, eulogize*
ἐγώ (ἐμοῦ, gen), *I, me*
ἔδαφος, τό, *pavement, floor*
ἐθελήσειε: ἐθέλω, 3 s. aor. opt.
ἐθέλω, *wish, be willing*
ἔθετο: τίθημι, 3 s. aor. mid.
ἔθνος, τό, *race, tribe, class*
ἐθρέψατο: τρέφομαι, 3 s. aor.
ἔθρεψε: τρέφω, 3 s. aor.
εἰ, *if*
εἰδέναι: οἶδα, infin.
εἶδος, τό, *appearance, form*
εἰδωλοποιία, ἡ, *creation of images, representation*
εἰδώς -υῖα -ός: οἶδα, part.
εἴη: εἰμί, 3 s. opt.
εἰκώς -υῖα -ός: ἔοικα, part., *like, similar;* (neut.) *likely, probable*
εἴληφα: λαμβάνω, pf.
εἰλήχατον: λαγχάνω, dual pf.
εἰληχώς -υῖα -ός: λαγχάνω, pf. part.
εἰμί, *be*
εἶμι, *come, go*
εἶναι: εἰμί, infin.
εἶπον: λέγω, aor.
εἰργασμένος -η -ον: ἐργάζομαι, pf. part. pass. of mid. verb

εἴρηκα: ἐρῶ, pf.

εἴρηται: ἐρῶ, 3 s. pf. pass.

εἴρω (pres. only occurs in Homer; fut. ἐρῶ), *say, speak*

εἰς (prep. + acc.: movement, time, purpose), *to, into, for, at, until, as far as, with respect to*

εἷς, μία, ἕν, *one*

εἰσάγω, *introduce, esp. bring into court*

εἰσηγέομαι, *introduce, propose*

εἰσηγήσατο, 3 s. aor.

εἰσπλέω, *sail in*

εἰσπλόος, ὁ, *entrance (for ships)*

εἴτε ... εἴτε (εἴτε ... ἤ), *either ... or, whether ... or*

εἰωθώς -υῖα -ός: ἔθω, pf. part., *accustomed, usual*

ἐκ, ἐξ (prep. + gen.), *from, because of*

ἑκασταχόσε, *at each end, in each direction*

ἑκασταχοῦ, *in each occasion*

ἕκαστος -η -ον, *each*

ἑκάστοτε, *on each occasion*

ἑκάτερος -η -ον, *each (of two); pl. each of two groups*

ἑκατόν, *hundred*

ἔκγονος, ὁ, *child, descendant*

ἐκεῖ, *there*

ἐκεῖνος -η -ον, *that, the former*

ἔκειτο: κεῖμαι, 3 s. impf.

ἐκέκτητο: κτάομαι, 3 s. plpf.

ἐκεχειρούργητο: χειρουργέω, 3 s. plpf. pass.

ἐκλέγομαι (mid.), *pick out for oneself, choose*

ἐκπλέω, *sail out*

ἔκπληξις, ἡ, *astonishment*

(εἰς ἔκπληξιν ἰδεῖν, *an object of astonishment to look at*)

ἐκπορίζομαι (mid.), *invent, provide*

ἐκρέω, *flow out*

ἕκτος -η -ον, *sixth*

ἐκτός (prep. + gen., adv.), *outside*

ἑκών -οῦσα -όν, *willing*

ἐλάττων -ον, *smaller, less*

ἐλαύνω, *drive*

ἔλαχεν: λαγχάνω, 3 s. aor.

ἐλέγχω, *test, criticize, reject*

ἑλεῖν: αἱρέω, aor. infin.

ἐλευθέριος -ον, *free-spirited, frank*

ἐλευθερόω, *set free*

ἐλεφάντινος -η -ον, *ivory*

ἐλεφάς, ὁ, *elephant*

ἐλέχθη: λέγω, 3 s. aor. pass.

ἐλήλυθα: ἔρχομαι, pf.

ἐλλείπω, *leave out, leave undone*

Ἑλληνιστί, *in the Greek language*

ἐλλόγιμος -ον, *famous*

ἔλοιεν: αἱρέω, 3 pl. aor. opt.

ἕλος, τό, *marsh, marsh-meadow*

ἐμβάλλω, *throw in*

ἐμεμνήμην: μιμνήσκομαι, plpf.

ἐμηνύθη: μηνύω, 3 s. aor. pass.

ἐμμελής -ές, *harmonious, in tune*

ἔμμονος -ον, *lasting, permenant*

ἔμπειρος -ον (+ gen.), *experienced in, skilful at*

ἐμπιμπλάμενος -η -ον (+ gen.), *filled with*

ἐμποδών (adv.), *in the way*

ἐμποιέω, *produce inside*

ἔμπορος, ὁ, *merchant*

ἔμπροσθεν (adv.), *before*

ἔμφρων -ον, *sensible, in one's right mind*

ἐν (prep. + dat.), *in; by means of*

Vocabulary

ἐνακισχίλιοι -αι -α, *nine thousand*

ἐναλλάξ, *alternatively*

ἐνάμιλλος -ον (+ πρός), *a match for, the equal of;* (+ dat.), *in respect of*

ἐναντίον, τό, *on the contrary*

ἐναντίος -α -ον, *opposite, contrary*

ἐναντίος, ὁ, *opponent, enemy*

ἔνδειγμα, τό, *evidence, token*

ἐνδείκνυμαι (mid.), *show, make plain:*

ἐνδειξάμενος -η -ον, aor. part.

ἔνδοθεν, *from inside (from inside the country); inside*

ἐνδύνω, *put on*

ἐνδύς -ῦσα -ύν, aor. part.

ἕνεκα (prep. + gen.), *for the sake of*

ἐνέλειπε: ἐλλείπω, 3 pl. impf.

ἐνενήκοντα, *ninety*

ἐνέστησαν: ἐνίστημι, 3 pl. aor.1 (trans.)

ἔνθα, *there*

ἔνθα μὲν ... ἔνθα δέ, *in one place, in another, in different places*

ἐνθάδε, *to this place*

ἔνθεν καὶ ἔνθεν, *on either side, on this side and on that*

ἐνιαυτός, ὁ, *year*

ἐνίστημι (trans. tenses), *place in*

ἐννοέω, *recognize*

ἔνοικος, ὁ, *inhabitant*

ἔντιμος -ον, *honoured*

ἐντός (prep. + gen., adv.), *inside*

ἐντραφῇ: ἐντρέφω, 3 s. aor. subj. pass.

ἐντρέφω, *bring up in*

ἐντυγχάνω, *meet with*

ἐξαιρέω, *set apart, reserve*

ἐξαίσιος -ον, *violent, extreme*

ἐξαρκέω, *be strong enough*

ἐξαρτύω, *equip*

ἐξετάζω, *examine closely, scrutinize*

ἐξῃρημένος -η -ον: ἐξαιρέω, pf. part. pass.

ἐξηρτυμένος -η -ον: ἐξαρτύω, pf. part. pass.

ἑξῆς, *in order, in series; next in series*

ἕξις, ἡ, *condition, type*

ἐξίτηλος -ον, *extinct, weakened*

ἔξω (adv.), *outside*

ἔξωθεν, *from outside, from abroad; outside*

ἐξωτάτω: ἔξω (superlative adv.), *outermost*

ἔοικα, *seem*

ἑορτή, ἡ, *festival*

ἐπάγω, *draw in*

ἐπάνειμι: ἐπανέρχομαι, *go back, repeat, recapitulate; ascend*

ἐπάνελθε: ἐπανέρχομαι, aor. imp.

ἐπανερωτάω, *ask again and again*

ἐπανιών -οῦσα -όν: ἐπάνειμι, part.

ἐπάνω (adv.), *above*

ἐπάρχω (+ gen.), *rule over*

ἐπαυξάνομαι (pass.), *grow up*

ἐπειδή, *when, since*

(ἐυθύς ... ἐπειδή, *as soon as*)

ἔπειμι, *approach, attack*

ἐπεμνήσθην: ἐπιμιμνῄσκομαι, aor.

ἐπέρχομαι, *come suddenly*

ἐπέταξα: ἐπιτάττω, aor.

ἐπεύχομαι (+dat.), *call down curses on*

ἐπί (prep. + gen.: place), *on, at; (time) at the time of;* (prep. +dat.: place) *on, upon;* (prep. + acc.: place) *on, towards, in the direction of, throughout, over; (hostile sense) against; (time) for, during*

ἐπιβάτης, ὁ, *chariot fighter, one who goes mounted*
ἐπιβατός, -ον, *accessible*
ἐπιεικής -ές, *good, noble*
ἐπιθεῖναι: ἐπιτίθημι, aor. infin.
ἐπιθυμία, ἡ, *desire*
(εἰς ἐπιθυμίαν ἔρχομαι/ἀφικνέομαι, *experience desire*)
ἐπικαλέω, *call by name* (mid.), *call in as a helper, call on*
ἐπίκλησις, ἡ, *designation, name*
ἐπίκουρος, ὁ, *mercenary soldier*
ἐπικρατέω, *become dominant*
ἐπιμείγνυμι (+ dat.), *mingle with*
ἐπιμέλεια, ἡ (+gen.), *attention to, practice* of
ἐπιμέλειαν ποιέομαι, *take care of, devote attention to*
ἐπιμιμνήσκομαι (mid.), *think of, mention*
ἐπιμνησθείς -εῖσα -έν, aor. part.
ἐπινοέω, *intend*
ἐπίπεδος -η -ον, *level*
ἐπίπροσθεν, *before, in front*
ἐπιρρέω, *flow on*
ἐπισκοπέω, *review, study*
ἐπιστήμη, ἡ, *knowledge*
ἐπιστήσας -ασα -αν: ἐφίστημι, aor. 1 (trans.) part.
ἐπιστολή, ἡ, *command*
ἐπίταξις, ἡ, *order, task imposed*
ἐπιτάττω (+ acc. of thing, dat. of person), *impose as a duty on someone, assign to someone*
ἐπιταχθείς -εῖσα -έν, pf. part. pass.
ἐπιτήδειος -α -ον, *suitable*
ἐπιτήδευμα, τό, *job, practice*
ἐπιτηδεύω, *practise, perform*
ἐπιτίθημι, *impose, inflict*

ἐπιχειρέω, *try, set about*:
ἐπιχειρήσειε, 3 s. aor. opt.
ἐπιχώριον, τό, *the custom, language of the country*
ἐπιχώριος -α -ον, *of the country*
ἐπιών -οῦσα -ον: ἔπειμι, part.
ἕπομαι (+ dat.), *follow, accompany, be dependent on*
ἐπόμνυμι, *swear*
ἐπονομάζω, *name*
ἔπος, τό, *word*
(ὡς ἔπος εἰπεῖν, *so to speak*)
ἐποχετεύω, *conduct (water by pipe)*
ἐπράχθη: πράττω, 3 s. aor. pass.
ἑπτά, *seven*
ἐπωνυμία, ἡ, *name, title, designation*
ἐργάζομαι (mid.), *make, do*
ἐργασία, ἡ, *workmanship*
ἔργον, τό, *work, job, action; pl., the works of war*
ἔργον (ἐστί + infin.), *there is a need of*
ἐρέψιμος -ον, *as roof timbers*
ἔρις, ἡ, *strife, dispute*
ἐρρήθη: ἐρῶ, 3 s. aor. pass.
ἐρυθρός -ά -όν, *red*
ἔρχεσθον: ἔρχομαι, *dual*
ἔρχομαι, *come, go*
ἐρῶ: εἴρω, fut; used as fut. of λέγω (past forms of ἐρῶ have no fut. significance and can be translated as equivalent forms of λέγω)
ἐσπουδάκει: σπουδάζω, 3 s. plpf.
ἕστασαν: ἵστημι, 3 pl. plpf. (intrans.)
ἔστησαν: ἵστημι, 3 s. aor. 1 (trans.)
ἔστησε: ἵστημι, 3 s. aor. 1 (trans.)

Vocabulary

ἑστίασις, ἡ, *feast, banquet*
ἑστιάτωρ, ὁ, *host, one who gives a feast*
ἔστω: εἰμί, 3 s. imp.
ἑστώς -υῖα -ός: ἵστημι, aor. 2 (intrans.) part.
ἔσχατος -η -ον, *furthest*
ἐτέθη: τίθημι, 3 s. aor. pass.
ἕτερος -α -ον, *other, another*
ἐτέτακτο: τάττω, 3 s. plpf. pass.
ἐτέτραπτο: τρέπω, 3 s. plpf. pass.
ἔτι, *still, yet, in addition*
ἑτοῖμος -ον, *ready, prepared*
ἔτος, τό, *year*
εὖ, *well*
εὔβοτος -ον, *rich in pasture*
εὐδαιμονία, ἡ, *happiness*
εὐδοκιμέω, *be popular, gain a good reputation*
εὐδόκιμος -ον, *famous*
εὐερκής -ές, *well-fortified, well-defended*
εὐθύς -εῖα -ύ, *straight*
εὐθύς (adv.), *at once, immediately* (εὐθύς ... ἐπειδή, *as soon as*)
εὔκαρπος -ον, *fertile*
εὐκρὰς -άς, *well-blended, of even temperature*
εὐκρασία, ἡ, *harmoniousness, temperateness*
εὐμαρῶς, *easily*
εὐμνημόνευτος -ον, *easy to remember*
εὐνομέομαι, *have good laws, be well-ordered*
εὔνομος -ον, *with good laws, well-ordered*
εὐπορέω (+gen.), *be well-provided with*

εὐπορία, ἡ, *capacity, opportunity*
εὑρίσκω, *find*
εὖρος, τό, *width*
εὔστροφος -ον, *manageable, easy to turn*
εὐφυής -ές, *naturally suited for a particular job*
εὔχομαι, *pray*
εὐψυχία, ἡ, *courage, brave spirit*
εὐώδης -ες, *aromatic, fragrant*
ἐφάπτομαι (+ gen.), *touch, handle, take hold of*
ἔφην: φημί, aor.
ἐφίστημι (trans. tenses), *place upon*
ἔχθρα, ἡ, *enmity*
ἐχθρός, ὁ, *enemy*
ἐχρήσω: χράομαι, 2 s. aor.
ἐχρῶντο: χράομαι, 3 pl. impf.
ἔχω, *have, hold; be*
ἐψυγμένος -η -ον: ψύχομαι, pf. part. pass.
ἔωθεν, *from dawn, early in the morning*

Z

ζάω, *live*
ζεύγω, *yoke*
ζητέω, *look for*
ζητητέον, verbal adj.
ζῷον, τό, *animal, living creature*

H

ἤ, *or*
ἦ (= ἔφη): φημί, 3 s. aor.
ἦ δ᾽ ὅς, *he said*
ᾖ: εἰμί, 3 s. subj.
ᾗ, *as*
ἡγεμών, ὁ, *leader*

ἡγέομαι, *lead; think:*
ἥγημαι, pf.
ἡδέως, *with pleasure*
ἤδη, *already, now*
ἥδομαι, *be pleased*
ἡδονή, ἡ, *pleasure*
ᾔειν: εἶμι, 3 s. impf.
ἦθος, τό, *character, disposition*
ἥκω, *to have come*
ἠλευθέρωσε: ἐλευθερόω, 3 s. aor.
ἡλικία, ἡ, *age, age group*
ἡμεῖς (ἡμῶν, gen.), *we, us*
ἠμέλουν: ἀμελέω, 3 pl. impf.
ἡμέρα, ἡ, *day*
(μεθ'ἡμέραν, *by day*)
ἥμερος -α -ον, *tame, cultivated*
ἡμέτερος -α -ον, *our*
ἥμισυς -εια -υ, *half*
ἠναγκάσθη: ἀναγκάζω, 3 s. aor.
 pass.
ἠνέγκατο: φέρω, 3 s. aor mid.
ἡνίοχος, ὁ, *charioteer*
ἤπειρος, ἡ, *continent, mainland*
Ἡράκλειος -α -ον, *of Heracles*
Ἠριδανός, ὁ, *Eridanus, a river in*
 Attica
ἤσαμεν: ἀείδω, 1 pl. aor.
ἥσθη: ἥδομαι, 3 s. aor.
ᾔσθησαι: αἰσθάνομαι, 2 s. pf.
ἡσυχία, ἡ, *rest, quiet*
ἡσυχίαν: ἄγειν, *be at rest, be*
 motionless
ἠσχημόνουν: ἀσχημονέω, 3 pl.
 impf.
ἠφανίσθη: ἀφανίζομαι, 3 s. aor.
ἠφανισμένος -η -ον: ἀφανίζομαι, pf.
 part.
ηὐξήθη: αὐξάνω, 3 s. aor. pass.
ηὗρε: εὑρίσκω, 3 s. aor.

Θ

θάλαττα, ἡ, *sea*
θαρρέω, *be confident, cheerful*
θάτερος -α -ον (= ἕτερος -α -ον)
 (ἐπὶ θάτερα, *in one direction, on*
 each side)
θαῦμα, τό, *surprise, source of surprise*
θαυμάζω, *wonder at, be surprised at;*
 (pass.), *be an object of surprise,*
 admiration
θαυμαστός -ή -ον, *surprising*
θεάομαι, *look at, view*
θέατρον, τό, *theatre, audience*
θεῖος -α -ον, *divine*
θεός, -ό, -ή, *god, goddess*
θερμός -ή -όν, *warm*
θέρος, τό, *summer*
θῆλυς -εια -υ, *female*
θηρευτής, ὁ, *hunter*
θηρεύω, *hunt*
θήσομεν: τίθημι, 1 pl. fut.
θνητός -ή -όν, *mortal*
θόρυβος, ὁ, *uproar, confusion*
θρέμμα, τό, *creature, nursling; pl.*
 livestock
θρεπτέον: τρέφω, *verbal adj.*
θρόμβος, ὁ, *clot of blood*
θῦμα, τό, *victim, sacrifice*
θυμοειδής, -ές, *spirited,*
 high-spirited
θυσία, ἡ, *sacrifice, festival, ritual*
θύω, *sacrifice*

Ι

ἰατρική (adj., τέχνη understood), *the*
 art of medicine
ἴδητον: ὁράω, dual aor. subj.
ἰδίᾳ, *privately, personally,*
 individually

ἴδιος -α -ον, *private, personal*
ἰδιώτης (as adj. + gen.), *inexpert in, layman in;* (as noun) *private individual*
ἰδιωτικός -ή -ον, *for private individuals*
ἴδωμεν: ὁράω, 1 pl. aor. subj.
ἱερά, τά, *offerings, sacrifices*
ἱερεύς, ὁ, *priest*
ἱερόν, τό, *temple, holy place*
ἱερός -ά -όν, *holy*
ἵζομαι, *sit down, settle*
ἱκανός -ή -όν, *adequate, sufficient*
Ἰλισός ὁ, *Ilissus, river in Attica*
ἵνα, conj. + subj. or opt., *that, in order that*
ἴοι: εἶμι, 3 s. opt
ἱππόδρομος, ὁ, *race-course (for horse-racing)*
ἴσμεν: οἶδα, 1 pl.
ἴσος -η -ον, *equal*
ἵστημι, (trans. tenses) *set up,* (intrans. tenses) *stand*

Κ

καθαγίζω, *dedicate, devote to a god (usually by burning)*
καθαίρω, *purify, purge*
καθάπερ, *just as*
καθειμένος -η -ον: καθίεμαι (pass.), pf. part.
καθεώρων: καθοράω,
καθίεμαι (pass.), *stretch down, come down*
καθίζω, *sit*
καθίστημι (trans. tenses), *bring, set in order*
καθίστημι εἰς, *bring into a certain state:*

καθίστημι εἰς πόλεμον, *engage in war*
καθοράω, *look down on, observe, perceive*
καί, *and, also, even*
καὶ μὲν δή, *and indeed*
καίτοι, *and yet*
κακός -ή -όν, *bad*
κακουργέω, *do harm, injure*
καλέω, *call on, summon*
κάλλος, τό, *beauty*
καλός -ή -όν, *beautiful, fine, noble*
κάμνω, *be weary, jaded*
καρπόομαι (mid.), *take the benefit of, reap the fruit of*
καρπός, ὁ, *fruit; crops, incl. grain*
κατά (prep. + gen.: motion), *down from, down into, down over; (place) below; (time) for, at;* (prep. + acc.: place), *over, throughout, in; (distributively)* e.g. κατὰ τόπους, *region by region;* καθ' ἐνιαυτόν, *year by year;* καθ' ἕκαστον, *in each case; (purpose) for; towards; (time) during, in the course of; (other meanings) in accordance with, in relation to*
καταβαίνω, *come down*
καταβάτης, ὁ, *foot soldier (one who dismounts)*
κατάβορρος -ον, *sheltered (from the northern winds)*
καταγηράω, *grow old*
καταγιγνώσκω (+ gen.), *condemn, pass judgement on*
κατάγω, *lead down, draw down*
καταδέχομαι (mid.), *receive, accept*
κατακλύζω, *deluge, inundate*

κατακλυσμός, ὁ, *flood*
κατακομίζομαι (mid.), *have something brought down*
καταλέλειπται: καταλείπω, 3 s. pf. pass.
καταλείπω, *leave, leave behind*
καταλύω, *destroy, overthrow; stay (as a guest)*
καταμελέω, *neglect, give no attention to*
κατανέμομαι (mid.), *divide among themselves*
κατανέμω (+ double acc.), *divide ... into*
κατανοέω, *observe, reflect*
κατανόησις, ἡ, *observation*
καταντικρύ (adv.), ἐκ τοῦ καταντικρύ (+ gen.) *opposite*
καταποθέν (adv.), *from any source above*
κατασκευάζω, *equip, establish, provide*
κατασκευασμένος -η -ον, pf. part. pass.
κατασκευή, ἡ, *equipment, fittings, construction*
καταστεγάζω, *roof over*
καταστήσας -ασα -αν: καθίστημι, aor. 1 (trans.) part.
καταφαίνομαι (pass.), *seem, appear, be obviously (something)*
καταχράομαι (mid.), *use, treat something (dat.) as something (dat.)*
κατέγνωκα: καταγιγνώσκω, perf.
κατενείμαντο: κατανέμομαι, 3 pl. aor.
κατεσκεύαστο: κατασκευάζω, 3 s. plpf. pass.

κατέστησε: καθίστημι, 3 s. aor. 1 (trans.)
κατευθύνομαι (mid.), *make something straight, have something made straight*
κατεχρήσατο: καταχράομαι, 3 s. aor.
κατήκοος -ον (+ gen.), *obedient to*
κατηρεφής -ές, *roofed over*
κατηύθυντο: κατευθύνομαι, 3 pl. impf.
κατιδών -οῦσα -όν: καθοράω, aor. part.
κατοικέω, *settle in, occupy, dwell*
κατοίκησις, ἡ, *home, dwelling*
κατοικίζω, *establish, set up a community*
κατοψόμεθα: καθοράω, 1 pl. fut.
καττίτερος, ὁ, *tin*
κάτωθεν (adv.), *from below; below; later*
κατῳκήκειν: κατοικέω, 3 s. plpf.
κατῴκισε: κατοικίζω, 3 s. aor.
κατῴκιστο: κατοικίζω, 3 s. plpf. pass.
καῦμα, τό, *burning heat; pl. embers*
κεῖμαι, *lie, be laid, be preserved*
κεκοσμημένος -η -ον: κοσμέω, pf. part. pass.
κεκραμένος -η -ον: κεράννυμι, pf. part. pass.
κεκτημένος -η -ον: κτάομαι, pf. part.
κεραμίς (adj.), *potter's*; κεραμὶς γῆ, *potter's earth: clay*
κεράννυμι, *mingle, harmonize, regulate:*
κεράσας -ᾶσα -άν, aor. part.
κεραυνόω, *strike with a thunderbolt*
κεραυνωθείς -εῖσα -έν, aor. part. pass.

Vocabulary

κεφάλαιον, τό, *main point, chief point*
κεφάλαιος -α -ον, *chief, principle*
κεχαρισμένος -η -ον: χαρίζομαι, pf. part.
κεχωρισμένος -η -ον: χωρίζω, pf. part. pass.
κῆπος, ὁ, *garden*
Κιθαιρών, ὁ, *Mt. Cithaeron (in Boeotia)*
κίνδυνος, ὁ , *danger*
κινέομαι (pass.), *move* (intrans.)
κίων, ἡ, *pillar, column*
κλῆρος, ὁ , *lot, allotment*
κληρουχέω, *obtain by lot*
κλητέον: καλέω, verbal adj.
κοῖλος -η -ον, *hollow*
κοινῇ (adv.), *in common, communally*
κοινός -ή -όν, *common, public*
κοινωνία, ἡ, *association*
κοινωνός, ὁ, *partner*
κολάζω, *punish*
κομίζω, *convey, transport*
κομισθείς -εῖσα -έν, aor. part. pass.
κόρη, ἡ, *girl, daughter*
κορυφή, ἡ, *apex, top, head*
κοσμέω, *organize, put in order; dress up, decorate*
κόσμησις, ἡ, *decoration, arrangement*
κόσμιος, -α -ον, *orderly, moderate*
κόσμος, ὁ, *order, universe*
κρατέω (+gen.), *rule over, conquer*
κρατήρ, ὁ, *mixing bowl*
κρήνη, ἡ, *stream, river, fountain*
κριτής, ὁ, *critic, judge*
κτάομαι, *obtain, master*
κτῆμα, τό, *possession, property*

κτήνη, τά, *pl. flocks*
κτησάμενος -η -ον: κτάομαι, aor. part.
κτύπος, ὁ, *din, shouting*
κυάνεος -εα -εον (contr. κυανοῦς -ῆ -οῦν), *dark blue*
κυβερνάω, *steer*
κυκλόομαι (pass.), *form a complete circuit*
κύκλος, ὁ, *circle*
κύκλῳ (adv.), *around, in a circle*
κύριος -α -ον (+ gen.), *having power, authority (to do something)*
κωλυτής, ὁ, *obstacle*
κώμη, ἡ, *village*

Λ
λαβών -οῦσα -όν: λαμβάνω, aor. part.
λαγχάνω, *take as one's lot*
λάθρᾳ, *secretly*
λαμβάνω, *take*
λαμπρῶς (adv.), *brilliantly, splendidly*
λανθάνω, *escape the notice of*
λέγω, *speak, say*
λειμών, ὁ, *meadow*
λεῖος -α -ον, *smooth*
λείπω, *leave, leave behind, abandon*
λειφθείς -εῖσα -έν, aor. part. pass.
λείψανον, τό, *remnant*
λελειμμένος -η -ον: λείπω, pf. part. pass.
λέλειπται: λείπω, 3 s. pf. pass.
λέληθε: λανθάνω, 3 s. pf.
λεπτός -ή -όν, *lean, thin*
λευκός -ή -όν, *white*
λεχθείς -εῖσα -έν: λέγω, sor. part. pass.

λῆξις, ἡ, *assigned area, allocation*
λίθινος -η -ον, *made of stone*
λιθόβολος, ὁ, *stone throw*
λίθος, ὁ, *stone*
λιμήν, ὁ, *harbour*
λίμνη, ἡ, *marsh*
λογισμός, ὁ, *reasoning*
λόγος, ὁ, *word, speech, statement, discussion, story, account*
λοιπόν, τό, *that which remains, esp. the time that remains, the future*
λοιπός -ή -όν, *left, remaining over, rest of*
λουτρόν, τό, *bath*
Λυκαβηττός, ὁ, *Mt. Lycabettus, in Athens*
λύω, *release, loose*

M
μάθημα, τό, *study, branch of knowledge*
μακάριος -α -ον, *blessed*
μακρός -ά -όν, *long*
μάλα (with adj.), *very*
(καὶ μάλα, *and indeed*)
μαλακός -ή -όν, *soft*
μάλιστα, *most, most of all; (with numeral) about*
(ὅτι μάλιστα, *as far as possible*)
μᾶλλον, *more*
μᾶλλον δέ, *or rather*
μαντική (adj., τέχνη understood), *the art of prophecy*
μαρμαρυγή, ἡ, *gleaming, flashing*
μαρτυρέω, *give witness, proof*
μάχη, ἡ, *battle*
μάχιμος -η -ον, *fighting, of warriors*
μέγας -άλη -α, *big, great*
μέγεθος, τό, *size, greatness*

μέγιστος -η -ον, *biggest, greatest*
μεθεῖτο: μεθίεμαι, 3 s. aor.
μεθίεμαι (mid.), *release oneself, free onself*
μεθύω, *be drunk*
μείγνυμι, *mix, combine*
μειζόνως, *to a greater extent*
μείζων -ον: μέγας, comp. adj., *greater, bigger*
μέλας -αινα -α, *black*
μελέω, *care for, give attention to*
μέλιττα, ἡ, *bee*
μελλητέον: μέλλω, verbal adj.
μέλλω, *be likely to, intend to; delay* (τί οὐ μέλλομεν; *why shouldn't we?*)
μέλος, τό, *limb; tune* (παρὰ μέλος, *out of tune*)
μέμνημαι: μιμνήσκομαι, pf., *remember*
μέν … δέ, *on the one hand, on the other* (τὰ μέν, τὰ δέ, *some things, others*)
μὲν οὖν, *indeed*
μέρος, τό, *share, portion, lot*
μέσον, τό, *middle point, mean* (εἰς τὸ μέσον, *in the open, publicly*)
μέσος -η -ον, *middle*
μεστός -ή -όν, *full*
μετά (prep. + gen.), *with; (prep. + dat.), with, accompanying; (prep. + acc.), after*
μεταδιώκω, *pursue, aim at*
μεταδόρπια, τά, *dessert*
μετακεχείρισται: μεταχειρίζομαι, 3 s. pf.
μεταλαμβάνω, *take in place of, instead; (+ gen.) have a share in, participate in*

μεταλλάττω, change, put forward in
    exchange
μεταλλεία, ἡ, mining
μεταφέρω, transfer, translate
μεταχειρίζομαι, handle, occupy,
    practise
μετείληφε: μεταλαμβάνω, 3 s. pf.
μετενεγκών -οῦσα -όν: μεταφέρω,
    aor. part.
μετενενηνοχώς -υῖα -ός: μεταφέρω,
    pf. part.
μετέχω (+ gen.), participate in, share
    in
μέτριος -α -ον, moderate, reasonable
μέχρι (prep. + gen., adv.), as far as,
    down to, until
μέχριπερ, so long as
μέχρι πρός, right up to
μή, not
μή οὐ (double negative), not
μηδείς -εμία -έν, nobody, nothing
μηκέτι, no longer
μῆκος, τό, length
μήν, truly, certainly
μηνύω, reveal
μήποτε, μή ... ποτε, never
μήτε ... μήτε, neither, nor
μητρόπολις, ἡ, mother city, capital
    city
μητρῷος -α -ον, of the mother
μηχανάομαι (mid.), arrange, devise
μίκρασπις, with a small shield
μιμέομαι (mid.), imitate, represent
μίμησις, ἡ, imitation, representation
μιμητικός -ή -όν, of imitators,
    imitative
μιμνήσκομαι (mid. and pass.),
    remind oneself of, recall,
    remember, mention

μνημεῖον, τό, remembrance,
    memorable quality
μνήμη, ἡ, memory
μνησθείς -εῖσα -έν: μιμνήσκομαι,
    aor. part.
μοῖρα, ἡ, portion, share
μονογενής -ές, only (child)
μόνον, only, solely
μόνος -η -ον, alone
μονόω, isolate:
μονωθείς -εῖσα -έν, aor. part. pass.
μόριον, τό, part
μουσική (adj., τέχνη understood),
    culture (music, literature, etc.)
μυθολογέω, tell stories
μῦθος, ὁ, story, traditional tale, myth
μυριάς, ἡ, unit of ten thousand
μυρίοι -αι -α, ten thousand
μυρίος -α -ον, numberless, infinite

N
ναί, yes
νᾶμα, τό, spring, stream
ναῦς, ἡ, ship
ναύτης, ὁ, sailor
νέμω (of shepherds), drive to pasture
νέμομαι (mid., of animals), feed,
    graze
νέος -α -ον, young, new
νεώριον, τό, dockyard
νεώς, ὁ (= ναός, ὁ), temple
νεωσοίκος, ὁ, dockyard, shipyard
Νηρηΐς, ἡ, Nereid, daughter of
    Nereus, sea-nymph
νῆσος, ἡ, island
νήφω, be sober
νομεύς, ὁ, herdsman
νομή, ἡ, foodstuff (for animals)
νομίζω, consider, regard:

νομιοῦσιν, 3 pl. fut.
νόμος, ὁ, *region; law, custom*
νόος, ὁ, *mind*
νοσέω, *be sick*
νόσημα, το, *sickness, plague*
νότος, ὁ, *south*
νύκτωρ, *by night*
νῦν, *now*
νυνδή, *just now*
νύξ, ἡ, *night*

Ξ

ξένια, τά, *friendly gifts, feast,*
   hospitality
ξενίζω, *entertain (as a host)*
ξενών, ὁ, *guest room, guest quarters*
ξηρός -ά -όν, *dry*
ξύλινος -η -ον, *of the woods,*
   wooden
ξύλον, τό, *wood, wooden club*

Ο

ὁ, ἡ, τό, *the*
ὄγκος, ὁ, *bulk, mass*
ὅδε, ἥδε, τόδε, *this; the following*
ὁδός, ἡ, *road, way*
ὅθεν, *from where, from which source*
οἵ, *where, in which direction*
οἴαξ, ὁ, *rudder*
οἶδα, *know*
οἰκεῖος -α -ον, *one's own, related,*
   suitable
οἰκειότης, ἡ, *relationship,*
   connection
οἰκέω (intrans.), *live, dwell,* (trans.)
   inhabit
οἴκησις, ἡ, *household, home;*
   (military) quarters
οἰκία, ἡ, *house, household*

οἰκοδομέομαι (mid.), *have a house*
   built
οἰκοδόμημα, τό, *building*
οἰκοδόμησις, ἡ, *building*
οἷον, *as, as if, just like, as it were*
οἷόνπερ, *just as though, as it were*
οἷος -α -ον, *such as, of what sort*
οἴσειν: φέρω, fut. infin.
οἴσοι: φέρω, 3 s. fut. opt.
ὀκτακισχιλίοι -αι -α, *eight*
   thousand
ὅλος -η -ον, *whole*
ὀλίγος -η -ον, *little; pl. few*
ὁμαλός -ή -όν, *level*
ὁμογενής -ές, *of the same family*
ὁμοῖος -α -ον, *same, similar*
ὁμοιότης, ἡ, *resemblance, likeness*
ὁμολογία, ἡ, *agreement*
ὅμως, *yet, however*
ὄνομα, τό, *name*
ὀνομάζω, *name*
ὀνομαστός -ή -όν, *notable, famous*
ὄντως, *really, in a real sense*
ὀξέως, *sharply, keenly, quickly*
ὀξύς -εῖα -ύ, *sharp, keen, quick*
ὅπλα, τά, *arms*
ὅπλα φέρειν, *bear arms, make war*
ὁπλίζω, *arm, equip*
ὁπλίτης, ὁ, *hoplite; fully armed*
   soldier
ὁπόσος -η -ον, *as much as (pl., as*
   many as), however much (pl.
   many)
ὁπόταν (+ subj.), *whenever*
ὅπου, *where*
ὅπως (+ subj. or opt.), *that, in order*
   that
ὁράω, *see*
ὀρεῖος -α -ον, *in the mountains*

Vocabulary

ὀρειχάλκινος -η -ον, *of orichalch*
ὀρείχαλκος, ὁ, *orichalch (unknown metal; usually the word means brass or copper in Greek)*
ὀρθός -ή -όν, *right, straight*
ὄρκός, ὁ, *oath*
ὀρκωμόσια, τά, *sacrifices made on taking oath*
ὁρμάομαι, *start a movement, come; rush, move eagerly, launch an invasion*
ὁρμή, ἡ, *assault, rapid movement*
ὄρος, τό, *mountain*
ὄρος, ὁ, *boundary, pillar to mark boundaries*
ὀροφή, ἡ, *roof, ceiling*
ὀρύττω, *dig, quarry*
ὀρώρυκτο, *3 s. plpf. pass.*
ὅς, ἥ, ὅ, *who, which; he, she, it*
ὅσος -η -ον, *as much as, how much; pl., as many as, how many (sometimes used as equivalent to ὅς, ἥ, ὅ)*
ὅσοσπερ -ηπερ -ονπερ, ὅσος -η -ον in emphatic form
ὅσπερ, ἥπερ, ὅπερ, *the very ... who, which*
ὄσπρια, τά, *pulse (type of vegetable, incl. beans, peas, lentils)*
ὀστέον, τό, *bone*
ὅταν, *whenever*
ὅτε, *when*
ὅτι, *that; because*
οὐ, *not*
οὐδαμῇ, *nowhere, not in any place*
οὐδαμόσε, *for no purpose*
οὐδαμῶς, *not at all*
οὐδέ, *and not, but not*
οὐδείς -εμία -έν, *nobody, nothing*

οὐδέν (adv.), *not at all*
οὐκοῦν (in questions inviting assent), *surely, then?*
οὔκουν, *certainly not; surely ... not*
οὔπω, *not yet, not at all*
οὐράνιος -α -ον, *heavenly, from the heavens*
οὐρανός, ὁ, *heaven, the heavens*
οὐσία, ἡ, *substance, property*
οὖσι: εἰμί, *dat. pl. part.*
οὔτι, *not at all*
οὗτος, αὕτη, τοῦτο, *this*
οὕτω(ς), *thus, so, in this way*
ὀχετός, ὁ, *pipe*

Π

πάγκαλος -η -ον, *very beautiful, splendid*
πάθος, τό, *experience, event*
παιδεία, ἡ, *education*
παίδευσις, ἡ, *education*
παίδευμα, τό, *pupil*
παιδεύω, *educate*
παιδία, ἡ, *amusement*
παιδοποιία, ἡ, *procreation of children*
παῖς, ὁ, ἡ, *child*
πάλαι (adv.), *of old, in former times*
παλαιός -ή -όν, *old, ancient*
(ἐκ παλαιοῦ, *from ancient times*)
πάλιν (adv.), *back again*
πάμμεγας -μεγάλη -μεγα, *very great, all important*
παμπληθής -ές, *in great number*
πάμπολυς -πόλλη -πολυ, *very great, very numerous*
πάμφορος -ον, *productive of all kinds*
πανήγυρις, ἡ, *festival*

παντάπασι (μὲν οὖν), *absolutely, entirely, exactly so*
πανταχῇ, *at every point, everywhere*
παντελῶς, *completely*
πάντῃ, *on every side, altogether*
παντοδαπός -ή -όν, *of all sorts, of every kind*
πάντοθεν, *from all places*
παντοῖος -α -ον, *of all sorts*
πάντως, *in every way*
πάνυ, *very*
πάνυ μὲν οὖν, *absolutely, certainly*
πάππας, ὁ, *father (one's own)*
πάππος, ὁ, *grandfather*
παρά (prep. + gen.), *from, issuing from;* (prep. + dat.), *beside, at, amongst, with, in the presence of, in the possession of;* (prep. + acc.), *beside, near, at the house of; beyond, in violation of, in transgression of, e.g.* παρὰ μέλος, *out of tune*
παραβαίνω, *commit an offence, do wrong, contravene:*
παραβεβηκώς -υῖα -ός, pf. part.
παραγγέλλω, *instruct, recommend*
παράδειγμα, τό, *sample, counterpart, parallel*
παραδέχομαι (mid.), *accept, receive from another*
παραδίδωμι, *hand over, transmit; hand down, lay down*
παραθαρρύνω, *encourage*
παραιτέομαι (mid.), *beg for, ask for a favour*
παραίτησις, ἡ, *request*
παραλαμβάνω, *take over, receive from another*

παραλειπόμενος -η -ον: παραλείπω, part. pass.
παραλείπω, *leave out, omit, neglect*
παράλλαξις, ἡ, *deviation, change*
παραμένω, *endure, last*
παραμυθέομαι, *urge*
παραμύθιον, τό, *encouragement; consolation, means of soothing*
παραπλήσιος -α -ον (+ dat.), *closely resembling, nearly equal to*
παρασχεῖν: παρέχω, aor. infin.
παράσχοι: παρέχω, 3 s. aor. opt.
παραχρῆμα/ ἐκ τοῦ παραχρῆμα, *on the spot, off the cuff, without preparation*
πάρειμι, *be present*
πάρεργος -ον, *subordinate, secondary, merely accessory*
παρέσχετο: παρέχομαι, 3 s. aor.
παρέχω/παρέχομαι (mid.), *supply, create*
Πάρνης, ἡ (Πάρνηθος, gen.), *Mt. Parnes*
παρών -οῦσα -όν: πάρειμι, part.
πᾶς, πᾶσα, πᾶν, *all, whole*
πάσχω, *suffer, experience, feel*
πατήρ, ὁ, *father*
παύω, *put a stop to, check; make an end of, annihilate*
πεδίον, τό, *plain*
πείθομαι (mid./pass.), *be persuaded by, obey* (+ dat.)
πείθω, *persuade*
πειθώ, ἡ, *persuasion*
πειράομαι (mid.), *try:*
πειρατέον, verbal adj.
πείσεσθαι: πείθομαι, fut. infin.
πειστέον: πείθω/πείθομαι, verbal adj.
πέλαγος, τό, *sea, ocean*

Vocabulary

πέμπτος -η -ον, *fifth*
πέντε, *five*
πεντήκοντα, *fifty*
πεπαιδευμένος -η -ον: παιδεύω, pf.
    part. pass.
πεπονθώς -υῖα -ός: πάσχω, pf. part.
πέρα (prep. + gen., adv.) *beyond*
περί (prep. + gen.), *around, about,*
    concerning; (prep. + dat.),
    around, about; (prep. + acc.),
    around, about
περιαλείφω, *overlay*
περιβάλλω, *surround, enclose*
περιβολός, ὁ, *enclosing wall*
περιγενόμενος -η -ον: περιγίγνομαι,
    aor. part.
περιγίγνομαι, *survive*
περίδρομος, ὁ, *circuit, edge*
περιειληφώς - υῖα -ός: περιλαμβάνω,
    pf. part.
περιερρυηκώς - υῖα -ός: περιρρέω,
    pf. part
περιέχω, *enclose, contain, surround*
περιήλειψαν: περιαλείφω, 3 pl. aor.
περιθέω, *run around*
περιίστημι (trans. tenses), *place*
    around
περικαθαίρω, *cleanse or purify*
    completely
περιλαμβάνω, *enclose, contain*
περιλείπομαι (pass.), *be left over,*
    remain, survive
περιλειφθείς -εῖσα -έν, aor. part.
περίοικος, ὁ, *inhabitant*
περιορύττω, *dig around*
περιορυχθείς -εῖσα -έν, aor. part.
    pass.
περιρρέω, *flood around, roll round;*
    (land) be eroded

περιρρήγνυμι, *break off all around,*
    isolate from surrounding area
περιστήσας -ᾶσα -αν: περιίστημι,
    aor. 1 (trans.) part.
περιτήκω, *wash away; cover with a*
    molten layer
περιτιθείς -εῖσα -έν: περιτίθημι, part.
περιτίθημι, *place around*
περιττός -ή -όν, *odd*
πέτρα, ἡ, *rock*
πεύσομαι: πυνθάνομαι, fut.
πέφυκα: φύω, pf., *be by nature such*
    and such; (+ infin.), *have by*
    nature the property of
πῇ, *how? in what way?*
πη, *somehow, in any way*
πη μάλιστα, *somewhere about,*
    approximately
πηγή, ἡ, *source, fount, spring*
πηγαῖος -α -ον, *from a spring*
πηλός, ὁ, *mud*
πίειρα (fem of πίων -ον), *rich, fat*
    (esp. of land)
πιθανός -ή -όν, *reliable, trustworthy*
πίναξ, ὁ, *tablet, writing-tablet*
πίνω, *drink*
πιστευτέον: πιστεύω, verbal adj.
πιστεύω (+ dat.), *trust, believe*
πίστις, ἡ, *pledge*
πιστός -ή -όν, *reliable, trustworthy,*
    credible
πιών -οῦσα -όν: πίνω, aor. part.
πλάγια, τά, *the sides (i.e. slopes, of*
    the Acropolis)
πλάγιος -α -ον, *sideways, at right*
    angles
πλανητός -ή -όν, *wandering*
πλασθείς -εῖσα -έν; πλάσσω, aor.
    part. pass.

πλάσσω, *make up, invent, fabricate*
πλάτος, τό, *width*
πλεθριαῖος -α -ον, *of a plethron (one*
  plethron = 100 feet in length)
πλεῖστος -η -ον, *greatest, most*
πλείων/πλέων -ον, *more*
πλεονεξία, ἡ, *greed*
πλέω, *sail*
πληγή, ἡ, *blow, stroke*
πλῆθος, τό, *number, amount; great*
  number, mass
πλημμελέω, *be out of tune*
πλήν (prep. + gen., conj.), *except*
πλήρωμα, τό, *total complement*
πλησίος -α -ον, *near*
πλησμονή, ἡ, *fullness, repletion*
πλοῖον, τό, *ship*
πλούσιος -α -ον, (+ gen.) *rich in*
πλοῦτος, ὁ, *wealth*
Πνύξ, ἡ (Πυκνός, gen.), *the Pnyx,*
  site of assemblies of the Athenian
  people
πόθεν, *from what source?*
ποθέω, *desire, miss*
ποιέομαι (mid.), *have something*
  made for oneself
ποιέω, *make, do*
ποίημα, τό, *poem*
ποίησις, ἡ, *poetry*
ποιητικός -ή -όν, *of poets, poetic*
ποιητής, ὁ, *poet, creative writer*
ποικίλλω, *decorate, ornament*
ποικίλος -η -ον, *varied, diversified*
ποιμήν, ὁ, *shepherd*
ποίμνιον, τό, *flock (esp. of sheep)*
ποῖος -α -ον, *what sort of?*
πολεμέω, *fight a war*
πολεμιστήριος -α -ον, *of war; neut.*
  pl., war equipment

πόλεμος, ὁ, *war*
πολιός -α -ον, *grey-haired,*
  venerable
πόλις, ἡ, *city, city state*
πολιτεία, ἡ, *state, constitution; pl.*
  political institutions
πολίτης, ὁ, *citizen*
πολιτικός -ή -όν, *political,*
  statesmanlike
πολλάκις, *often*
πολλαχοῦ, *in many places*
πολυβόρος -ον, *voracious*
πολύς, πολλή, πολύ, *much, great; pl.*
  many
πόντος, ὁ, *sea*
πορεύομαι, *travel, come*
πορεύσιμος -ον, *navigable, passable*
ποταμός, ὁ, *river*
πότε, *when?*
ποτε, *at some time, at any time, ever*
ποῦ, *where?*
που, *somewhere, anywhere; perhaps,*
  I suppose
πούς, ὁ, *foot*
πρᾶξις, ἡ, *action, achievement*
πραότης, ἡ, *mildness, gentleness*
πράττω, *do, act:*
πραχθείς -εῖσα -έν, aor. part. pass.
πράως, *gently, humanely*
πρέπει (+ dat. and/or infin.), *it is*
  fitting, appropriate (for someone,
  to do something)
πρεπόντως, *in a fitting, appropriate*
  way
πρέπων -ουσα -ον (part. as adj.),
  fitting, suitable
πρεσβύτατος -η -ον, *eldest, oldest*
πρεσβύτης, ὁ, *old man*
πρίν (adj., conj.), *before*

Vocabulary

πρό (prep. + gen.), *before, in front of; on behalf of*

προαγαγεῖν: προάγω, aor. 2 (προήγαγον), infin.

προάγω, *lead on, induce*

πρόγονος, ὁ, *ancestor, parent*

πρόειμι, *go forward, advance*

προθυμία, ἡ, *enthusiasm*

πρόθυμος -ον, *eager, enthusiastic*

προθύμως, *eagerly, enthusiastically*

προΐστημι (intrans. tenses + gen.), *be outstanding among, be the leader of;* (+ dat., *in some respect, because of something*)

προλέγω, *say in advance*

προμήκης -ες, *oblong, rectangular*

προπάππος, ὁ, *great-grandfather*

προπολεμέω (+ gen.), *make war on behalf of, be defender, guardian of*

πρός (prep. + gen.), *(position), on the side of, towards; (source), from, at the hand of;* (prep. + dat.), *near, close to; in addition to, in comparison with; (movement), towards;* (prep. + acc.: movement), *to, towards, against; (position), close to; (purpose), to, for, with a view to; (other meanings), in relation to, with reference to*

προσάγω, *lead to*

πρόσβορρος -ον, *facing the north*

πρόσειμι (εἰμί), *be present in addition, be also available;* (εἶμι), *approach, come, be brought*

προσέοικα (+ dat.), *resemble, be like*

προσετάχθη: προστάττω, 3 s. aor. pass.

προσεύχομαι (+ dat.), *pray to*

προσεχρῶντο: προσχράομαι, 3 pl. impf.

προσῄειν: πρόσειμι, 3 s. impf.

προσήκει (+ dat. of person), *it is fitting, appropriate for*

προσήκων -ουσα -ον (part. as adj.), *fitting, appropriate*

πρόσθεν (prep. + gen., adv.), *before*

προσοικέω (dat.), *live beside*

προσομιλέω (dat.), *converse with, negotiate with*

προσπεριβάλλομαι (mid.), *put round oneself in addition*

προσπεριβεβλημένος -η -ον, perf. part.

προστάς -ᾶσα -άν: προΐστημι, aor. 2 (intrans.) part.

προστάττω, *command, impose a duty*

προστυγχάνω, *(person) meet; (thing) come to hand*

προστυχών -οῦσα -όν, aor. part.

προσφερής -ές, *similar, like*

πρόσφορος -ον (+ dat.), *suitable for*

προσχράομαι (mid., + dat.), *use, apply in addition*

προτείνω, *project, stretch forward*

πρότερον (neut. adj. as adv.), *before, formerly*

πρότερος -α -ον, *before, former, earlier in time*

προτιμέω (+ gen.), *prefer one person to* another; (+ infin.), *prefer to do something*

προτιμητέον, verbal adj.

πρόφασις, ἡ, *ground, reason, excuse*

προχόω, *pile up, deposit*

πρύμνη, ἡ, *stern (steering position in ancient ship)*

πρῶτα, πρῶτον (neut. pl. and s. adj. as adv.), *firstly, at first*
πρῶτος -η -ον, *first*
πυκνός -ή -όν, *closely packed*
πύλη, ἡ, *gate*
πυνθάνομαι (mid.), *learn, discover*
πῦρ, τό, *fire*
πύργος, ὁ, *guard house*
πυρώδης -ες, *fiery*
πῶμα, τό, *drink*
πῶς, *how?*
πως, *in any way, somehow*

Ρ
ῥᾴδιος -α -ον, *easy*
ῥᾷον (adv.), *easier, more easily*
ῥᾷστα, *most easily*
ῥᾳστώνη, ἡ, *ease, facility*
ῥαψῳδία, ἡ, *public recitation*
ῥεῦμα, τό, *stream, flow of water*
ῥέω, *flow, run*
The following parts of ἐρῶ (*I will say*) should be translated as if they were the equivalent parts of λέγω (*I say*):
ῥηθείς -εῖσα -έν, aor. part. pass.;
ῥηθήσεσθαι, fut. infin. pass.;
ῥηθησόμενος -η -ον, fut. part. pass.;
ῥητέον, verbal adj.
ῥίζα, ἡ, *root*
ῥώμη, ἡ, *strengthen, vigour*

Σ
σαφής -ές, *clear*
σεισμός, ὁ, *earthquake*
σεσωσμένος -η -ον: σῴζω, pf. part. pass.
σέσωται: σῴζω, 3 s. pf. pass.

σημεῖον, τό, *sign, token*
σίδηρος, ὁ, *iron*
σῖτος, ὁ, *food*
σκέπτομαι (mid.), *examine, consider*
σκεῦος, τό, *implement*
σκεψάμενος -η -ον: σκέπτομαι, aor. part.
σκιαγραφία, ἡ, *outline, drawing (in black and white)*
σκοπέω, *observe, consider, think about*
σκοπός, ὁ, *aim, purpose*
(ἀπὸ σκοποῦ, *purposely, on target*)
σκοτεινός -ή -όν, *dark, obscure, hazy*
σκότος, ὁ τό, *darkness*
σμικρός -ά -όν, *small*
σμικρῶς (adv.), *to a small extent, a little*
σός, σή, σόν, *your* (s.)
σοφιστής, ὁ, *sophist, itinerant teacher or intellectual*
σοφός -ή -όν, *wise*
σπένδω, *pour libations (i.e. drink offerings to a god)*
σπέρμα, τό, *seed*
σπουδάζω, *take seriously*
σπουδή, ἡ (+ gen.), *attention to, seriousness about*
στάδιον, τό, *stade, (unit of length, about 200 yards)*
στακτός -ή -όν (+ gen.), *oozing out from, exuded by*
στάσις, ἡ, *political strife*
στέγασμα, τό, *roof*
στέγω, *keep out (water)*
στέγων -ουσα -ον, part., *non-porous*
στενός -ή -όν, *narrow*
στερεός -ά -όν, *solid*

Vocabulary

στερέω (+ acc. of person, gen. of thing), *deprive of*
στερηθῶμεν, 1 pl. aor. subj. pass.
στήλη, ἡ, *pillar, column, monument for inscriptions*
στολή, ἡ, *robe, garment*
στόμα, τό, *mouth; (in sea), strait*
στρατόπεδον, τό, *army*
σύ (σοῦ gen.), *you (s.)*
συγγενής, *relative*
συγγενής -ές, *natural, innate, related*
συγγιγνώσκω, *pardon, excuse*
συγγνώμη, ἡ, *pardon, excuse; indulgence; understanding (i.e. sympathy)*
συγκαίω, *burn up, set ablaze*
συγκλείω, *enclose, complete a circuit*
συλλαγχάνω (+ dat.), *to be joined by lot with*
συλλέγομαι (mid.), *come together*
σύλληξις, ἡ, *association by lot*
συλλήξομαι: συλλαγχάνω, fut.
συμβαίνω, *happen, fall out; (+ infin.), turn out to, result in* (τὰς ἀεὶ συμβαινούας τύχας, *their current fortunes, i.e. their fortunes as they fell out at any time*)
συμμείγνυμαι (mid. + dat.), *make love to*
σύμμετρος -ον, *in proportion*
σύμπας -πασα -παν, *all together; (with noun) the whole of*
συμπίπτω (+ dat.), *happen to*
συμφέρομαι (pass.), *agree with, correspond with*
σύμφυτος -ον, *inherited, innate, natural*

συν (prep. + dat.), *with, together with*
συναγείρας -ασα -αν: συναγείρω, aor. part.
συναγείρω, *summon, call together*
συναθροίζω, *gather together*
συναθροισθείς -εῖσα -έν: συναθροίζω, aor. part. pass.
συναπόλλυμαι (mid.), *perish together*
συναρμόζω, *fit together, harmonise*
συναρμοστέον: συναρμόζω, *verbal adj.*
συνδιαιτάομαι, *keep house together, live together*
συνδοκεῖ (+ dat.), *it seems good to someone else, is approved by someone else*
συνδοκιμάζω, *examine, judge, together with others*
συνέβη: συμβαίνω, 3 s. aor.
συνέκαυσε: συγκαίω, 3 s. aor.
συνέκλειεν: συγκλείω, 3 s. impf.
συνέπεσε: συμπίπτω, 3 s. aor.
συνεπίσπεσθε: συνεφέπομαι (aor. συνέφεσπόμην), 2 pl. aor. imp.
συνέπομαι, (+ dat.) *correspond to*
σύνερξις, ἡ, *junction, forcing together*
σύνερξις τῶν γάμων, *contraction of marriages*
συνέστη: συνίστημι, 3 s. aor. 2 (intrans.)
συνετέτρητο: συντετραίνω, 3 s. plpf. pass.
συνέτρησαν: συντετραίνω, 3 pl. aor.
συνεφέπομαι (mid.), *follow together*
συνηθές, τό, *custom*
συνηθής -ές, *accustomed, usual*
συνηνέχθης: συμφέρομαι, 2 s. aor.

συνίστημι, (intrans. tenses) *come
    into existence, be formed,
    establish itself*
σύννομος -ον, *gregarious, living in
    herds*
συνοικέομαι, (pass.) *be densely
    populated*
συνοικέω, *live with*
σύνοικος -ον, *familiar, closely linked*
συνομολογέω, *agree with*
συνουσία, ἡ, *meeting, party*
σύνταξις, ἡ, *arrangement*
συντάττω, *draw up, marshal*
συντετραίνω, *dig a channel*
συντόμως, *briefly, concisely*
συνῳκεῖτο: συνοικέομαι, 3 . impf.
συνωρίς, ἡ, *pair of horses*
συσσίτιον, τό, *mess hall. common
    dining hall*
σφάλλομαι (pass.), *trip up, reel,
    stagger*
σφαττω (= σφάζω), *cut a throat,
    make a sacrafice*
σφεῖς (σφῶν, gen.), *they*
σφενδονήτης, ὁ, *slinger, one who
    shoots with a sling*
σφόδρα, *very (with adj. or adv.);
    sheer (with noun); very much,
    very well (with verb)*
σχεδόν (adv.), *almost, near, rather*
σχεῖν: ἔχω, aor. 2 (ἔσχον)
σχέσις, ἡ, *style*
σχῆμα, τό, *form, appearance*
σχίζω, *divide, split*
σχολή, ἡ, *leisure, ease*
σχολὴν ἄγω, *be at leisure*
σῴζω, *protect, keep safe*
σῶμα, τό, *body*
σῶς, σῶν, *safe, surviving*

σωτήρ, ὁ, *saviour, preserve*
σωτηρία, ἡ, *preservation, deliverance*
σωφονίζω, *discipline, make someone
    self-controlled*
σωφρονισθείς -εῖσα -έν, aor. pass.
    part.
σώφρων -ον, *moderate,
    self-controlled*

T

τάξις, ἡ, *order, arrangement*
τἀπιταχθέντα = τὰ ἐπιταχθέντα
τάττω, *order, lay down; appoint,
    station*
ταῦρος, ὁ, *bull*
ταυτῇ, *in this way*
τάφρος, ὁ, *ditch*
τάχα, *soon, presently; perhaps*
ταχύ, *quickly*
τε (following word referred to), *and*
τε … καί, *both… and*
τεθράφθαι: τρέφω, pf. infin. pass.
τεῖχος, τό, *wall*
τεκμαίρομαι (+ ὅτι), *to draw an
    inference from the fact that*
τεκμήριον, τό, *proof*
τέκτων, ὁ, *carpenter*
τέλεος -α -ον, *perfect, complete*
τελευτάω, *come to an end, die, finish*
(τελευτάω εἰς, *come to an end at*)
τέμνω, *cut, cut down, dig*
τεταγμένος -η -ον: τάττω, pf. part.
τέταρτος -η -ον, *fourth*
τετμημένος -η -ον: τέμνω, pf. part.
    pass.
τετράγωνος -ον, *quadrilateral, with
    four sides (or angles)*
τῇδε, *in this place, here*
τηκτός -ή -όν, *fusible*

Vocabulary

τίθεμαι (mid.), *make, place, allocate*
τίθημι, *place, lay down, assume,*
    suppose
τιμή, ἡ, *honour, position of honour*
τίμιος, -α -ον, *honoured, valuable*
τις, τι, *some, any, a certain* (τι, *at all,*
    in any way)
τίς, τί, *who, what?* (τί, *why? how?*)
τμηθείς -εῖσα -έν: τέμνω, aor. part.
    pass.
τό (+ gen.), *the class of, the subject of*
τοι (emphatic particle), *let me tell you*
τοιόσδε -άδε -όνδε, *such as this*
τοιοῦτος -αύτη -οῦτο, *such, of such*
    a kind
τοῖχος, ὁ, *wall*
τοξότης, ὁ, *archer*
τόπος, ὁ, *place*
τορνεύω, *use a turning lathe*
τοσοῦτος -αύτη -οῦτο, *so great*
τραφείς -εῖσα -έν: τρέφω, aor. part.
    pass.
τρεῖς, τρία, *three*
τρέπομαι (mid. and pass.), *be*
    turned, face (in a certain
    direction)
τρέφομαι (mid.), *rear for oneself*
τρέφω, *bring up, rear*
τριήρης, ἡ, *trireme*
τρίπλεθρος -ον, *measuring three*
    plethrons (one plethron = approx.
    100 feet)
τριστάδιος -ον, *measuring three*
    stades (one stade = approx. 600
    feet, or 200 yards)
τρισχίλιοι -αι -α, *three thousand*
τρίτος η -ον, *third*
τρόπαιον, τό, *trophy (symbol of*
    victory set up after battle)

τρόπος, ὁ, *way, manner*
τροφή, ἡ, *nutrition, nourishment,*
    basic maintenance; training,
    upbringing
τροχός, ὁ, *wheel, ring, circle*
τρυφή, ἡ, *luxury*
τυγχάνω (+ part.), *happen to, chance*
    to; (+ gen.) *obtain*
Τυρρηνία, ἡ, *Etruria*
τυχεῖν: τυγχάνω, aor. infin.
τύχη, ἡ, *luck, chance*

Υ

ὕβρις, ἡ, *unprovoked violence,*
    violent ambition
ὑγίεια, ἡ, *health*
ὑγρός -ά -όν, *wet, liquid*
ὕδωρ, τό, *water, source of water*
ὕλη, ἡ, *wood; woods*
ὑμεῖς (ὑμῶν, gen.), *you pl.*
ὑμνέω, *celebrate in a hymn, praise*
ὑπαίθριος -ον, *open air*
ὑπάρχω, *be available, be at the*
    beginning
ὑπέρ (prep. + gen.), *on behalf of;*
    over, above (place); (+ acc.)
    beyond
ὑπερβάλλω, *excel, exceed:*
ὑπερβεβληκώς -υῖα -ός, pf. part.
ὑπερέχω, *stand out, be prominent;* (+
    gen.) *rise above*
ὑπερηφανία, ἡ, *arrogance,*
    extravagance
ὑπεροράω, *disdain, look down on*
ὑπό (prep. + gen.), *by, because*
    of; from under; (+ dat.) *under*
    (position); (+acc.) *under (with*
    verbs of motion)
ὑποδέχομαι (mid.), *receive*

ὑποζύγιον, τό, beast (of burden)
ὑποθέσθαι: ὑποτίθεμαι (mid.), aor.
    infin.
ὑπομιμνήσκω, remind
ὑπομνήσω, fut.
ὑπόπλοος, ὁ, underground passage
    (for ships)
ὑπόπτερος -ον, winged
ὑποστέγος -ον, roofed over
ὑποτεθείς -εῖσα -έν: ὑποτίθημι, aor.
    part. pass.
ὑποτίθημι/ὑποτίθεμαι (mid.),
    propose (a subject), imagine,
    suppose
ὕστερος -α -ον, later (time), further
    back (place)
ὑφαίνω, construct, make
ὑψηλός -ή -όν, high
ὕψος, τό, height

Φ

φαίνομαι (pass. + part.), be evidently
    (something); (+ infin.), seem to be
φανερός -ά -όν, clear, obvious
φάρμακον, τό, drug, medicine
φατέ, φασί: φημί, 2 and 3 pl.
φέρω, bring, bear; φέρομαι (mid.),
    obtain, get for oneself; (pass.), be
    carried, borne
φήμη, ἡ, resort, message
φημί, say
φθίνω, waste away, diminish
φθόνος, ὁ, grudge
φθορά, ἡ, destruction
φιάλη, ἡ, flat bowl, cup, saucer
φιλαθήναιος -ον, pro-Athenian
φιλία, ἡ, friendship
φιλοκαλός -ον, loving the beautiful,
    the fine

φιλοπόλεμος, war-loving, warlike
φίλος -η -ον, dear, friendly
φιλοσοφία, ἡ, philosophy, love of
    wisdom or intellectual enquiry
φιλόσοφος -ον, philosophical,
    thoughtful
φιλόσοφος, ὁ, philosopher
φιλότιμος -ον, ambitious, assertive
φιλοτεχνία, ἡ, craftsmanship,
    artistry
φιλοφρόνως ἔχειν πρός, be
    well-disposed towards
φιτύω, produce (a child)
φοβέομαι, be afraid
φράτηρ, ὁ, member of the same tribe
φρόνιμος -η -ον, intelligent, sensible
φρόνημα, τό, thought, idea,
    judgement
φρουρά, ἡ, guard, garrison
φυλακή, ἡ, guarding, guardianship
φύλαξ, ὁ, guardian, defender
φύσις, ἡ, nature
φύσις, ἡ, τῆς ψυχῆς, character,
    temperament
φύτευσις, ἡ (= φυτεία, ἡ), plantation
φωνή, ἡ, voice, speech, noise, tongue,
    language
φῶς, τό, light

Χ

χαλεπός -ή -όν, difficult,
    burdensome, harsh
χαλεπότης, ἡ, difficulty
χαλκός, ὁ, bronze
χαμαί, on the ground
χαρίζομαι (mid., + dat.), do a favour
    to, please; (+ acc.) do as a favour,
    give freely
χάριν (+ gen.), for the sake of

Vocabulary

χάριν ἀποδοῦναι (ἀποδίδωμι, aor. infin.), *express gratitude, return a favour*

χάριν φέρειν, *do a favour*

χάρις, ἡ, *favour, gratitude*

χεῖλος, τό, *lip, edge*

χειμερινός -ή -όν, *of winter, for winter use*

χειμών, ὁ, *winter; storm*

χειροποίητος -ον, *made by hand, artificial*

χειρουργέω, *make, build*

χθές, *yesterday*

χίλιοι -αι -α, *a thousand*

χλόη, ἡ, *young shoot, stalk (esp. of grain)*

χράομαι (mid. + dat.), *use*

χρεὼν ἐστί, *it is necessary, one must*

χρῆμα, τό, *thing, pl. wealth, goods, property*

χρήσιμος -η -ον (+ πρός), *useful, serviceable for*

χρῆσις, ἡ, *use*

χρόνος, ὁ, *time* (διὰ χρόνου, *after such an interval of time*)

χυλός, ὁ, *juice, gum*

χῶμα, το, *sediment, topsoil*

χώρα, ἡ, *place, land*

χωρίς (adv.), *separately, apart*; (prep. + gen.), *apart from, without*

Ψ

ψιλός - ή -όν, *bare*

ψυχή, ἡ, *soul*

ψυχρός -ή -όν, *cold*

ψύχω, *make cool, put out (fire)*

Ω

ὦ (used with vocatives), *e.g.* ὦ φίλε, *my dear*

ὧδε, *thus, in this way*

ᾠκεῖτε: οἰκέω, 2 pl. impf.

ᾠκοδομοῦντο: οἰκοδομέομαι, 3 pl. impf.

ὡπλίσμεθα: ὁπλίζω, 1 pl. pf. pass.

ὥρα, ἡ, *period of time, season; pl. climate*

ὡραῖος -α -ον, *in season*

ὡς, *that; how!; about, approximately*

ὡς + superlative, *as ... as possible*

ὥσπερ, *just as, as if*

ὥστε, *so that*

Index of Ancient Passages

This index includes passages in Greek and Latin literature cited in connection with Plato's Atlantis story; it does not include the core texts for the story (Plato *Timaeus* 17a–27b and *Critias*) which are presented or discussed throughout the book.

General Index

In the case of modern scholars, only the most salient references are included.